END OF TERM
REPORT

Paddy O'Hanlon

Published by Paddy O'Hanlon Publishing Ltd
©2011 Paddy O'Hanlon Publishing Ltd

ISBN: 978-0-9570320-0-2

Designed by April Sky Design www.aprilsky.co.uk
Printed by W&G Baird Limited
Front cover image: iStockPhoto

END OF TERM REPORT

Paddy O'Hanlon

Acknowledgements

Paddy sadly passed away before this book was ready for publication. I do not intend to try to complete a list of acknowledgements on Paddy's behalf because I cannot be sure who might inadvertently be left out.

This page is simply to recognise those who were involved directly in the publication of this most important of Paddy's work.

Firstly, Brian Feeney his friend and fellow politician, who has completed a superb edit of the work which is both sensitive, respectful and protective of Paddy's distinctive style of writing.

His cousin Rory O'Hanlon was both a best friend and a close political counterpart and always an inspiration.

Rory McShane, executor of Paddy's affairs, was along with myself and Rory O'Hanlon charged by Paddy in the days before his death to ensure that this work was published appropriately and at the right time and has been at the centre of the project.

Wesley Johnston of April Sky Design has been a pleasure to work with – flexible, always good humoured and professional to his fingertips.

Paddy had not chosen photographs to accompany the text and we were greatly assisted by the librarians in a number of publications. All were unfailingly helpful and a credit to their professions – Kathleen Bell of the Irish News, Paul Carson of the Belfast Telegraph and finally Irene Stevenson and Mary Sheridan of the Irish Times.

David Torrans of No Alibis Bookshop was a great help to Paddy with a previous publication and was equally giving of his expertise with this project.

Ultimately to our publishers in the US – the American Irish Historical Society – Chris Cahill (Executive Director) and Meghan Walsh (Editor). Paddy loved the United States and would have been delighted to have two such committed and enthusiastic advocates of his work.

Gary Mills
Director
Paddy O'Hanlon Publishing Ltd

To Absent Friends

FOREWORD

At the outset it is important to corroborate what Paddy O'Hanlon says in the introduction to this book. During autumn 1996 Paddy, Eugene Grant QC and I began to meet at irregular intervals usually in the Europa Hotel, Belfast. The purpose of these meetings was to report back on the tasks Paddy had given Eugene and me and to pool our thoughts. At other times Paddy met Eugene and me separately to incite us to greater effort.

Eugene was engaged in dealing with Lord Williams of Mostyn QC a Labour spokesman in the Lords. They had met originally when Eugene was acting in his capacity as a representative of the Bar Council of the North but by 1996 the main aim was to persuade Willams to encourage the Labour party to talk to Sinn Féin in the run up to the British general election expected in summer 1997. My task was to contact Sinn Féin to tell them what we were up to and to convey the messages Eugene was receiving from Williams.

After the election we continued to meet with Paddy setting Eugene to work on criminal justice matters. In my case we met a few times at my house where he interrogated me about policing, local government boundaries and European examples of politico-ethnic conflict. His interrogations became more urgent as winter drew on. We all exchanged written summaries. He talked vaguely of handing the results over to the Irish government. Neither of us knew he had been given any commission.

In my case I must confess that when he handed over his completed paper to an official from Foreign Affairs in my house I thought it was a futile exercise and that we would never see any return. Instead I was amazed to see familiar wording months later in the Good Friday Agreement.

A decade later in 2009 following Paddy's untimely death I was delighted when members of his family asked me to edit what amounts to his autobiography: delighted because I was a witness to what he produced but also because I had been a close friend and admirer over thirty years.

In life he never achieved the recognition he deserved so now it is especially important to place on record the role he played in providing what became the outline draft of the Good Friday Agreement. He distilled a lifetime's thought and experience into his proposals.

Brian Feeney
September 2010

INTRODUCTION

Very few people know how the Good Friday Agreement was put together, or what is in it. It is time to reveal the truth. The detailed blueprint of the Agreement was written by Paddy O'Hanlon, a founder member of the SDLP.

He agreed to write a document after a meeting in late 1997 with the SDLP's Seamus Mallon MP and Alex Attwood and a representative of the Department of Foreign Affairs at a time when the all-party talks at Stormont had already settled into a weary pattern. He told the SDLP representatives that it could not be an SDLP document because it would have no legs if it were. It had to go to the Irish government who needed ideas from a Northern source in the context of a Northern solution. The meeting agreed to this approach.

O'Hanlon focussed on six key issues: policing, the criminal justice system, judicial appointments, political prisoners, a voting system for the proposed assembly and a fail-safe mechanism to operate during periods of suspension of the proposed power-sharing executive. These were the major roadblocks to peace in the North.

The completed document was handed over to a senior civil servant from Foreign Affairs in the home of Brian Feeney, the most influential political journalist in the North and a close friend of O'Hanlon's, in the presence of Brian Feeney in mid-December 1997.

Paddy demanded that the origin of the document should be concealed until there was a full-blooded power-sharing executive in the North otherwise the purpose of the exercise would be frustrated. The Department of Foreign Affairs agreed. It has remained a closely guarded secret for more than ten years.

His proposals on policing, the criminal justice system and judicial appointments appeared in two discussion documents from the British government with a foreword by Mo Mowlam MP the British secretary of state for Northern Ireland dated 2 and 4 March 1998, six weeks before the final Agreement talks took place. O'Hanlon's proposals had been transferred from the Irish government to the British government and were presented to the parties from the British side who had the necessary reserved powers in these matters which solely affected the North.

Paddy O'Hanlon's proposals are at the core of the new policing arrangements, the new criminal justice system and the judicial appointments system in the North. Political status, the new voting system and the fail-safe mechanism for future breakdown exactly as he envisaged were agreed at the talks in April 1998. He retained the original documents and there were witnesses at every stage of the procedure as indicated above. There is a full-blooded power-sharing executive now.

Martin McAllister

PREFACE

Anne came from Portadown in County Armagh, home of Drumcree Church and the Garvaghy Road, a fraught place where the minority were made very aware of the Orange Order and the special role of Unionism in the history of Northern Ireland, a place where tradition went soul deep in both communities. We spent time in Wexford in July 1996 at the home of her aunt, Tess Fallon. Anne was at a late stage of her battle with cancer. We walked on the beach at Wexford every day and talked about many things that were dear to both of us. We always discussed the Orange Order march in Portadown due in a few days time. The march was allowed on certain conditions by the Garvaghy Road residents in 1995 and I took the view that it would be stopped on this occasion in 1996. Anne believed that it would be forced through, that the ancient certainties would reassert themselves.

Anne was right: she nearly always was. An armour-plated JCB appeared at Drumcree and the police let the massed ranks of the Orange Order and their supporters march down the Garvaghy Road on 11 July amid scenes of humiliation and triumphalism. Images of policemen removing Garvaghy Road residents by force from the route of the march to allow the Orange Order through were relayed around the world, resulting in widespread rioting in nationalist areas for several days. The North was on the verge of Civil War. It was the worst of times politically, as bad as I remembered, as bad as the early Seventies and the hunger strike year of 1981.

Years in politics had failed to educate me about the political realities of life in Northern Ireland and the role of tradition. I felt absolutely powerless as I watched events unfold. Anne died of cancer on 8 August 1996. She left the world with a reinforced memory of ritual sectarianism and the defeat of hope. I vowed, in the aftermath of her death, that I would take every opportunity at my disposal to change the situation. I had no idea how that might work. I left politics in 1982 in pursuit of a law degree and a career at the Bar of Northern Ireland and limited my political activity to canvassing at election time. I wanted to help so I watched for an opportunity, in memory of my Amazing Grace.

Chapter One

I was born in Drogheda on 8 May 1944 and lived for the early part of my life in the small seaside village of Blackrock in County Louth, now the southern boundary of Dundalk. The locals may not agree with my description. They are of independent spirit and consider Dundalk to be an extension of Blackrock. There were green fields for miles to the north when I was growing up, out past The Crescent and the golf course and the marshland that soaked up the shallow sea, out past the mysterious house that lay on a curve of the road, the Cooley Mountains in the distance and Dundalk in plain view, out of bounds for the bare-footed.

Blackrock was my playground. The strand lay outside the front door of our house and the home of Brigid MacDermott Roe who came from Ballinafad in the west of Ireland. She ran a number of boarding houses that were jammed in the summer months, at a junction in the road that ran away to Haggarstown and the main Dublin Road. She was always 'Dermy' to us. The water curved in once a day along a deep channel that lay in the thin mist, a hundred yards out in front of the house. I watched the ceaseless roll of the water from the first gleam in the distance to the splash of the sea on my feet. The tide trickled through my toes and I felt a joy that never left me.

A greyhound called Pups took me to the national school each day, a placid creature who waited until I entered the gate at the top of Sandy Lane before she returned home. She was always there when school was out in the evening. Pups took it easy on the return journey, down Sandy Lane past the pitch and putt course and the Nissen hut with hard wooden forms for seats where the movies were shown weekly. Into the village street, past the Neptune and Malocca's, where the best chips in the world were sold, and Uncle Tom's Cabin and the necklace of small houses that lay below the parish church, peeping out at the strand and the sea. In those years I spent my life on that stretch of sand below the road to Dundalk, lost in the paddle pools that lay around the black rocks, searching for pinkies and small crabs until the lazy shallow sea rolled back into my life along the gash in the foreshore. The water was perfect for small people, never too deep and a weak current near the shore. There was once a storm that carried a huge ship close to the black rocks on a wall of water but it was sucked out to sea again and came to rest on the marshland further down the coast. There was a Church of Ireland rectory near The Crescent, where rounders were played in high summer when the ministers visited and sported themselves, after coming from Bangor, County Down in a bus.

Most of the time I ran between the house and the strand, down the stone steps to the narrow beach and up along the steep wall to the road. I can still feel the metal wire on my hand, bolted to the wall and attached to the telegraph pole by the roadside. I climbed up the wire forever when I was young, scrambling up the wall and down on the busy road, growing stronger with the years. The strand was a safe place to play. The great danger was diving into the sea at full tide and cracking your skull on the sunken rocks. A landing craft from the second world war, known locally as a 'duck', was stuck in the sand a short distance from the shore. It landed for the last time in Blackrock and bedded into the foreshore, empty and forlorn and beyond use. We played around the duck until the water came in and made us run. A playground the size of a beach is a privilege and not many children are so lucky. I remember it fondly, a sand-kicking waterway with tide and wet rain and the warm beat of the sun on bare backs and exploring for miles before running home for tea to my mother Margaret, who was always called Peg, and Dermy.

I watched my father with the curiosity of the young when he was getting ready in the morning. He sat on the bed and began the ritual, a sock on the foot of his good leg and a cloth over the stump, then the rest of his clothes after the artificial limb was in place. Soon he was upright and ready for the day. I checked the legs of the other fathers outside the school during the morning round. All fathers might be the same, one good leg and another made of sponge and hard material. I knew that he was different after watching legs for a while. I asked a few questions about the leg when I was small but he gave me fairy tales so I let it be. I found a body on the beach once and it chased the leg question out of my head. The man had two legs and he was dead: one leg and alive was better.

My father was a butcher by trade with a shop in the Square in Dundalk. He left in the morning and came home in the evening and I settled into school and strand. After tea one evening when I was eight years old the news came. Both of my parents were from the village of Mullaghbawn in South Armagh and they wanted to go home. My father had sold the business and we moved to a new house in the centre of the village in 1952. The new home lay between the homes of my much loved grandmothers, Bridge House and Maphoner House, a wee sprint away in both cases and I loved to spend time in both places.

It took time to settle in. No sea sound and a new start, a green valley below Slieve Gullion with a saucer of drumlins called the volcanic rim that swept away to Forkhill and Dromintee. A tiny river that once served the linen trade ran through the village. It matured into a river by the time it reached Forkhill and went down to the sea after that.

Bridge House faced the river near the crossing point. The pub was in the family for fifteen generations, or so they said. A short race from home took me through the busy yard full of livestock and beer barrels and the tools of the undertaker's trade and into the public house. Grandmother Sarah lived there with a number of uncles who never married and my aunts Bessie and Sadie. Grandmother Sarah in full control, indulgent of grandchildren and human nature, excited talk about farming and football and the curse of emigration, fond memories of Tilley lights and hurricane lamps and huge men in brown boots and dungarees bound with binder twine or held up with galluses, four square to the counter with cloth caps tilted to the Kildare side. Men to be left home at closing time when Uncle Barney was busy and bowls of soup for the bar beaten. Grandmother Sarah oversaw it all with a gimlet eye and a warm heart. There were two pubs in the family business and they employed my uncles and aunts and a number of local people. The second pub in the family was further up the road and catered for the locals who wanted time out from Bridge House, a small dark place that consisted of a bar and a sort of snug and a television room that we camped in after school. The pub lacked some facilities but there was always 'Mrs Greenfield', the whole way to Dundalk if you needed to visit the toilet.

Maphoner House, my mother's maternal home, was an attractive white-washed house with an ample garden and a gravelled driveway nestled at the top of a narrow lane. It was home to Grandmother Tess and my uncle Louis. Grandfather Felix died in 1947, the year of the big snow. There were empty rooms upstairs and I asked about them. I was told that my uncles and aunts had gone away and to stop asking questions. I was happy enough. There were more rooms to explore when the grown-ups were downstairs. My two grandfathers were dead and I was blessed with my grandmothers. I am sure there were days when they salted me but I have no memory of it. All I remember is running to each house and being happy there.

As for my siblings, Marie, Gerard and Frances were born in the Sorth, Eilish, Siobhan and Deirdre in the North after the return to Mullaghbawn. My father opened for trade in a small building down from Bridge House, only at weekends. I remember the sides of beef arriving from Newry on a Friday afternoon and he did a steady trade over the weekend. There was always a joint of beef on the table on Sunday. It was not the best of times. It was an age of poverty and we were poor with the rest. The weekend trade kept a roof over our heads and the world turned.

The first years in Mullaghbawn are a whirl of memory. Threshing day, the engine roaring and a blizzard of sheaves, rats running for their lives from the base of the rick when the bottom was lifted, shirts pickled with dust and sweat on a blazing day. Long rows of tables loaded with plates of meat and steaming vegetables and a huge pot of potatoes. Men in from the local farms to lend a hand because thrashing machines were scarce and there were other farms to visit, banter and loud laughter and plugs of tobacco and a penny for the chiseler making a nuisance of himself. Secret delight and money in my fist and away to Maggie Rice for a ginger cake.

There were trout in the river that we hunted in dry weather when the water ran low. There was a chance of catching a mountain trout in the small pools of water that gleamed like the rock pools at Blackrock.

The wonder of Christmas Eve: setting the candles, two or three to a window, upstairs and downstairs, and pulling back the curtains for safety, touching the wax stalks gently to make sure they were secure and waiting for the signal. The parochial house was first to light the way of the Saviour. Soon the valley was flickering candle flame, burning in every home in the icy calm of a winter night.

When I was a teenager digging graves with Patsy McKeown in the lee of the church, close to the bones and the dust of eternity. Early morning in the farmyard at Bridge House with a job to do, up the steps to the loft, where the shiny apples lay in wooden crates and the coffins were stacked in tidy rows, to wake Mickey Quinn. It was not a wake in the traditional sense, a blow on a stiff door and the light filtering in when it creaked open. He always answered on the first call, a coffin lid rose slowly and the head appeared, ready for the new day. Filling stout straight from the barrel on the six prong machine, watching the flow until the bottle was full and punching the caps on, hands stained brown with Guinness when the barrel was empty. I was asked in later life why I never smoked and I said that the stale smell of smoke in the morning put me off. The questioner said it was a pity that the stale smell of drink did not have the same effect.

I was very shy when I was young. I remember the terror I felt when I was named as an altar boy. I did not want the job but I was forced to do it. A week of preparation and I was told to present myself. I remember the first morning when I lifted the latch and entered the holy of holies. A place of mystery, a robing room for the servers and a sacristy for the priest, the smell of incense and the tumble of communion wafers into a ciborium. A battle with the surplice and the soutane and into line before the priest. The door opened and I was on. The quiet ritual of the Latin mass and a first look at the congregation, a Tuesday morning before school and a weekday crowd was in. My mother in a distant pew, looking pleased. It was not a disaster, I banged the bell at the right times and never dropped a book. I faced the congregation without blushing when we went from kneeling to sitting. I served for a couple of years and it was a benefit. Running through the fields and over the tree trunk that bridged the river near the church, through the graveyard and up the steps to the sacristy. Sunday mass and a change of mood. I faced the crowd and relaxed, comfortable with the scrutiny and my performance, picking out pals in the crowd. Serving mass is a boon for shy people. It grounds them and gives them confidence. I ended my serving career at the consecration of the foundation stone of Aughanduff Church in 1955, server to Cardinal D'Alton at the height of my powers as an altar boy. As it was in the beginning, I rang the bell in Mullaghbawn church at the right moments and communion was served to the parish of Forkhill by Cardinal D'Alton and me, or should that be by me and Cardinal D'Alton?

My maternal grandparents were principal teachers in the parish. Tess Crowley came from Adrigole on the Beara peninsula. She took the brave decision to come north after qualifying, to teach in a small school at Clonalig on the northern side of the border and married Felix Grant. She was the seminal influence on my young life. I got the Eleven Plus examination a year early because of her influence and I went to school in Newry as a day boy. Saint Colman's College is a boarding school set in acres of ground at Violet Hill that included the residence of the Bishop of Dromore. Children do not question the system that surrounds them. They simply experience it and I experienced life in a seminary college. The school was geared towards the education of the Catholic middle classes and the needs of Maynooth and we were never allowed to forget that fact. The Eleven Plus system was more equitable than the old network and it flooded the grammar schools with children from all walks of life. It changed the culture of the grammar schools because it changed the background of the pupils who gained entry. The President of St Colman's was a fan of daily humiliation. Maybe he believed it was good for the soul? He lined up the day boys when they arrived every morning and inspected their shoes. We lined up and he passed by and poked a stick vaguely at unpolished surfaces and scruffy leather and pointed out a tale of hard times.

I soon realised I had a learning difficulty. I had no idea what I was doing at Violet Hill. I was not unmannerly or rude. I just drifted away. I was as feckless as this narrative will make me and totally out of kilter. My father said I was bone lazy and a dreamer and that was the nub of it. I had no ambition, I just wanted to live. I had a severe aversion to school work from the moment I arrived in the place. Maybe it was an internal thing and maybe it was the turnover in my life? Blackrock to Mullaghbawn, Irish to English (for we grew up speaking Irish at home), Eleven Plus and St Colman's College, constant motion, constant change and three new sets of faces in four years. I avoided the lurking fear that stalked me, a lot of smart guys in the class and I was petrified of working hard and finding out I was not as clever as I wanted to be.

By the second year we were prisoners of the system but we held on to the use of reason. We were growing and changing and beginning to look around us and we began to think for ourselves. It was the year Hungary was invaded by the Russians (1956) and the classrooms were agog with the news. The IRA began a border campaign and the local area was in the spotlight. We South Armagh boys were pestered in school about bomb explosions and telephone boxes. We were expected to be experts so I repeated the gossip I heard in the bar at home. We were border cubs and proud of it, close to danger and close to normality on the same day.

The heroes were the smugglers, the men who ran the roads and evaded the B men and made a living on the sly. There was a story told about a man who crossed the border at the Customs Post at Jonesborough once a week, wheeling a barrow load of sand. The Customs men searched the sand for weeks looking for smuggled items before they gave up. They never got it : the man was smuggling wheelbarrows. I began to listen to news bulletins and read the newspapers. There were attacks on barracks and the deaths of young men and a telephone box was blown up in Mullaghbawn. The IRA campaign was a bigger topic than smuggling in Bridge House, where I did my turn behind the bar. I heard the gossip and the sober discussions but there was mention of earlier risings. It imposed like warm drizzle until I was wet with the word of politics and the history of the O'Hanlon clan.

The O'Hanlon was chieftain of Orior for hundreds of years, the Pale on the south side and The O'Neill on the north. The O'Hanlon was the traditional ally of The O'Neill but the power of all the chieftains was greatly reduced between 1560 and 1650. Confiscation and plantation followed various acts against the crown. In 1566, The O'Hanlon sided with The O'Neill in an insurrection in which The O'Hanlon lost his life in the course of a government offensive. Thomas Chatterton was given a Royal Charter over O'Hanlon land and, when the project failed, Sir Eochaidh

O'Hanlon regained some of the lost land in 1587. It was a time before nationhood was a potent force, a time when local warlords, including the O'Hanlons, held sway over vast tracts of the country. There was no concept of nationality and the main concerns were territory and position. There was a great deal of feuding and fence mending and a court in London for the settlement of disputes.

Eochaidh was a knight and the ancient title of The O'Hanlon was abolished to underline the change in the relationship with the English crown. The other chieftains made similar arrangements. The O'Neill became the earl of Tyrone. The clans changed sides at will in the following years but they came together at the Battle of the Yellow Ford where the English forces under the leadership of Henry Bagenal were defeated and Bagenal was killed. One of the Irish captains was Turlough O'Hanlon, a son of Sir Eochaidh, who put the English cavalry to flight. Their baggage and 200 horses were captured and three of their officers slain.

The native Irish were knights and earls when they were stretched on the rack of history. They tried everything to save their territory but they were broken on the wheel. After the battle of Kinsale in 1602, a number of the chieftains sailed down Lough Swilly from County Donegal with O'Neill in 1607. It was a very significant date in the history of the island but I have a thing about the wording. The conferring of earldoms was an English idea, conferred on The O'Neill first in 1542 as earl of Tyrone and on Rory O'Donnell from Donegal as earl of Tyrconnell after the treaty of Mellifont in 1603. The phrase - the Flight of the Earls - probably comes from an English source in that the use of the word 'earls' at first instance implies an English hand and 'earls' is inaccurate in any case because there was only one earl on the ship. 'Flight' is hardly the appropriate word to describe the event. 'The Leaving of the Chieftains' has a ring to it but there is better wording out there to describe the occasion. Some Irish historian should attempt a more appropriate title for the event because it is important. It changed the nature of politics on the island forever. The result of the leaving was a decision to implement a policy of Plantation.

The O'Hanlons did not leave Ireland with O'Neill. Eochaidh Óg joined his brother in law, Cahir O'Doherty, the Chieftain of Inishowen, in an uprising in 1608. O'Doherty was killed and the rebellion was short lived. Eochaidh Óg spent some months in the local forests in a rearguard guerrilla campaign before he surrendered and was deported to Sweden. He was already stripped of the right to succeed because he had fought with O'Neill in the Nine Years War which ended at Mellifont in 1603. By 1610, Tandragee Castle, the seat of O'Hanlon power, was in the hands of Oliver St John and the power of the clan began to wane. Under the Cromwellian confiscation, the O'Hanlons were dispossessed of their remaining lands and were granted no relief after the Restoration in 1660. It was the beginning of a long slow decline and a scattering of the clan.

I have no idea if my ancestors included the chieftains of Orior or Redmond O'Hanlon, the rapparee. I can document the family tree in various ways. A tombstone in the local graveyard dated 1860, records back to 1773. An oral reach through my cousin Rory O'Hanlon, Fianna Fáil TD for Cavan/Monaghan and former Ceann Comhairle of Dáil Éireann, father of the comedian Ardal O'Hanlon, takes me back to the mid-seventeenth century. Too many generations have passed since that time. It is likely that every O'Hanlon in South Armagh can lay claim to the blood, and blood there was in full measure.

The night came when talk in the bar drifted round to the War of Independence and the Civil War. I was shovelling coal on a roaring fire when the craic started in the circle of men surrounding the blaze. I was still listening when it ended at closing time. The years have brought me closer to the facts than the fiction. My grandfather, Bernard O'Hanlon, died of pneumonia in 1915. He owned two spirit stores, a grocery, a hardware store and a farm. The obituary notice said that he employed a large number of local people and paid them a generous wage. The notice went on to say that a number of the employees had worked for his father before him, a good sign in the circumstances. Another line in the obituary seems to chime with my experience of the O'Hanlons. It said that Bernard O'Hanlon was straightforward to a fault. I had a flash of recognition as I read the line in the obituary. It is a family trait and remains that way today.

Sarah O'Hanlon did not have her troubles to seek after the death of her husband. There were educational needs to sort out and Bridge House to run and nine children to rear. She was determined that the children would have a good education and she made it happen. Uncle Mick went to Blackrock College in Dublin and my father followed him there. The Easter Rising brought another complication. There were too many sons and a daughter coming to the attention of the local Specials, the embryonic RUC, as the War of Independence progressed.

My father was enrolled in Blackrock College in Dublin in 1918 and stayed for a year. He set out to return to the college at the beginning of the next school year but he left the train at Dundalk along with Paddy McCoy and they made their way back to Mullaghbawn. He enrolled as a student at the Agricultural College in Ballyhaise with a view to a life as a farmer. The Civil War was raging when he came home on holidays in the summer of 1922. He took part in the raid on Dundalk jail with the IRA Fourth Northern Division, led by Frank Aiken, on 28 July 1922.

He was almost eighteen when he came to Dungooley Cross on the Louth/Armagh border with the local IRA unit, less than a month later. They ran into an ambush manned by Free State soldiers. He was hit a number of times and was lucky to survive. After he was captured the soldiers left him lying beside an outhouse while they searched the area: his loss of blood was severe. Finally, they took him to Dundalk Infirmary where his leg was amputated above the knee. The shock effect of the amputation was severe enough to kill a person in the age before antibiotics but he survived and grew strong again. Although his wounds were almost healed he was still in hospital and therefore still at risk, but not from infection or infirmity.

His status was unclear. Was he under arrest or was a charge pending? Nobody knew what the authorities would do. He was captured bearing arms and there was a consequence, a danger of execution. It was an anxious time. He worked on his mobility and worked out the best way to avoid a military court was to make his escape. The plan took weeks to prepare. A nurse in the hospital, Bridie Agnew, disguised my father in a nursing uniform and smuggled him out. It was a risky venture because of his lack of mobility and his state of health but Bridie Agnew pulled it off. The family were waiting to take him to Mullaghbawn.

Tom Rodgers, who was wounded at the taking of Dundalk barracks, escaped in a similar manner and emigrated to America. Bridie Agnew served time in a Dublin prison as a result of her activities. She emigrated subsequently and married Tom Rodgers in America. As for my father, it took a long time to recuperate at home. There was no return to active service and there were other consequences. It was gently pointed out by the family that a one-legged man was vulnerable at the nervous end of a cow and the days at Agricultural College were over. Getting used to crutches was trial enough but there was the farm after that. Mobility was essential in the bar and on the farm. There was a need to consider other careers after you lose a limb.

My Uncle Michael was a medical student in Dublin during the War of Independence and he joined the IRA in college. In November 1920, he was a member of 3 Company, 3 Battalion Dublin brigade and took part in the attack on British agents living in Dublin whose names and addresses had been leaked to Michael Collins by his intelligence network. Mick was a member of the unit that entered a house at 28 Upper Pembroke Street: five British agents were shot dead at this location. After the mission was accomplished, he walked across Dublin and dumped his gun at a safe house in Swifts Row near the Ha'penny Bridge, made for Amiens Street railway station and took the train to Dundalk. He was met by the family pony and trap and taken to Mullaghbawn. It was the morning of what would be known as Bloody Sunday. In retaliation for the killings of the agents British forces entered Croke Park that afternoon and opened fire on a crowd at a Gaelic football match, killing fourteen civilians. Three prisoners were killed that night in Dublin Castle by their British captors.

Mick was IRA organiser in Cavan during the Civil War and was arrested in possession of a firearm in November 1922 and taken to Tintown One, a Curragh internment camp run by the Free State. Tintown One was built to accommodate 600 men. Tintown Two held almost 2000. There were four huts in Tintown One and Mick was appointed O/C of one of them. Peadar O'Donnell was the overall O/C. The objective from the beginning was to escape, by tunnelling under the wire. Peadar O'Donnell was moved to Mountjoy Jail during the construction of the tunnel and Mick replaced him as O/C of Tintown One. Seventy-three men escaped on 24 April 1923 including my uncle Mick, a record for an internment camp in Ireland. Mick walked across the flatlands of the Curragh of Kildare after his escape and crossed the River Liffey. He made for Dunboyne in Meath where he took refuge. Mick then took to the fields and walked home to Mullaghbawn.

Frank Aiken declared a ceasefire on 30 April 1923 and ordered the dumping of arms on 24 May bringing the Civil War to an end. The Northern authorities never inquired about my Uncle Mick when they raided Bridge House. The reason seems to have been that there was a photograph in his bedroom of Mick at Blackrock College, posing with the rest of the college rugby team. It seemed to allay suspicion. He returned to UCD and finished his medical degree after the Civil War. It is said in the family that he returned on the order of Frank Aiken who was keen that he finished his studies rather then enter politics. Mick went to Shrewsbury after he qualified as a doctor and took a break from Irish affairs. He met Daisy there and they married. He returned to Ireland at the invitation of Frank Aiken, to a position in the Irish Army. His son is Rory O'Hanlon, who has been a TD for thirty years and has held various ministerial ranks. He finally served as Ceann Comhairle of Dáil Éireann.

Uncle Barney was quartermaster of the local IRA unit and was forced to go on the run. Uncle Pete went to Belfast where he was apprenticed to his uncle who was a publican. He was involved in republican activities there. Aunt Bessie was a member of Cumann Na mBan and was very active in the War of Independence and the Civil War. The Specials suspected her of carrying dispatches in the course of her duties. We made a discovery in the Fourth Northern Division file in the archives in Collins Barracks when Rory and I visited a couple of years ago, a letter from Mick to my father who was recovering from his wounds at Bridge House. It is a snapshot of a point in time and it states:

Hut A
Tintown No 1
Curragh
1ˢᵗ March 1923

Dear Paddy

Just a line to let you know that I have arrived at the above address and having a fairly good time here. We are allowed papers, parcels etc so we are as well off here as on the Argenta [an internment ship in Belfast Lough]. My brother Pete and Johnnie McCoy are in No 2 camp. We can walk up and down twenty yards about (barbed wire and sentry in between) but dare not talk or signal to one another across without serious risk.
I hope the ploughing is going ahead. I am sorry I cannot give you a hand this Spring. I hope you don't get fed up with the extra work but the weather is not too bad. Did anything happen Gerry lately? I heard the other day that he was in bad health. You might remember me speak of Peadar O'Donnell, Tirconnail, he is in the same hut with me.

With the best of wishes etc etc to everybody.

Yours
M 'Hanlon

It is a treasured possession, a record of a family moment in a Civil War that divided families. The O'Hanlons of Mullaghbawn were lucky that way. They saw it out together. The family did not do bigotry or sectarianism. They were stubborn to the point of public despair and over-loyal to organisations and individuals at times but they refused to hate on the grounds of race, colour or creed. I hope that I inhabit the same world. O'Hanlons who served in the War of Independence and the Civil War are buried in the family plots in Mullaghbawn graveyard, not in the Republican plot. There is no coded message in the choice, it is just the way we are as a family.

The RUC were still raiding our premises in the winter of 1923, after the Civil War had ended in the Sorth. The family were viewed as bitter Republicans by the authorities, according to the correspondence between the family solicitor and the RUC. A letter of 16 April 1923 from the District Inspector claims that:

> Mrs O'Hanlon has seven sons, two of which were arrested by Free
> State troops and are at present in custody. A third son is a cripple
> having lost a leg in a fight between Free State soldiers and Irregulars at
> Dungooley, the remaining four sons are quite young. She also has two
> daughters, the eldest - Bessie – was suspected of carrying dispatches for
> Frank Aiken and McCoy, the Irregular leaders in the locality, and was
> frequently seen coming from Dundalk..

Uncle Mick escaped from Tintown One eight days later, I have no date of release for Uncle Pete from Tintown Two.

A letter of 23 July 1923 from the same RUC source claims that:

The house was a meeting place for the blackguards of Mullabawn and Forkhill.

My father loved animals and the family had relatives in the Sorth. Contact was made and he moved to Nugent's Stud Farm and worked there for some years. He paid a visit to England when Mick was settled in the medical practice. He was fitted for a leg in Shrewsbury and made rapid progress and was able to discard the crutches in quick time. He dabbled at flapper tracks for greyhounds, developed a rich breeding strain in racing dogs in the forties and joined his brother Jem in a mobile butcher's shop.

Chapter Two

W e went back to stay with Dermy at Blackrock during the summer holidays throughout the teenage years. The late teens and twenties went to the Pavilion Ballroom at the head of the Blackrock strand but we younger ones owned the skating hall. We came together for the afternoon hop and we lived in the house of rock and roll. It was a special place, the floor a blur of girls and boys in the spangled light doing lazy circles of the hall, loud raucous music and the magic of the first touch. Lazy nights by the lapping shore in large groups, listening to the waves and the airwaves, testing the edges of mystery with the sound of the hit parade on the warm air. Dodgem cars and swing boats beside the skating hall for the summer, all the fun of the fair. Summer girls with winter hearts in the restless crowd and 'Love letters In The Sand', getting the heart broken early because it saves time. An invasion of Belfast people on 15 August, escaping to the seaside for a day at the nearest southern point. Careless days and I was still careless, despite the new influences in my life.

School was not working for me, or the church, or society in general, and I was in need of help. I was lost and rudderless and my parents lost heart. Football cured the boredom and the lack of direction and it carried me along until the realisation that when nothing else worked for me, the GAA worked for me. When nothing else made sense to me, the GAA made sense to me. When nobody spoke to me about identity, the GAA spoke to me about identity. The local pitch was crowded with young men catching the ball in their hands and banging off each other. There were five sides from Lurgan in the Armagh first division when I started playing club football for Mullaghbawn, an amazing statistic considering that they came from a small nationalist enclave in the most hard line Unionist territory in Ulster. I came to know the reason in the following years. Playing GAA was a caste mark, a badge of identity, a means of survival in a hostile climate, the only peaceful way to identify with core principles of culture and tradition in the days of maximum bias. If you want to talk about identity, you need to know who you are.

There were no class divisions in the GAA and the ritual was played out every Sunday. The village team togged out for the league match and the team was announced. Bricklayers and farmers, teachers and unemployed men, all one in spirit, playing for the pride of the village. The classless aspect of the game conditioned my politics and the organisation conditioned my life. Nobody ever sat me down and told me what to think or lectured me about history. The GAA taught me about discipline. It did not kick into my general life and habits for many years but it was there when the time arrived. Coaches put manners on kids. You obey instructions or are shown the gate after the general warning to shape up. You want to play football so you obey the rules. Nobody talked about sanctions, there was no need. I refused to imagine a life without football so I shaped up. I learned about winning and losing, how to take a tumble and the need to play for the team. I came to realize that Gaelic football is not about victory laps and autographs. It is about loyalty, commitment and a sense of place. The Olympic spirit lives in Mullaghbawn and every village dreams of a county final or a day in September in Croke Park. The game belongs to the men and women who have power without the glory, who lift the lottery tickets and drive the cars. They may not realize it but the power endures and informs and lives in all of us.

The Fifties were well christened before the Tilley light was dimmed forever in Mullaghbawn. Electricity surged over the rim of the valley in 1956 and changed everything. A switch on the wall replaced the safety match and there was word of the first television in the village. Radio Luxembourg let in the world and the music of Perkins and Holly and a guy from Ferriday, Louisiana. Suddenly I was a strut of the pylon generation. The music was a deluge and it swept all before it including my quiff. I had a duck's ass haircut held down by Brylcreem and a head like a rook's nest, full of shit and sticks. Radio Luxembourg exposed me to the outside world. The radio was king and unrest was everywhere, in Hungary and other strange sounding places with faraway names. There was rebellion on the radio called popular music and it was rocking in South Armagh.

The clergy hated Radio Luxembourg and rock and roll. They called it 'the devil's music', alleged it was putting the young bucks astray. They never got it. The programmes came flooding in and informed our world. It was better than the alternative, a man in clerical garb poking around in the dark places at the rear of a building, disturbing courting couples, rooting out occasions of sin and reading culprits out from the altar. They were expert at putting the clerical hat over the projector in the parochial hall when the man kissed the woman in the weekly western, substituting a bright fantasy in a hushed room for a minor rush. I knew a South Armagh boy who was caught with a girl behind the parochial hall by a priest. His stock rose with his peers when the detail was read from the altar. Shadow beats substance in the fertile mind and fertility was an issue. There was a great irony involved in the condemnation. The version given in church was inaccurate. The boy wished it was true but he kept his silence. Among his peers he was a made man. His real crime in the eyes of the church was knowledge. Marty Wilde did not sing flat for my generation. He floated down the airwaves and he made sense: 'Each night I ask the stars up above - why must I be a teenager in love?' A simple message about feelings and emotions and it was coming from the radio. It was only rock and roll but I liked it. Marty was more real to me than a priest in the dark behind the parochial hall.

Emigration was a big issue in the pub when I was growing up. A third of the fathers were in England because there was no work at home and there was an ugly gash in the social fabric of Mullaghbawn. The men left the farms and made for Belfast. They boarded the *Duke of Lancaster* and sailed for England. They left Ireland in thousands and unsettled in the back streets of Birmingham and London.

There was no reward for good works, just a ganger's boot in their arse swung by an Irish leg. They followed casual work, living from day to day. They came home at Christmas and disturbed the nest, dour men with set faces who left stubble in the sink and spoke as strangers. They saved the street face for the local pub. They stood four square, coxcomb faces reddened by strong drink, flecked with razor glaze, starched white shirts, keeping the best side out, speaking in fractured accents that stuttered round the Isle of Man before sinking in the Irish Sea. They struggled with the local drawl, alien now, accent tempered by a Liverpool slide, secretly proud of the leavening, dazzling the natives. Mighty. Never better. Plenty of work and good digs. The single men talked romance, glittering ballrooms and plenty of women and secret promises under a full moon. They cobbled together the money for the Christmas job and flooded the village with tales of 'Merrie England', not drunk just merry. Not much older than me and wise in the ways of plenty.

They thronged the pubs after nightfall and cashed the cheque, sought word of permanent jobs and slipped into the cycle of the soft pint and the hard road. A crash at the top of the house with other men on the piss, the big sub and the foreman's fist and the alcohol in place of a lonely room, unemployed for months and a vast thirst, steeping the home sickness in vineyard slops. It was hard to rise from Mrs Greenfield or escape from some rag and louse and go to work. Survival was ambition in aspic, everything would be better tomorrow and you create your own peace. Many wanted to call Ireland but there was nobody there, aliens in two countries now. They moved from building site to building site but they never moved on from the bed sits of north London or Birmingham. In the end, a drift to the margins with a banging, clanging, raging in the brain tuned to loss of home, loss of country, loss of family and loss of self.

There were nine in my father's family and ten of the Grants so I know about emigration. The O'Hanlons stayed in Ireland: all the uncles and aunts I have mentioned already plus Jem and Sadie in the family business and Joe and Jack who had medical practices in the area. The Grants had a different story. Uncle Vincent and Aunt Josephine died before we returned to Mullaghbawn and emigration took most of the rest. I saw very little of Gerry, Harry, Joe, or Kevin when I was growing up, or my Aunt Bernadette who married Tommy Gracey and went to Australia; gone before I knew them. My Uncle Louis and my mother were the only Grant children left in Ireland after my Aunt Sheila died. I still miss them all.

The touching of the forelock returned to my mind when I joined the civil rights movement and had my first encounter with the political system. Unionist politicians displayed an implacable will. They were obsessed with power and were a presence in most parishes in the North. They were full of arrogance and pride, just like the Catholic clergy in the rural parishes. I never checked if Unionist politicians only visited the big houses on their patch but it made sense. Clergymen spent their lives talking down to people during the worst days of discrimination, talking about the dead Christ instead of the risen Christ. The church assured the people that it was all in our best interests but I wonder. There was still the GAA, classless and concerned, sometimes brutish but life is like that, interested in people and making it better, trying to find potential and developing it, building the confidence of kids as they prepared to face the world. Did the church in the small parishes do this? Did they look for potential or did they prepare us to be super Catholics in a Protestant state?

I had a gift for football. My Uncle Joe played for Ulster Colleges when he attended Saint Patrick's College in Armagh and the gift passed. Joe went to England when he left college and rarely returned to the village. I had a spurt of growth that left me strongly built and a member of the Armagh minor team for two years. In time I realised that all games are simple: players make them hard. Music was a different matter. I was comfortable with a ball in my hand but I made strange with a guitar. The McAllister boys from Crossmaglen were different. Peter and Martin were comfortable with guitars and the music flowed effortlessly. They did their level best to teach me. I tried hard but my fingers were heavy and clumsy on the strings and the sound was strained and stilted. There was precious little music in me but I learned to pass myself.

Things got no better at school. The poor reports kept coming and my mother was mortified and I refused to search for improvement. Better not to try than face the reality of failure: always have an excuse position. My mother talked to me, showed me the letters from the dean of the college threatening drastic action but it was lost on me. I promised change and a new attitude but I was lying. Frank Feely, the only teacher I had any time for, described my approach once within earshot, and he was right. Do nothing for the whole year and try and pass the exams in the last three weeks. Anything to avoid the hint of stupidity. Pass is a relative term. The clang when I scraped through some exams could be heard in Mullaghbawn. It seemed like victory to a teenager as lazy as bog water.

I made the various teams in Saint Colman's College and it took a huge effort. Team football was for boarders and there was little encouragement for day boys. The training was after school in the meadow below the college. Fifty minutes of training and practice and a scatter up the stairs to the trough near the quadrangle to wash the mucky bits, a wipe with a sweaty jersey and into the school clothes. Down the avenue at the double to make the Crossmaglen bus, darkness falling and twelve hundred yards to go, gasping for breath and sweating on the run down the Mall, no relief until I was safe on board. The alternative was a two hour wait if you missed the connection. I played for the school teams and we missed out on a Hogan Cup in my last year in the school. Making the bus was the only connection I made in those years. Playing for the team was a mighty effort compared to homework but I never went there. Football and music were enough and I was happy at my work.

I was a complete mess when I left Colman's. I had no slant on life that made me an anarchist or turned me into a fan of Attila the Hun. I just hated formality and convention. Contact with any establishment caused a type of chemical reaction in me. I was intent on destroying myself and I made a good start. I did not have a poor self image or difficulty with relationships and I was not loud in debate. The secret was in me and unknown to me and I was not on my own. A lot of kids were searching in an aimless sort of way, looking for reasons for their lives. The search for purpose was a slow burn. School and the church did not do it for me and I needed a lead. It was not a matter of limping for life. It was more a matter of how fast was I limping? I was off the pace but not out of sight. There was a tradition of education in the O'Hanlon family that seemed to end with me. Three of my uncles on the O'Hanlon side were doctors but there was a small ray of hope. Michael did not finish medicine until the War of Independence and the Civil War were over and Joe and Jack tried other avenues before they qualified. Joe was a Garda on the beat in Dublin when he commenced study and Jack was in the Irish Army. There was a tradition of education on the Grant side as well. My only hope was a late development like Joe and Jack but I took no comfort there.

Truth to tell, Saint Colman's worked for the majority of pupils and that is a matter of record. The majority of the boys accepted the Colman's system. They worked hard and got the grades and joined the professions open to Catholics in the North at the time or went to regions or countries, after qualification, that believed in merit. I was glad that nobody applied the merit test to me. I never bought into the education system and that was a personal choice. I suppose it was an attack on my belief system if I had a belief system at that age. The chance of an education was presented to me and I refused it. There were certain aspects at Colman's that never warmed me. The place was suffocating: too many priests, too many sung Masses in the college chapel, too many visits from the various religious institutions seeking vocations. Colman's had a rigid regime that spilled over into brutality and worse at times but that was the way it was. I always considered it a hostile environment and I was a day boy: God knows how the boarders felt. The school musicals were always Gilbert and Sullivan and I found the elocution lessons, available for the senior students on a bought-in basis, bizarre, a pathetic attempt to ape the accent of the ruling elite in Belfast who happened to be hard-line Unionist. I left the college as a harmless individual, a rebel without a clue. It was all about control, I know that now but it never occurred to me in the time I was a failure at St Colman's.

My mother told me that the sun always danced on Easter morn in joyous memory of the Resurrection. I opened my eyes when the day came and watched the celebration: giddy sun rays scudding across the wall of the bedroom and a dawn chorus in the huddle of trees, piping them to the dance. I climbed the sacred mountain in the teenage years along with the kids from the village after the parade to the Republican plot was over. Our ancestors climbed the mountain with us towards the cradle of Irish mythology. We lit the gorse when we reached the summit in memory of the Paschal fire lit by Saint Patrick above the Boyne valley, seen on the hill of Tara where the High King lived. Swards of Leinster before us and a sight of Tara on a clear day, Ulster all around us and the silver sheen of Dundalk

Bay at our feet. No other mountain in Ireland like it, source of our legends and our beginnings. The last time Gullion erupted, the Mourne mountains were formed. We stopped at the lake on the summit and planned our sport for the day.

The wind blows cold on a mountain top when Easter is early so we ran about in the thick gorse where Setanta played as a young boy until we were flushed and gasping for breath. Hard-boiled eggs and minerals for lunch and a trip to the Caille Beara's cave. Setanta became Cuchulain on Slieve Gullion and Deirdre of the Sorrows grew up on the mountain in the cave of the druidess, Levarchan. Look away to Armaghbrague and remember the Red Branch cycle of tales or search for the children of Lir at Tullyvallen where Aoife changed her daughters into swans. We learned as we played where the legends lived and it never left us. We are the myths and the mountain and we always will be.

Landlords came to our valley in Plantation times. Local squires like Jackson got a mixed press: over-praised in the 'Boys of Mullaghbawn' because indolence is not akin to honour or reason but he was sainted compared to Johnston the Tory hunter. They planted the valley and they took profit from the linen industry and the sweat of the people. There is a special place on the road to Forkhill, best seen in mist, a stretch of giddy green upland with a hunting lodge on top, caught against the volcanic ring, built by Squire Jackson when he had a grip on the land. It is a Disney moment, a broad panning camera shot at the start of a fairy tale or a ripping yarn about rapparees and redcoats.

Reality is different. John Mason, the Collector, paints a broad picture in the Revenue Returns of 1796. There were 8,423 Catholics in the parish, nearly all Irish speaking, 406 members of the established church and 104 Dissenters. There were 38 houses in Forkhill, all thatched save two and 10 dwellings in Mullaghbawn, all thatched. Bernard Smith and Alexander Murdock had a licence to sell spirits in Forkhill at the time. Some of the Dissenters, who had been planted from County Antrim on a part of the Jackson estate, spoke Gaelic. Bernard O'Hanlon, Brown Seal Master, in 1799 states that 2,543 persons were wholly engaged in the linen industry in the district and 2,970 were part time. Every farmer was employed in the linen trade on holdings from two to twenty acres. I tumbled about in the last showes in the local scutch mill when I was growing up, all that was left of the linen trade, decommissioned in the late Fifties.

Gaelic poets lived and worked within the ring of Gullion when Irish was spoken by the people. *Aisling* poems in the main with Ireland in the form of a woman, young and beautiful or old and haggard, omens and visions for the fertile mind. *Ag Úirchill an Chreagáin* is a poem of simple innocence, an alternative *aisling* that is superior to the polished vision songs of later years. The Stuart Pretender is not mentioned or the hope of foreign help to free Ireland but it is an *aisling* at the deep core. MacCuhmaigh lamented the flight of the O'Neills in many poems and the destruction of Glassdrummond Castle. He lies in Creggan graveyard, an example of poetic justice. MacCuarta invoked older literary traditions in north Leinster and south Ulster. He worked off the vast reservoir of culture and folk lore

END OF TERM REPORT

and celebrated it through his literary skills. Ó Durnin was steeped in the same rock pool, his authorship of Mná na hÉireann is little known and it is a personal favourite. It was put to music by Sean Ó'Ríada and recorded by Kate Bush in Irish. Her mother came from Waterford and the performance is inspirational. Donal Lunny produced and he was in top form. Tradition is ever changing, ever adapting and the poets knew it. Tradition never sleeps and it never dies.

The legends live here in South Armagh. Moss gathers on the walls of Jackson's hunting lodge that holds the dark lady, hares turn into supple women, fairies leave glass slippers in the path of the imagination and shades swirl in the gathering darkness near the fairy tree in the bog. I fingered yellow pictures in wizened frames in my youth and the stone skeletons at the end of secret *loanins* spoke to me. I touched walls that shielded the dead generations from the north wind and fingered the rough surface for the pattern of their existence. Their heat was removed from me but their life beat lingered in ancient ashes and strange carvings on a half door. The enchanted land never forgets. She waits for the footfall of the people who left her, the men and women who parted her hair in ancient times. I lay amongst the crumbled walls and listened for their voices. The cold stars glowered through the tattered roof and I imagined a hissing hearth and the warm gush of voices when the thatch was sound, song and laughter and a few verses from the bard at the heel of the evening.

Art MacBionaid came later, no less celebrated than the other poets. He preserved the traditions in his writing and it was sorely needed. His vision of Ireland as a weak, crazy old woman in *Triamhain na hEirinne* is not misplaced. The language was in decline in the area. Gaelic Ireland was in retreat and MacBionaid kept a lonely vigil. He kept the literary traditions of south-east Ulster in a safe place until help arrived. There is a great need of poets and the craft of poetry. Their poems and songs and balladry danced before us on the road to Gullion on a bright Easter morning and they lit the way home in the semi-darkness. The poets were safe on Gullion because they were of the spirit breed. MacCumhaidh, MacCuarta and Ó Dornin were of their time. They sang of the hedgerow and the hill and the sacred mountain and they kept the spirit alive. The oral tradition was freedom and poetry was the password, the bread of liberty and wild dreams. Sometimes dreams happen and sometimes they turn into nightmares and we were not to know.

I made a speech at the Republican plot in Mullaghbawn graveyard in 1962. I followed the accordion band down the road from the parochial hall on Easter Sunday and spoke after mass when the time was right. It was probably poor stuff but it was what it was. It was not the last time I spoke on Easter Sunday in Mullaghbawn but the experience that day changed me. A question was growing in my mind as I wandered home after the meeting. What was the purpose of the ceremony? Certainly it was an act of remembrance, an opportunity for the local community to celebrate the lives and deaths of local men and women who joined the struggle for freedom. It was a day to stress the goal of liberty and duty but was it a celebration? People had reason to celebrate in Tullamore and Tralee but Maghera and Mullaghbawn were a different story. The IRA border campaign came to a close that year, at the high water mark of Unionist discrimination, because of a lack of public support. The Unionists were busy celebrating the fiftieth anniversary of the signing of the Covenant against Home Rule in 1912. The Catholic population took the view that armed rebellion had failed in the past and it had failed again. They were trapped in a society where neither political nor extra-political means could change their condition from subjects into citizens.

The North was missionary work in the southern mind. They lost us like they lost the emigrants through a mixture of apathy and guilt. There was suffering up there but there was suffering nearer home as well. The Treaty debates rarely mentioned the North and the Civil War was fought over the Oath not the evil that Partition was about to impose. The period after the Civil War was a struggle for survival so southern politicians concentrated on nation building and forgot about the severed part. The North appeared at election time to boost a flagging campaign and flagging was the key word. We got a dose of long distance republicanism and they got elected. I was never a fan of the white charger syndrome that emerged at polling time, fiery speeches and an image of a Taoiseach at the border with a sword in his hand, promising to free us from our shackles, speaking of a people united and free. It was a classic come-on. Southern politicians did it because it was therapeutic for them, not for us. Maybe it was not a white charger either. King Billy had a monopoly on that form of transport on northern gable walls and bragging rights in that area. The North was an interest free zone where Dublin was concerned. It disappeared off the map after the election, out of sight and out of favour. The southern government watched from afar, powerless to help, unable to stand still. The harsh truth was that partition worked for everybody except northern Nationalists. Southern Nationalists had the freedom to choose and so had the Unionists. This is not a question of fault. People deal with the situation as they find it.

Chapter Three

Students at Queen's University needed special skills. There was a need to know the safe drinking places or you ended up with your head in your hands. Belfast was a sectarian city and I did not need the hassle so I went off to UCD. It was the obvious choice, only down the road and the makings of a good Gaelic football team. We lived in the village of Fairview on the Malahide Road instead of the Village in Belfast, a commune of like-minded people next to the White House bar and we settled for a liberal education. I walked past the stands on enrolment day, including the Law Stand, and put my name down for Commerce. I am not saying that I would have attended law lectures but it was an outside chance and I blew it. The university was stuck in a time warp. There was a West Brit feel to the place and the GAA club struggled for space on the notice boards. The rugby set had overall control of the main hall, the imperial claw was still raking the back of the local population and poverty and the church were everywhere. It was hard to tell who was Taoiseach. Sean Lemass was in power with the help of Archbishop John Charles McQuaid.

College was a litmus test of society at the time and we refused to turn blue so we registered for degree courses, collected our scholarships and beat it back to the Malahide Road. Academic pursuits had a part to play in the development of the whole man but there were other forms of intelligence. The mission statement lasted a month. I dumped it in a litter bin one night with a greasy chip wrapping on the way from the pub to the flat. The motto on our coat of arms was basement flat with White House rampant. We toured north Dublin and flatland and heard the sound that was coming from the tap rooms and we were on first name terms with the barmen while the money lasted. Our university scholarships were a lot of money per term by Dublin standards and we pissed the bulk of it away: the rest we squandered on food and chasing women. We were so far away from the university, we might as well have been at Queen's.

Sedition was all around me. All was not well at Radio Luxembourg. Whispers of foul deeds and half truths and the end of innocence, rumours about live disc jockey presentations by a team of resident announcers on the station, partly recorded at their UK studios at 38 Hertford Street in London W1. It was a 'quare gunk' as they say in the North. I had imagined presenters sitting in the Grand Duchy or performing live on a landline to Luxembourg. It became a hot debate on the way to dances and it was never the same after that. I switched loyalty to a pirate radio station when nobody was looking. I was a Radio Caroline man at university without a radio and I loved the Magic Roundabout like the rest of the students. You need to show signs of development when you reach the third level.

Paddy Walsh from Mayo convinced me that I should commit to one college institution so I lined out for the Junior and Intermediate teams on a regular basis in first year. I played for the Armagh county team before I played for UCD seniors. The remedy came when we played Donegal in a National League match in Armagh that autumn and Paul Kelly and Bernard Brady were in action for the other side. A few days later, I found my name on the first team when I checked the GAA notice board in Earlsfort Terrace. The Sigerson Cup was imminent, the inter-university football competition, the holy grail for college and I was told to turn up for training. Autumn is a bonny time, mist like yellow floss in the college quadrangle, dim figures in pools of light, portcullis windows and warm fires and a hint of frost in the air. Sigerson training in the small open space behind Earlsfort Terrace and away to the student pubs after the slog for a couple of pints, long-scarved, long-winded and desperate for craic. Most of my degree course lectures were given in Earlsfort Terrace but I rarely went there. Too much like hard work for my liking.

I still played with my home club when I was home. The Bawn were cruel to watch before we started to win. We togged out behind a ditch, dumping our clothes under a whin bush and played hard in the bitter rain that streamed off the face of Gullion. I remembered the pain of losing and hoarded it like a miser because I wanted to remember the feeling. We won the Armagh Senior County Championship in 1964, a big achievement for a small village with a limited pool of players. I needed a pain-killing injection on the morning of the match to get me through. Uncle Jack looked up when he finished injecting my ankle and told me. 'It will not fix you but it will smarten you.' I failed to get the point then but I get it later. We won comfortably on the day against the Wolfe Tones from the Lurgan area. We stood around the bonfire that night and felt the rush and the quiet pride of the local people. The first time that Mullaghbawn were county champions and it was the end of ambition. We were immortal in several townlands, the greatest fame of all.

I played Sigerson Cup for the next two years under the sceptical eye of Eugene Magee. He never played much himself and he was not given to praise but players always knew that he was on their side, a great trait in a manager. We won the Dublin Senior championship, beating Round Towers in the final on a summer night in Croke Park, the year after the Bawn won the county championship in Armagh. My recollection is that the Sixty-Four championship finished in Sixty-Five in Dublin so I won two championship medals the same year. Football is a great release, a journey around yourself, a visit to sinew and spirit, a call on talent, character and work ethic. It is also about freedom and expression. I remember a moment in the Dublin final, a ball in the summer sky above the Hogan Stand, tumbling slowly towards the UCD square. Players running beside me, a spring upwards to the dropping leather and a feeling of pure joy as my feet left the ground that I remember to this day. The end of my football career was nigh. I felt the knee go in a county march and I never recovered. Knee ligament trouble was a major problem in those years. If it did not show up on an X-ray there was nothing wrong with you. Joe McNulty said, not unfairly, that if I wanted the injury to heal it would have happened. Maybe he was right. Then again, I was badly wounded and there was no quick fix. Even today, the recovery period is a year.

I took the guitar with me when I left Mullaghbawn and convinced myself it was the life for me as soon as I hit Dublin. It was a form of escapism or a fantasy and I was good at these things. The lifestyle combined all my excesses, lotus eating every night of the week with my brother Gerard, Paul McConville and Frank Moore, music, beer and women. It was the time of the folk boom in the city, basement clubs crammed with bearded fellows smoking pipes and playing the down home intellectual for the pretty girl at their side, drinking in the old culture amid the candle wax and wonky microphones, quiet applause at the end of a saga of love and loss, Sweeney's Men and the Emmet Folk and the Spicelands. I made noises like a musician but it did not last long. I appeared at a student concert in the Aula Max and went on stage for a couple of numbers. I performed all right. No bum chords and I was always a decent singer and nobody sent for the good music police. I tucked the guitar away and settled down near the stage. Some group provided a wedge before Paul Brady and Donal Lunny. They did not come on after me and I am glad, the contrast would have been embarrassing. My music ambitions ended with the first chord they played but there was an upside. I know good musicians when I hear them and I looked around for a career change.

I finally made a connection. It was a scholarship free year and drink needed to be bought. I was a night telephonist in the main exchange in Exchequer Street, crowded into a room with strange looking geeks who all wanted to be somewhere else. The exchange felt like the departure lounge in Star Wars. There was a stirring of personal awareness in the place of the dislocated, and it disturbed me. I was amongst my own, 24-carat gold dropouts with time on their hands in search of a reason to believe. Telephony was legitimate employment if I was interested in the workings of the machine or in running the Department of Post and Telegraphs but I was just doing the time. It was a comfort, not a joy. Walking home at three in the morning to a student flat was the real deal and the price of a drink in my pocket. It was a kind of life and I found it all quite hysterical.

A special memory were the Dubliners and the midnight concerts in the Grafton cinema after the pubs closed, less comely maidens and dancing at crossroads, more dark urban myth and local bother. It was a sort of Beggars Opera, a mixture of street theatre indoors and vibrant political forum. The atmosphere was Hill Sixteen on the big match day, light years away from rock and roll and I was entranced in it. Nothing po-faced here. The audience kept up a constant banter with Ronnie Drew between numbers. The fact that it was fuelled by drink was a bonus and I learned a rake of Dublin street songs. Raucous taverns in Dublin village, a blast of booze and better amplification and a torrent of political debate: Thomas Davis, the Young Irelanders, the birth of the Irish state and the wee North.

I discovered Thomas Davis the year that electricity came to our village and it had the same effect. The first touch was a wrinkled old volume in the family home with a name I have long forgotten but I have never forgotten Davis. He did not impress in the early years, a stutter of a boy and an obscure youth who went to Trinity College as a first resort. The student was a book in breeches in the college grounds, a thick-set young man in a fear-naught coat shambling about the cobbles in search of a lecture, useless at handball or hurling or the drinking art. There was nothing of the coxcomb about Davis and the plain people took to him. He walked for hours in the streets of Dublin, watching the mill of activity, taking occasional notes, stopping for music in the local alehouses. He vanished across the Irish Sea when he finished Trinity, raw bacon when he left and London cured when he returned. Changed by his travels, an original voice uttering opinions with fervour and conviction. He founded the *Nation* with Gavan Duffy and John Blake Dillon when he went to practise at the Irish Bar.

The aims and objectives of the *Nation* were set out in bold type in the first edition. To create and to foster public opinion in Ireland. To make it racy of the soil. Davis opened with an editorial that contained the following sentence. 'There are, in truth, only two parties in Ireland: those who suffer from her national degradation and those who profit by it.' I sat up and paid attention. James Clarence Mangan dedicated the voice of the *Nation*.

> We announce a New Era - be this our first news
> When the serf-grinding landlords shall shake in their shoes,
> When the ark of a bloodless and mighty Reform
> Shall emerge from the flood of the popular storm.

A friend told Davis that the publishing venture was impossible. Davis told him never to use that foolish word again.

The *Nation* broadsheet was a cause wrapped around his personality that impacted at the ground level with the native Irish. He knew the elements of identity and he wrote about them; about Irish music and poetry, separation and self reliance, nationalism and the Wild Geese and the slavery of colonisation, the curse of landlordism and the evil of bought men. It was not blood that made you Irish but willingness to be part of the Irish nation. He loved justice and valour, generous life and proud death and recalled the memory of great men. The words of Davis - according to the *Nation* - were sudden flashes in the serious mind, like electric current smiting a dusty coil of wire. Talk about identity if you know who you are and work miracles when you can. Poetry was a focal point of his writing because he believed in a ballad tradition that kindled hope and softened the edges of despair. 'A Nation Once Again' and 'The Sack of Baltimore', 'The West's Awake' and 'Bodenstown Churchyard' or 'Tone's Grave' as he called it. Davis raised the native tongue up and placed it before the nation like a Phoenix when the Liberator was making them stale. Davis had no rivals, only disciples and he shone through the power of his mind. It was a national tragedy when he died young.

The end of football at twenty-two left me with more time on my hands so I became a strolling player. Third floor apartments in Victorian piles and a crush of people, students and useful members of society and Mursheen Durkan fought with Mick Jagger in the drunken haze. The faces at the parties were changing. My old mates were qualified and gone back to the sticks and I was a party relic in a corner of a room. The party scene was changing and it was a harder sell. Always be on top of the music, always be cool, always be aware of the new trends. The boys were gone, including my brother. No cigar and no degrees but they got a liberal education and scattered to the four winds in search of something. Michael Mooney was the first to leave. He got a job in Brooks Thomas in the glazing department and I watched him go with a rising sense of panic. I met Jimmy Snee walking up Leeson Street in 1967, about three months before the final exams. He was a long time friend who had taken time out for other things and he salvaged me. He was a good student and had copious lecture notes for the final year. His parents were back in Galway and he needed company so he invited me to stay with him in Leopardstown Avenue and study for the final exams. It was an act of great generosity to take me into his home and I never forgot it. I left UCD with a pass Degree in Commerce after five years. It was better than no degree at all. I was tired of the student life so I left Dublin and went home to Mullaghbawn.

I got a job at Abbey CBS in Newry as a relief teacher, and took classes for maths and English. The school was a complete revelation to me. There was a great feel in the corridors, a relaxed relationship between teachers and pupils that I never experienced in Saint Colman's College. There was no fear factor in the Abbey and no repression. The teachers were seeking to advance potential not crush it. I remember individual teachers in St Colman's with affection but I pass on the rest. Maybe it was the time away and maybe St Colman's had moved on also. There were war stories about the past in the Abbey and I do not doubt them but I came at a better time and I was happy to be there. The relief job extended through Christmas but events were on the move outside the school window.

Sixty-Eight was moving year. The world was in motion, not just the Hippies in San Francisco. The streets were full of the post-war generation, celebrating an end of food coupons and austerity and the Beatles and Dylan were the soundtrack of our lives. 'I Can't Get No Satisfaction' sang the Stones and it chimed with the times. There was a ripple of unrest across Europe and America was immersed in the Vietnam war. A flood of change in Czechoslovakia, student uprisings in western Europe and North America and a cultural revolution in China. It was the year Martin Luther King was assassinated and a civil rights movement took hold in Northern Ireland. The world was in a post-war state of mind. Politics was shedding a skin, trying to rid itself of mistakes made at the Potsdam conference. The United States and the Soviet Union were in competition and everybody took sides, two forms of imperialism intent on a play off. War by proxy was the way forward and millions of civilians died in the cause of capitalism and communism, far away from America and Russia. There is an African saying: when elephants fight the grass gets trampled. The policy was not peace, just another location in the world where ideas clashed with deadly effect.

The Prague Spring began in the middle of winter. Alexander Dubcek replaced Novotny as Communist Party chief on 5 January 1968. He introduced a liberal programme of reform and annoyed his imperial masters who invaded Czechoslovakia on 20 August 1968. It was the week of the Democratic convention in Chicago. Anti-Vietnam war protestors invaded the city and tensions were high. They arrived on the day that Russian tanks moved against Dubcek. Mayor Daly ordered out the riot police. They used crushing force, beating protestors, journalists and onlookers without discrimination and they did it in the full glare of the television cameras.

Marchers convened in Derry on 5 October 1968 in support of one man one house, one man one job, one man one vote and an end to gerrymandering and the Special powers Act, freedom of speech and freedom of assembly. Television was the most lethal weapon of the age. A Telefis Eireann cameraman Gay O'Brien pointed a lens down Duke Street in Derry when the RUC were baton-charging marchers and he changed our world forever. It was simpler in earlier centuries, no television crews with a camera in your face when you pulled the trigger in an Irish town or on a line of enraged locals against a mosque wall or in a remote gulag, assisting in the drive to make the world safe for imperialism. The civil rights marches in the North were on television and the message was everywhere. Demonstrate, protest, organise: you know it makes sense. Events in Derry had a seismic impact on politics in the North and the local activists began to believe. The questions were asked and Unionism had no answers. One other notable event lives in my memory of 1968. Olympic year in Mexico. A guy called Bob Beamon almost jumped out of the long jump pit in winning gold. The jump was so long that the official measuring device available was not able to record the distance. It seemed to represent the vaulting ambition of the world-wide revolution and, on the local level, the civil rights movement in the North.

It was over a year since the movement had taken to the streets and dramatic things had happened. Splits in the Unionist hegemony, leading figures in the local parliament retrieving hoary old IRA effigies from the spare room and dusting them down, interest at Westminster in the civil rights movement and constant pressure on the British Government to break the convention in the House of Commons and permit debate on Northern Ireland affairs. I joined the Peoples Democracy, a Queens University based organisation, when they arrived in Newry in November 1968. It was not an ideological thing. They were the first pro-civil rights organisation to visit us. Tom Keane, a friend from South Armagh was elected chairman of the local Civil Rights Association at a public meeting in the Town Hall and I was elected Press Officer. Half the staff room at the Abbey was involved in the Civil Rights movement, some were members of existing political groupings and the rest were raw amateurs. I place myself with the latter group and I needed to learn fast so I embarked on a crash course in the history of Unionism to discover the cause of all the fuss.

Carson resigned from the Unionist leadership in February 1921, after the Government of Ireland Act was passed. He had some advice for his successor.

> From the outset, let us see that the Catholic minority have nothing to fear from the Protestant majority. Let us take care to win all that is best among those who have been opposed to us in the past. While maintaining intact our own religion let us give the same rights to the religion of our neighbours.

> I Colvin *Life of Lord Carson* Vol. 3 p.400

A Council of Ireland was envisaged by the Government of Ireland Act to encompass representatives of both parliaments on the island and Carson identified with it. The Unionist population did not share his view and neither did Sir James Craig, the new Prime Minister of Northern Ireland. Craig worked to a simple formula. An individual was a Unionist or a subversive, ergo all Catholics were disloyal and would be treated accordingly. The Unionists acted with great urgency. Their altered electoral boundaries meant that Unionism controlled all but two of the local government councils within two years of the imposition of Partition. The failure of the Boundary Commission in 1925 was a bitter experience for the minority and alerted them to the permanence of the border.

In relation to the employment of Catholics:

> Sir Edward Archdale Minister of Agriculture from 1921 to 1933, apologised to a Unionist meeting for the fact that there were four Catholics on his staff of 109. He added that three were employed before 1921.

> *Northern Whig* 2 April 1925

The views of Archdale were a rallying call for the exclusion of the minority from positions of influence in the affairs of the state. His words brought little comfort to my father. When the Civil War ended, he gritted his teeth and lifted his crutches and faced the long night of Unionist discrimination. There was no relief for his generation, no jobs, no liberty and no hope. There was always a boat at the quay bound for the New World or Britain, or internment if you were angry enough to complain in public about the Unionist Party.

Unionists challenged the authority of Westminster in the affairs of the North of Ireland.

They drafted a Local Government Act (Northern Ireland) proposing the abolition of Proportional Representation in local government elections in the region and submitted it to the imperial parliament. The Westminster government advised the king to withhold Royal Assent. The advice of the Government was not taken and Royal Assent was granted. The major democratic tool in a divided society was withdrawn from service. Proportional Representation in Northern Ireland parliamentary elections was abolished in 1929 and absolute power was in the hands of the Unionist Party who replaced the possibility of a representative parliament with the veneer of democracy. Unionist candidates in successive parliamentary elections were returned unopposed in forty to seventy per cent of the seats. There was a creeping hubris that marched side by side with the dream of a Protestant parliament for a Protestant people, hence the following newspaper report.

> Sir James Davidson, a Unionist Senator and Orange Grand Master of Belfast asked when will the Protestant employers of Northern Ireland recognise their duty to their Protestant brothers and sisters and employ them to the exclusion of Roman Catholics.

Northern Whig 28 August 1933

The new system of majority rule was a licence to discriminate against a significant section of the population. Over a period of time, the local parliament became sovereign in all but name. Stormont legislated at will and a convention arose at Westminster that the sovereign parliament did not discuss the internal affairs of Northern Ireland. The northern parliament was never meant to be sovereign but that became a reality and Northern Ireland experienced fifty years of one party sectarian government. Unionism was about order and power, not about peace and good government. The arrogance of power reached its high water mark in 1962 when the Unionist Government declared a special public holiday called Jubilee Day at the high water mark of Unionist discrimination. The Orange Institutions and the Ulster Unionist Council organised a monster demonstration to celebrate the Jubilee of the signing of the Covenant in 1912, a public holiday to glorify Unionist hegemony and bad faith. It was a studied insult to the minority population, a public holiday to mark to celebrate bondage, a memorable example of insensitivity and inhumanity.

Christmas 1968 was coming and Terence O'Neill made his 'Ulster at the Crossroads' speech. There was a march in the New Year from Belfast to Derry by the Peoples Democracy via Burntollet Bridge. We called a march for Newry as a result of the assaults on that march by Unionist extremists, including off-duty members of the B Specials. The Newry march was a shambles with the exception of the stewards, drawn from the local GAA clubs and highly dependable. Thousands turned up in Newry on the day and we let them down. There was no working PA system and we blew it tactically. The march route was blocked at the Savoy cinema by the riot squad but the bridge into the banned area around the town hall was wide open. We stopped the march at the police barrier and held a meeting. The tenders were placed beyond the police barriers and the hotheads walked into the trap. The labour exchange was occupied and some tenders were burned. The Unionist press had a field day and I felt that we had let down the Citizens Action group in Derry.

The Town Hall was packed to the rafters for the meeting that we called in the aftermath of the march. We outlined our failures in great detail and tendered our resignation en bloc as a committee. Nobody wanted to know. The blame was directed at the Unionists and the British and we were re-elected by acclamation in a new guise as the Newry Civil Rights Association. We resigned en bloc from Peoples Democracy after the meeting. University students have a unique view of politics but it gets lost in the gloom of a ghost town like Newry. Belfast rule by the student population was still Belfast rule and Newry preferred a local variety. Joining the Civil Rights Movement identified the area with the broader plan but we retained the necessary autonomy of action.

To run or not to run was the topic at lunchtime in the staff room every day. Debate was heated and the pros and cons were well aired. Should the civil rights movement remain aloof from a corrupt system or was there a need to engage? The discussion was complicated by abstentionism. It was almost a decade since the last IRA campaign ended but there was support for that organisation on the staff and in the streets of Northern Ireland. The substantial Sinn Féin influence in the local community did not support the aims and objectives of the Civil Rights Association. They looked upon the CRA marches as a recognition of the state, a campaign for internal reform and a betrayal of traditional republicanism. They were not engaged in any material way in the struggle for civil rights, although I recall prominent members of Sinn Féin today who supported the CRA in the late Sixties. There were also some people in attendance at marches who had the whiff of militancy about them but they made no significant impact and they drifted away in time. Folk memory helped them make their decision. They were convinced on past experience that the effort would fail and that was not an unreasonable attitude in the circumstances. The link with family tradition was broken when I joined the Civil Rights movement and it came at a personal cost. Many people in South Armagh took it badly that I forsook the old ways. They viewed it as a form of desertion but I toughed it out. I never had a sliver of doubt that my father supported my efforts in the CRA.

The bulk of the Civil Rights activists wanted to take the struggle into Parliament but there was opposition within the Civil Rights movement itself. A minority wanted the movement to remain outside Parliament and continue as a pressure group. The abstentionists were happy with the split in the movement and they were vocal on the point. Minority representatives had attended Stormont before and nothing had changed as a result. Why should the Civil Rights Movement be different? They could have said the same about IRA campaigns since the formation of the state. I was in favour of attendance, bringing the struggle on to the floor of the chamber at Stormont. The civil rights movement had a ground swell but it needed to change tack. Above all else they had given the minority population self respect and that has its own reward. More was needed. The marches had cracked the monolith but there was a problem. Marching was a tactic not a principle and the situation was changing by the day. Support on the streets throughout the North was still strong. There was a price to pay if we continued to march. The day would dawn at an assembly point when we would find a meeting where there used to be a march. An opportunity presented itself to effect change directly. There was a need to confront the government we were complaining about on a daily basis. If we did not run in the election, we were guilty of political cowardice.

A number of activists met in the public bar of the Boulevard Hotel over a quiet pint. It was an opportunity to canvass views on the subject of the election. A consensus emerged very quickly and some people left when the trend became clear. We were on the streets complaining about Stormont rule. It was time to challenge the source. Recognition of the parliament was not an issue at the meeting. The Unionists ignored us and we were damned if we were going to ignore them. It was time to take the struggle to the seat of power. I ended up as the Independent candidate in the election for compelling reasons. I was likely to be out of a job shortly and my uncle Jack was willing to put up the election deposit. The exact amount escapes me but it was substantial at the time. I sought a mandate from my constituents in my election manifesto, the right to join a new political party if it emerged in the aftermath of the election. Ivan Cooper and John Hume ran in Derry as Independents as well. I won the South Armagh seat by a margin of two thousand votes. Certain things were factors in the victory: the popularity of the Civil Rights movement and the family name, playing for the County Gaelic side gave me instant recognition amongst the young. It was a dramatic change in fortune. I went from an ancient student at UCD to the youngest member of the new Parliament. I was twenty-four years of age and a political novice. It worried me more then than it does at the moment.

The swearing-in ceremony was due at Stormont so I left early. I wanted to drive by the shipyard on the way to the Newtownards Road. Lunchtime at Titanic quarters, workers coming through the main gate of Harland & Wolff and rushing down the cramped streets with outside toilets like the Falls Road. An industry in decline and the great crane called Goliath newly arrived, straddling the stocks and the city. Different in the old days. Teams of draught horses hauled the clean metal from the foundry to the building dock; sparks and white heat as the propellers for the Titanic were made. They laid the keel on the slipway and they built from the base. They hammered in time with their passion, Protestant men in a Protestant shipyard and the words of Carson aflame in their minds, preparing to sign the solemn Covenant to defeat, by all means necessary, the conspiracy to set up a Home Rule parliament in Ireland. Sweating men in the firelight, shadows on the flame, tempered by the sparks and scrabbed by the firethorn. The riveters sat, way up on the high steel, dreaming of Fenian blood and Protestant victory. They hammered down the snub end in time with the political pulse, making thunder for a Protestant God. The shell of a vessel towering above the stocks was safe in the grasp of Goliath, midwife to the modern miracle that makes iron and steel float. It was time to go to Stormont. I started the motor when the crowd was gone and moved away from the great crane.

Things were quiet on the Newtownards Road, no band to greet me and the building playing hard to get. I never visited Stormont before my election to the House. Men with an evangelical zeal were in control of the House, constantly on the case of the anti-Christ in the form of minority members of the House, settling old scores like a day out at Scarva where the battle of the Boyne was replayed every year by the Orange Order. They kept holy the Boyne water and the Covenant men and the year of 1912. They hated the IRA but the *Clyde Valley*, the old ship that ran in the UVF's guns in 1914, was a glorious memory.

Stormont peered out of the trees as I approached and looked down at me when I reached the main entrance. Parliament buildings on a hill in East Belfast, far removed from the minority heartlands, a comfort for Orangemen when the location of parliament was changed to a Fenian free zone, sepulchre white and distant and in total command of the heights, remote from the fleeing vehicles on the main road and the local housing estates and resentful of intruders. It looked like a gig where the minority were barely tolerated. I drove slowly through the entrance and stopped at the security hut at the bottom of the hill. My mind was full of prejudice and it showed. I sneaked a look at the House of No as the security guard examined my papers. Carson on a plinth astride the wide avenue, monumenting over me, right arm raised in exhortation of the Protestant people who controlled Belfast city, a Dublin man in a red-brick town. He signed the Covenant against Home Rule with the fountain pen used at the trial of Oscar Wilde. He was gazing towards the shipyard where the *Titanic* was built without guilt. The *Titanic* was alright when it left the yard. The ship went down and the Orange Order corked to the surface and ruled the land with a rod of attrition. The English gave the Unionists a lethal toy called local power to play with and left for a while.

I put the car in gear and moved up the incline to have a closer look. A mock castle lurked in the woods, a Grimm reminder to the plain people when they walked in the grounds of fairyland. The figure of Britannia cast against the leaden skies on top of a wedding-cake building where the icing was in Protestant hands, a baby Versailles made of Italian marble and Mourne granite and built to last forever. The voice of James Craig chased me down the years.

> I have always said that I am an Orangeman first and a politician and a member of this Parliament afterwards...all I boast is that we have a Protestant Parliament and a Protestant State..

He was prime minister when he went on the record. There were Catholic riots in Belfast after Partition. Craig agreed with Michael Collins and Winston Churchill, when they met in 1922, that the Royal Ulster Constabulary would be reorganised to safeguard Catholics and he promised to increase Nationalist recruitment to give fairer representation in the force. He pledged that the Northern Ireland Government would make every effort to secure the return to work of Catholics expelled from Belfast shipyard. He was still working on his promises when he died in 1940.

A plump shower was falling as I locked the vehicle and hurried to the main entrance. No word of Ulster at a crossroads in Parliament buildings, no sign of a tricolour about the place and a monastic silence - hardly the right word - and the soft-shoe shuffle of feet. Down the stone steps past the members' lobby, cubby-holes jammed with Order Papers and letters and I looked for my name. Into the central hallway with the ornate ceiling, gold chandelier with a German eagle rampant, a present from the Kaiser to George V when the Somme was a tranquil river. The table on which the Act of Union was signed was somewhere in the building but it was not of major moment. Unionism had a more intimate relationship with the Crown now. Travertine marble columns on the way to the Senate chamber, gold-tooled dispatch boxes and comfortable benches and inlaid arabesques in the ceiling, lauding the great industries that funded discrimination. Past the Library and the Vote office, past an early portrait of Queen and consort and a sombre study of George IV and his wife. A warren of corridors and roomy lobbies, ornate stairwells and a chamber where the Commons met, ciphers with closed faces, the Ancient Order of the Sliced Pan. There was a hiatus between the dogma of freedom, religion and laws and practice. Northern Ireland held the record for one-party rule in a democracy. No Catholic was elected to Parliament as a Unionist since the formation of the state.

The first day in a strange land, a squad of captains and other ranks mainly captains, a sniff of aristocrats and back benches crammed with frozen city burgers, some lawyers and doctors and a scattering of working class representatives. There was a whiff of the schoolyard about it, a lot of swagger and loud voices and looking from under the eyes, a hint of menace if you draw near, clusters in distant corners looking at the new boys and planning mischief, waiting for the school bell to ring and class to begin. I felt a lot happier. County Gaelic football was a great education. You meet very few dainty footballers at that level and a swollen lip is part of the price that you pay for wearing the colours. Let the games begin.

I climbed the stairs after I was sworn in, the archdukes of discrimination tracked me down the corridor, glowering at me from the panelled walls in the Strangers Dining Room so I glowered back. There was no reaction from the Unionist Prime Ministers on the wall who discriminated without reflection and retired without remorse. I doused the glower and turned away because the room was well named. I was a stranger still and my glower was required elsewhere. I wandered into the Members Dining Room. Bright carpets and fresh flowers everywhere, tables

END OF TERM REPORT

creaking with banded china and crested porcelain on crisp Irish linen, a chill factor for a border cub. The waiters ignored me as I cased the silverware so I opened the French windows and walked outside.

The wind bored through my coat and chewed at my kidneys. The sun smiled wanly through a haze of cloud, just above the horizon. I attempted a first for the Catholic minority and looked down on East Belfast. There was prosperity under the window. The road was well fed, the advance factories were serviced and the estates were quiet during working hours. There was little prospect of change in the heartland where personal freedom on the baptism issue and a livelier style of hymn singing were radical innovations. The structure of Protestant society shouted stability. Neat, compact, compartmentalised, centred on the kirk and the secret societies and the eternal Unionist Party, Goliath in full view from the terrace, vast against the skyline, running the boundaries of his domain, a daily reminder and a warning. Power lay in the shipyard, not in a room full of crested crockery and the building was designed with this in mind. Ulster might be at a crossroads but Unionism would follow the traditional route. I walked back into the dining room. Goliath was old Testament and I wanted to believe in the new.

Chapter Four

There was little time for reflection. The situation deteriorated quickly and reached boiling point in August 1969 after the Apprentice Boys Parade in Derry. Days of rioting in the Bogside and the trouble spread to other parts of the North, including districts with a history of sectarian conflict. I spent a day in the Falls area of Belfast with Paddy Kennedy a local Republican Labour Stormont MP. I watched Shorland armoured cars mounted with Browning heavy machine guns patrol the area. The RUC fired tracer rounds from these guns at Divis Towers, a Catholic housing complex in the mistaken belief that there were snipers in the walkways. Patrick Rooney, a nine-year-old boy asleep in the flats was shot dead. I went to Dublin with Paddy Kennedy and Paddy Devlin a Northern Ireland Labour Party Stormont MP from the Falls to ask the Taoiseach Jack Lynch for guns. Lynch did not meet us and we got no guns but the demand concentrated minds on the gravity of the situation. Bombay Street in the Clonard district of West Belfast and houses in adjacent streets were in flames next day and refugees poured over the border into the South of Ireland.

There is a major question that arises out of that visit to Dublin and I will address it. I supported the civil rights movement but I am not Mahatma Gandhi. I defended myself on a number of occasions from physical attacks by my political enemies and I would not make a cup of tea for a thief if I found him in my house. There is a very thin line between defence and attack, between participants and civilians, and it is too easy to cross it. Add a little more and you end up with the fraught history of the world.

There were big changes in direction and ideology by Sinn Féin and the IRA in the aftermath of the August violence. The leadership of both organisations was criticised by the rank and file for failing to defend Catholic areas from Loyalist violence in 1969. A Provisional Army Council was established in advance of the 1970 Ard Fheis when the factions went their separate ways. Those who did not leave with the Provisionals called themselves the Official republican movement in the hope of demonstrating some authenticity or authority. The Provisional Army Council commanded the loyalty of the national organisation within months, with the exception of parts of the Lower Falls and Markets district of Belfast, Derry, Newry, Dublin and Wicklow, areas where the Official movement held sway.

I use the term Provisional movement or Provisionals in this account, in the interests of accuracy, unless I am certain of the role of a component part. Besides, it was hard to politically define anybody after the Kingsmill massacre. The people who carried out the atrocity did not believe in fraternity. I abhor the use of the terms Republican and Nationalist in press statements. They have no meaning in a definitive sense and are used as a crude propaganda tool. I use the word minority instead, purely as a descriptive term.

The foundation of the SDLP was an inevitability. Parliament meant cooperation between different groups and individuals, especially when the total numbers were small. Debates needed to be covered and policy papers needed to be written. It was not possible to fulfil the limited tasks without a rota system. Gradually, a relationship developed between Ivan Cooper, John Hume and me and Paddy Devlin, Austin Currie and Gerry Fitt. Discussions on a new party began shortly after the election in 1969. Cooper, Hume and I came from the civil rights movement and ran as Independents. Gerry Fitt was Westminster MP for West Belfast as well as a Stormont MP and leader of the Republican Labour Party. Currie was elected from East Tyrone as a member of the Nationalist Party in 1964. Paddy Devlin was chairman of the Northern Ireland Labour Party in 1968. We had informal talks with the four other Nationalist Party members who were serving in Stormont but nothing emerged from the discussions. My great regret was that talks with Paddy Kennedy came to nothing. He was a talent, a passionate intelligent man who had a real contribution to make.

The first real meeting about the formation of the new party took place in the Knocknamoe Castle Hotel outside Omagh. We searched for common ground and agreed on tactics in Parliament. We continued to meet in the Members Bar and dining room at Stormont. Edward Heath had come to power at the head of a Conservative government in June 1970 and the Labour party in Britain wanted an alignment with a grouping in Northern Ireland. There was some discussion about the name and there was some ribaldry in the press and amongst our enemies about the final choice. The party was accurately named. In those days the Labour party in Britain sang the *Internationale* at the end of their party conference, called each other 'Comrade' and wore red ties. That did not make them a socialist party. They were mainly social democratic with the Tribune group tagged on at the end.

The Conservative Party stretched from the 'hang them and flog them' brigade to one nation Toryism. It was the same situation in Ireland. Fianna Fáil were vaguely centrist with a slightly constitutional right wing that occasionally howled at the moon. Fine Gael stretched from the old Blueshirt tradition to the just society and Irish Labour were mainly social democrats. We were the Social Democratic and Labour Party because we were mostly social democratic in outlook but there was room for people of a socialist disposition. We gathered in Donegal and we sealed the deal in the Ostan Gweedore on a balmy night in August 1970.

Our timing could have been better but must is a great master. Structure was lacking in minority politics in contrast to the Unionist Party which was a way of life amongst the Protestant population. The Nationalist Party attempted to copy Unionism but it was an impossible task. The Unionist Party ran the machinery of government, the Nationalist Party bore the consequences of failure to effect real change at parliamentary level. They had no power at their disposal and the population knew it. There was another factor. The Nationalist party was not organised and that was a fatal flaw. Organisation was implicit in the success of a political party, proper branch structures, an executive and the other trappings of efficiency like party offices. We were also full-time politicians and we were prepared to work at it. We were non-sectarian in motivation and social democratic in outlook. Our ambition was to attract the descendants of Roddy McCorley and William Orr to our ranks in spite of the emerging storm. We hoped that the descendants of the United Men, the radical Presbyterian tradition, would be attracted to the new party, but that was a big ask. There had been a transformation in Unionism since the United Irishmen rose. There is still a dissenting tradition in the North and they marched with us in Sixty-Eight but they were small in numbers and well scattered.

Political life reduced itself to a familiar pattern. Welfare Tribunal Appeals at the local labour exchange in the late morning and I was always there. I never took money for the service and the constituent countered with the offer of a drink. Counter is a very good word in the circumstances and it was rude to refuse. Face time with the voting public was an important aspect of the job and there was no need to insult the man so I followed him there when the Tribunals were finished. Sometimes there was a crowd when I arrived and I made sure I got round them all. I forgot about afternoons after a while, almost sober when the night shift began with a political meeting in a local hall and a post mortem afterwards. Colour and nervous energy and wide ranging debate at a restless meeting, whiskey sloshing into a glass in aftertime, sucking down the diesel and feeling the power, getting drunk for the second time in a day. The afternoon hangover begins to lift but the shakes remain so you stand like a sparrow with your feathers all wet, a small-time MP with a big-time attitude and people prepared to listen to every word. Another glass of the good stuff goes down and the host hits you again. Soaring arrogance and raised voices in a crowded room and the genie escapes again. A mush of emotion in the cigarette smoke and the mist comes down. Later. Singing and bare feet in a private house and a frantic search for a guitar, left-handed if possible, upside down at a pinch. Loud singing and great patriotism, prepared to die for my country not once but several times. A house shivering with noise so I stumble outside, the feel of wet grass on my face as I pass out.

Awake to birdsong and forced to rise and return to a silent house. Bodies on the floor of the living room like the last scene in Hamlet, stoned and asleep and out of it. I stumble around strange rooms in search of a drop of liquid, anything runny at a pinch. The stylus on the record player in the corner scratches at a buckled groove. So much terror, so much emptiness, shaking in the half light and alone in the world. Forced to look down at the sleeping town of Newry. Could you not watch one hour with me? Priceless that, coming from a guy who has spent a few hours face down in the garden. Dawn steals through the summer haze and I walk the floor, talking to the stylus, before I collapse into an empty armchair. I begin to dress, following my clothes along the Via Dolorosa, shoes in the living room and socks in the hall, jacket on the front lawn along with an empty bottle. I climb into my car and drive into the town. I need to get ready for the Tribunals later today.

Life becomes a habit and my habit is nagging me so I crawl out of bed in search of the cure. Three hours since I passed out and the drink has not died. I trash the house for a rozaner and all I find is an empty whiskey bottle. I curse my luck and pull my clothing from the heap on the floor and get ready for the street. I keep a weather eye out for a mobile patrol as I drive across the town in the direction of the Clinic, afraid to guess at the blood alcohol reading if I am stopped on the road. Eerie morning and the sun is cranking over the horizon, red as a Bloody Mary or maybe that was my eyes? The Clinic is in sight and the mood improves. I am not in search of medical help but it is medicinal. No chance of an examination when I get there. It is not that kind of clinic. Head for the hospital in search of medical help, all I want is a cure. I climb gingerly out of the vehicle, full of piss and wind, unsure of a suitable body motion. The punters are arriving at an early morning shebeen that allows the sick and disoriented to drink themselves bad again. I wait until the street is empty and approach the entrance. A furtive rap and the noise of feet in the hallway, the lock turns and a head appears when the door opens. The consultant looks up and down the street before he looks at me like the first time. I croak at him and he scowls, more charity in a spit but he stands back and allows me in.

The smell of stale tobacco and drink fumes fight it out with my need of salvation. Tears fill my eyes and I lean against the damp wall until the feeling passes. I enter the lounge area when my stomach settles. The dregs of the town in the horrors are scattered around the place, waiting for quality time with the consultant behind the counter so I join the queue. I hold some money aloft and wince at the barman when my turn comes. The consultant gives me an optic examination before he pulls out a tumbler and pours out a cure. I hold up a second finger and he pours again. I knock back the first drink and stumble towards a distant pew. The barman retreats to hygienic distance, safe from the sound and smell of decay. I sit alone, unable to speak and me a public representative, riding the tremor that hits when the first sour mouthful goes down, ignoring the pink rat in the corner of the ceiling. The rat smiles and eats the ratlings and spits the tails across the bar. I cover the rim of the second glass with a furtive hand and stare straight ahead, ignoring the grinning rodent and the severed tails in the bottom of the tumbler.

The patients suffer in library silence and wait for the first tickle. Dawn becomes day and you notice the neighbours at last. Good guys, great pals, ready to listen and drink a pint if you happen to leave it. We swap war stories and medical reports and open the hurt register. No complaints about the booze unless the barman stops serving, but there is an ocean of badness out there and it needs sorting. Throats are cleared and whisper turns to hum and the electric soup kicks in. Conversation is repetitive in the Clinic, a bit like a television in a foreign hotel room tuned into the porn and money channels. Discourse slurs like an engine with damp plugs and reaches rev level in the fullness of time or should that be the timeness of full? The day stumbles onwards until numb turns to normal and the moment arrives. A man in the corner clears his throat and sings a snatch of Danny Boy.

On 3 November 1971, Mr Brian Faulkner, in the course of a Stormont debate, made the observation that enemies of Ulster considered the Stormont Parliament to be:

A useless and discredited institution, that was morally and politically bankrupt.

The enemies in question may have understated their case but the quotation has an enduring resonance. There was a price to pay for the street protests. Single party governments, who misrule for fifty years, do not go quietly and they do not go graciously when faced with the inevitable.

I represented the Civil Rights movement at the Bloody Sunday Inquiry in Derry and London and I had the opportunity to study the G Bundles, Intelligence documents discovered to the Tribunal by the British Government relating to that time. I prepared a report called the G Bundle Analysis and submitted it to the Tribunal. I think it is worth a read. The following extract from the submission shows how far the roles of Stormont and the Westminster Government had reversed over half a century in the legislative field and other areas. The dates and references are related to the Bundles. I hope I assisted the Tribunal.

August 4th 1971 G 4.49
This is a letter from J T A Howard-Drake to H F T Smith, the UK Representative, marked Secret. It is a message from the Home Secretary to Mr Faulkner which the Home Secretary wished to be delivered immediately. The text read as follows.

I said I would set out the position as clearly as I can. The decision whether to proceed to Internment is yours to make under the constitution, but it is our mutual understanding, particularly in view of the involvement of UK forces, that such a decision would be agreed beforehand with us. You had yourself often said, and I have supported this view, that you would be guided by the recommendations of the security authorities. As I understand it the GOC is not in present circumstances recommending internment on military grounds. This of course is the basis on which he would advise Ministers of either government who would be responsible for the decision. It would be for them to take into account the political considerations which are numerous and complex. I understand that the pressure for internment is considerable and I agree that it may well become necessary. I have stated in public that we would raise no objection to internment if we were satisfied on the advice of the security authorities and after consultation with you on the wider aspects that this would help in the campaign against the IRA. I have further stressed that no prior announcement would be possible or desirable. This remains our position.

The letter is the template for the working relationship between Stormont and the Westminster government in relation to security in the period prior to direct rule. It is the procedure adopted in relation to every future military initiative against the minority population. The message was sent the day before Brian Faulkner met the Westminster Northern Ireland Sub Committee known as Gen 47 and five days before Internment was introduced. It is a coded message. It points out that the GOC is not recommending Internment on military grounds, which should have been the end of the debate in the context of the criteria listed earlier in the letter, and it suggests a way round the problem. It would be for Government ministers to take into account the political considerations, which are numerous and complex in his view.

The decision to introduce Internment was a political decision taken by Brian Faulkner. The conventional Unionist view was that Internment seemed to have worked on all previous occasions through the invocation of the Special Powers Act (SPA). Mr Faulkner was appointed Minister of Home Affairs in 1959 and strongly supported Internment during the 1956-1962 IRA campaign. In reaching his decision on this occasion, he failed to recognise the political changes that had taken place since the last outbreak of the Troubles. Internment without trial was an ultimate challenge to liberty. It was not acceptable as a tool of government and it was intolerable as a policy. Internment without trial was a reserved matter. It imposed international obligations on the Westminster government but the sovereign government turned a blind eye, gritted its teeth and endured.

August 5th 1971 G 5.51
At the GEN 47 meeting, Mr Heath indicates to Mr Faulkner that

> ..if Internment is tried and did not succeed in improving matters.. the only further option is Direct rule.

He goes on to lay down the procedure, to be followed in future dealings between HMG and Stormont in the context of Security Initiatives.

G 5.52.
> If Mr Faulkner as the responsible Minister were to inform them that it would be his intention to proceed to early Internment, HMG would concur and ensure the necessary Army support with the Foreign Secretary to handle international repercussions.

Because there was a conflict between the Army view and the view of Mr Faulkner on the advisability of Internment, the official Press Statement after the meeting read:
> ..in the light of security advice and after consultation with the UK Government..

It is necessary to refer to the meaning of certain words, as used by Brian Faulkner at meetings with GEN 47. 'Ulster' was a place where Protestant people lived. The 'decline in public confidence', a reference in the overall correspondence, means the public confidence of the Unionist population. The 'general public' meant the Unionist population. The language of exclusion was used as a backup to the politics of exclusion. The exchanges recorded throughout highlight the Unionist mindset at the time. GEN 47 agreed to Internment after Mr Faulkner addresses the 'wider aspects' and the language used is the language of the Howard-Drake letter.

Internment without trial was introduced in the early hours of the morning of 9 August 1971 with the arrest of 342 Catholic men. The list of detainees was extracted from RUC Special Branch files that were wildly inaccurate, partisan and out of date. A number of detainees, including a former chairman of NICRA, were subjected to the 'white noise' and sensory deprivation techniques, used by the Army as counter-insurgency methods in other colonial theatres. A classmate in St Colman's and a good friend, Gerry McKerr, was subjected to the 'white noise' treatment. I visited him on the Maidstone when he was taken there.

Internment was a political and military disaster and was certain to fail. Operational Directive 4/71 at Paragraph 1(a)(3) at G 27.197, by Brigadier MacLellan, records that:

> The subsequent introduction of Internment, followed in its turn by the erection and dismantling of barricades throughout the Bogside and the Creggan, all combined to lead to a situation in which the security forces were faced by an entirely hostile Catholic population..

There were four immediate consequences of the policy of Internment. A massive civil disobedience campaign which took the form of a rent and rates strike, an escalation in the level of paramilitary violence instead of the decrease that Faulkner predicted, a withdrawal by minority representatives from all areas of public life and the first meeting of the Assembly of the Northern Irish people in Dungiven which was initiated as a symbolic alternative to Stormont and a sign of the complete alienation of the minority. Internment forced the British government to seek a derogation from the European Convention on Human Rights. Executive power lay with Ted Heath who held, with his government, a reserved power in the relation to security and should have used it. Faulkner was allowed to wield a political cudgel called internment with disastrous consequences for the North.

Harry Thornton, a resident of Silverbridge South Armagh working in Belfast died on 7 August 1971, two days before internment was introduced. He was shot outside Springfield Road barracks in Belfast by a British soldier on sentry duty after a car backfired in the street. South Armagh had been relatively incident free. I always considered that internment and the shooting of Harry Thornton drew South Armagh into the conflict.

7 October 1971 G 17.119/1

There is a meeting of GEN 47 on this day. Mr Faulkner makes use of a review of the social and economic position to convey the fact that the permanent secretaries in all the Northern Ireland departments of the civil service, were also concerned that the security situation should be tackled at once as the first priority. He mentions this in his initial comments because he wants HMG to realise that the civil service in Northern Ireland has a political view and that it was a major factor in the Direct Rule equation. He was also indicating that the views of the civil service and the Stormont regime on the primacy of the security problem were coincident. It is noteworthy that HMG did not ask Mr Faulkner why the senior civil servants, as a group, held starkly political views and that the political views expressed were sectional and partisan. This intervention by Faulkner highlights another reality. There were no meaningful jobs for Catholics in the Northern Ireland Civil Service. His words provide clear evidence that the civil service, in Northern Ireland in 1971, was as politically committed to the Unionist cause as the most right-wing member of the Unionist Party. Mr Faulkner indicates at G 17.122 that he:

> would not contemplate, leading or serving in a Government of Northern Ireland which included Republicans, whether or not they eschewed the use of violence in bringing about a unified Ireland..nor would he serve in a Ministry composed according to Proportional Principles..

Mr Faulkner is bluntly stating that he will not share power with Catholics. It was the view of his administration, the view of the Unionist Party and the view of the Unionist electorate.

At G 17.122 Mr Faulkner makes the observation, in the context of any British government initiative in that direction that there were Catholics of a constitutionalist view and that he might air a proposal in future talks for a Minority Council composed of representatives of interest groups whose chairman might have a seat in the Cabinet. Mr Faulkner seems to be indicating that Catholics of a 'Constitutionalist' view might serve on a Minority Council – a type of 'political homeland' – along with other interest groups. Mr Faulkner is not offering a seat in the Cabinet and he is aware that, if the post was created, the Chairman in Cabinet would be in a minority of one on every voting occasion. The prospect of a Catholic chairman was beyond remote.

The net result of the meeting is a mandate for a military initiative and HMG approval for a major push against the IRA by the British Army. A balancing political initiative is put on the back burner. Direct rule is not canvassed by the British Government even though Internment had been a disaster. There would be no evidence of clear signs that both Governments were working towards a realistic political settlement which should reasonably satisfy the desire of the minority to have their interests represented..

The following measures were agreed by HMG and Mr Faulkner on that day.

Legislation aimed at deducting benefit from individuals involved in the Civil Disobedience Campaign which was a protest against Internment. Legislation providing for a local means of taking over from non-co-operating Local Authorities, who had ceased to function as a protest against Internment. The sending of three extra Battalions who were to be used to support an increasing effort against terrorists in Belfast, the better control of the Border and a programme of cratering border roads – 84 in number - and humping 20 unapproved roads and a reassertion of control in all parts of Derry. The additional 3 Battalions had the prime objective of clearing the main trouble areas of Belfast, and secondly for border operations. The Derry problem had lower priority – the no-go areas - but the precise method of use of the troops should be left to the GOC (G 17.126). Mr Faulkner had failed to move Derry up the priority list but 3 extra Battalions were in the Province for tactical disposal. Other measures included the speeding up of recruitment to the UDR to the force maximum strength of 10,000. Local commanders were to be given a discretion in making arrangements for the vigilante groups, who were Protestant and Unionist in complexion, to make contact in an emergency situation.

In his history of the development and organisation of the *Ulster Unionist Party 1882-1973*, p. 163 Appendix 3, John F Harbinson comments upon the Consultative Document produced by Brian Faulkner.

> In October he [Faulkner] presented his proposals for the reform of the Northern Ireland Parliament in a further attempt to retain Unionist control. The 'Green Paper', as it was called, revealed a frightening lack of understanding of the real nature of the problems facing Ulster Unionism. The proposals were for: Functional committees of Parliament. An enlarged House of Commons and Senate. The possibility of elections under Proportional Representation. An Executive or Cabinet, based entirely or almost entirely, upon the party which had a majority in the [Stormont] House of Commons. The only outcome of such proposals could be a return to the situation prior to 1969, namely a Parliament dominated by Protestants and Unionists. It was not only a document lacking in statesmanship, but in the circumstances under which it was produced, it was a document that bordered almost on the criminal.

The record of the 7 October meeting is a record of betrayal, of exclusion and of nihilism. It is one dimensional in terms of the political situation in Northern Ireland and signals acute political revisionism. Faulkner speaks the language of the master race and HMG listens, intervening occasionally to ask him about his Consultative Document, which they know is fatally flawed. The Minute of the Meeting (G 15.89) records the clinical dismissal by Brian Faulkner of the hopes and aspirations of a large proportion of the northern Irish people. Internment has failed and he wants another turn of the security screw. It was Jubilee Day Mark 2. In the eyes of Unionism, he did not go far enough. The Nationalist population were not responsible for the policy of exclusion, perpetrated by successive Unionist Governments who wielded the political weapons of bad housing, institutional and geographical unemployment and gerrymandering in support of a sectarian agenda and used Internment to stifle protest about that policy. The Catholic community were not responsible for the sectarianism that attended Loyal and Orange parades through Catholic towns each summer since the formation of the state.

It is appropriate to ask why a British prime minister, who was a 'One Nation Tory' and who had fought in the Second World War, did not distance himself from the 'exclusive brethren' message that Mr Faulkner was delivering. Instead, he opted for a tactical approach based on the need to stave off Direct Rule. HMG refused to take direct responsibility for the political slum called Northern Ireland at this stage. They allowed the Unionist population to turn an army sent to protect the Catholic community from the excesses of Loyalist extremists in August 1969, and watched as they steered the army in the direction of their own political and military ends. Unionist objectives, at this time, included internment and the myriad military 'support systems' canvassed and approved in the course of this meeting. Mr Faulkner cloaks extremism and inhumanity in the jargon of democracy at this meeting in abstract terms. It is chilling because it is so workaday and the British Government went along with it.

The high tide of the Civil RIghts Movement was over but the aftershock was mighty as can be seen from the record of the Faulkner/Heath meeting. The Civil Rights record of achievement was extraordinary by any standards. Complete success in the propaganda war, bringing widespread pressure from throughout the world on the Stormont administration, and a clear victory in the moral crusade. NICRA took to the streets in the late Sixties and broke the mould forever. One of two great seminal movements in Irish history, they substituted non – violence for violence and radically altered the nature of the political debate. Their platform was very simple: strong on the human and civil rights, the right to a vote, a job, a house and an end to repressive legislation. The political strategy was genius. There was no need to ask for revolutionary reform off a reactionary government. Just look for social justice and the monolith will crumble because of internal intransigence.

There is an eternal argument about who brought down Stormont. I prefer to let the facts speak for themselves. Six Unionist Prime Ministers held power at Stormont prior to direct rule, three of them serving for 42 years, 1921-1963. The civil rights movement began in the period when Terence O'Neill was prime minister and three Prime Ministers relinquished office between 1969 and 1972. It happened because of the civil rights movement, the ordinary people who walked the walk. The brief existence of NICRA was a light that shone on the dark places. It pierced the darkness and positively exposed a great wrong. It became the assertive embodiment of civil liberties for everyone.

There is a story told to me by a prominent Unionist about an encounter between Basil Brooke near the end of his time as prime minister, and Terence O'Neill. The man was present in a room in the Sixties when Terence O'Neill came in. It was shortly after the Twelfth and Brooke asked how proceedings had gone in his neck of the woods. O'Neill gave him a full account of the day and the fields he attended. Basil Brooke walked to the window and looked down over the neat lawns of Stormont. He turned around suddenly and said:

> I worry about the turn that events are taking, Terence..I fear the worst if the coat-trailing and the bally-ragging of the Loyal and Orange Orders does not stop..it will do me for my time but I worry about yours..

It has a certain ring to it, a bell tolling in a distant spire, the opinion of a man who knew about survival to a man who did not.

Chapter Five

Things were dire in 1972, a puddle of myth and disputed history laced with the poison of centuries, divisions so wide and deep that there was a danger of drowning in the flood of bad will. Dead bodies began to appear in the streets of Belfast and on the apron of an Irish bog. History repeats itself with one vital difference: the repeater holds more bullets in modern times. Bloody Sunday occurred on 30 January. Twenty-seven Civil Rights marchers were shot by the 1st Battalion of the Parachute Regiment. Thirteen people, including six minors, died immediately and a man died some four months later as a result of injuries received on the day. The activities of the paratroopers were the greatest recruiting sergeant for the IRA in the course of the Troubles. The crowds were gone from the streets and young men checked out the location of the local recruiting hall. Resistance was cranked up on all sides. When the system runs out of reforming zeal and the gunmen run out of patience, the inevitability is blood. The Unionists dug in for the long haul and the minority rearmed where they could. Dialogue was fading as a favoured tool. The mood on the streets turned murderous and seemed to say:

If you can't convince a man by argument, you should try a brick.

I was driving up the Dublin Road out of Newry on 22 August 1972 when I heard a huge blast, dirty black smoke and rising panic. When I neared Cloghogue Bridge, milling people and abandoned cars and a shredded building where the Customs House used to be. I pulled into the side of the road and come to a halt, stepped out of the car and approached the scene, I was the Member of Parliament for the area and I was entitled to see. A man with a beard staggered by, smoke-blackened and shirtless and out of it, banshee sounds in the distance signalled that help was on the way. The smell hit me, a cocktail of spent fuel and after-burn and other things that choke the nostrils, blood everywhere like a massive speckled cape, covering the remaining walls and the surviving pieces of ceiling. Life blood is dark red and slippery. I try not to fall or vomit or turn away, stepping around the body parts on the floor of the building. I am losing it. Too much for a single mind in a forgotten part of the planet. The world spins and I struggle for control and I lean against the crimson wall. I reach a gutted area and I go no further, frozen by the scene, afraid to move in case I step on the heart of a human being.

The fire brigade arrive. They jump down and move into the rubble and begin their new trial, sweeping up after us, putting body parts into body bags, cutting us out of the chaos we cause. I follow them when I am brave enough, sorry I bothered. A light is swinging gently in the breeze from a buckled strut above my head and I have an insane urge to disconnect it. I turn around and leave the building and slump down on the roadside wall. The Army and the RUC arrive and cordon off the area. I wipe vaguely at the blood on my hands and clothing and the tears come. I rise when I am able and do my best to help. Finally, I drive out the Forkhill Road.

I was scarcely in the door at home when the phone rang. A strained voice on the other end of the line, a man informing on himself, placing himself at the scene of the slaughter, saying that the newsreader was a liar, saying that nine were dead in the bomb blast not eight. The newsreader was getting to him and I let him finish before I asked what he wanted from me. He claimed he was the driver of the getaway car and he wanted me to contact the authorities. He said that the bomb was made of weeping gelignite, that the sound of the alarm set it off when his comrades entered the building. I told him to make the call himself. He cursed loudly and the phone went dead. I went into the bathroom and wiped vaguely at my hands, covered in Customs House blood. Somewhere somebody was drafting an IRA statement, claiming responsibility for the blast, using remote terms like fortunes of war. I contacted the hospital and relayed the information when I was up to it and they rang me back next day. The information was correct, they counted the limbs at the hospital and came up with an odd number.

Another incident. I was at a meeting in another town on 28 February 1973. There was word of a fatal incident in the Derrybeg estate in Newry involving a young boy called Kevin Heatley aged twelve and the Royal Hampshire Regiment who were the resident army unit in Newry and South Armagh at the time. I grabbed the car keys when the phone call came and ran out into the night. There were two checkpoints on the way to Newry and they found things in the car boot that were missing for years. The radio was carrying a press statement by British Army Headquarters in Lisburn as I reached the scene of the incident, claiming that Kevin Heatley was shot in the course of a gun battle after rioting in the area. It was well past midnight, a biting wind blowing down Main Avenue when I got there. The removal of the body had not diluted the vigil. The estate was up and seething. They stood in groups on the street corners, hunched up against the cold, waiting and watching. Old faces and faded blue strides, lawnmower haircuts and rippling tattoos, safety pins and local hero symbols, waiting for justice on Main Avenue and all they got was me. A string quartet was playing Mozart on a tinny gramophone somewhere, not a requiem but it served. A bigger crowd visible further up the avenue, gathered around an empty space. There was blood on the ground and the body was gone so eye witnesses told me what happened.

The estate had been quiet during the evening and remained that way when the soldiers came back towards midnight. The patrol took up positions in the doorways of the shops and the flats and hunched down. A group of boys and girls were under a street light further up the avenue ignoring the winter cold, taking the last few drags out of the evening. A lone soldier walked into the middle of the street and fired a shot from the hip at the group of kids. Kevin Heatley, who was sitting on a low wall was shot in the temple and never spoke again. The witnesses were adamant that Kevin committed no act that justified the shooting, that no gunmen were present in the estate and no rioting was taking place at the time.

END OF TERM REPORT

They claimed that the soldier opened fire without warning and without reason.

A man approached me as the crowd broke up and asked to speak to me privately. I followed him back to his home. Frankie Finnegan, a TV engineer, was in his living room at the material time, recording an educational module on his tape recorder. The particular module was broadcast for the first time that evening on the BBC, and was on air when the shooting occurred. He played the tape for me, sparse street noise was the backdrop to the voice of the lecturer, occasional voices, some loud and some far away, the purr of a car engine passing up Main Avenue. Then, a single gunshot and distant cries but no further shots in the following minutes. There was no gun battle and no rioting in Derrybeg at the time and place involved, if it was a first time broadcast that night. Mr Finnegan was prepared to make the recording available to me as long as his anonymity was protected. I agreed for a compelling reason. The security forces took a dim view of anyone who witnessed the murder of a young boy and refused to remain silent. They were equally harsh on people who provided supportive evidence like tape recordings. Sad really, unable to publicly identify himself to a legal system that should have protected him.

The yellow card instructions issued to every soldier indicated that they could use reasonable force to prevent a crime. Opening fire is only allowed if the other person is committing or about to commit an act likely to endanger life and there is no other way to prevent the danger. The army claimed that they had come under fire but the tape recording cast grave doubt on this. There was a failure to observe army regulations and a death resulted. I called a press conference for Derrybeg Community Centre at noon before I went home. The press conference took place as arranged and I played the tape recording to the international media. The news bulletins carried the story and the Army went on the back foot in relation to the facts surrounding the shooting. The timing of the recording and the content has never been contradicted to my knowledge by the army or any other agency.

I had other decisions to make. There was no confidence locally that the Royal Ulster Constabulary would investigate the crime impartially and there were reasons for this view. No British soldier had been convicted of a serious offence since the beginning of the Troubles, no charges resulted from the criminal events on Bloody Sunday the previous year, just a report from Lord Widgery compounding the minority belief that there was supreme bias in the legal system. Bloody Sunday was still fresh in the minds of the people. I was aware that the Royal Military Police had taken the statements of the soldiers involved on Bloody Sunday and handed them over to the RUC. It was the tradition in the colonies. It was likely that the statements in relation to the present atrocity would be taken the same way.

It was difficult to get locals to testify against the police or army. Attracting the attention of the security forces was a dangerous game. It branded the eye witnesses as troublemakers in the eyes of the establishment and made them a target for the duck patrols when they toured the estate. Many civilians were charged with rioting after they made a statement against the military or police. Their reward was a place on a sighting list or on a big brother computer for use at check points or the subject of an early morning raid, followed by a day in court where a string of witnesses swore your freedom away. I had no confidence that the RUC, who had abdicated the right to take statements from the Army personnel involved, would prosecute the case with the necessary zeal. A large number of Derrybeg citizens indicated their willingness to put on record what they saw and attend court in due course. I arranged a meeting with the RUC and indicated that I would take statements from eye witnesses to the shooting and hand them over to the RUC afterwards. They told me it was not the proper procedure so I asked them how they could exclude locally taken statements when the Royal Military police were excluding the police from the investigation of the incident. The RUC were not happy with my approach to the case but I refused to change my position. The RUC acceded to my request with bad grace: there was nothing else they could do.

I was in the estate next day, preparing for the statement taking. A barbed wire mood on the streets and significant Army activity in the area. I spent two hours in the Community Centre, setting the process in motion, before I went back outside. There was a duck squad on the pavement on Main Avenue across from the shops, waiting for me. I was walking towards my car when I noticed a soldier taking aim at me with a baton round gun. I had been hit by a rubber bullet round before when we were trying to stop the rioting in Hill Street in Newry on the night after three local men were shot dead by the Army beside the local Post Office. We were sitting down between the Army and the stone throwers at the time. The soldier meant to hit me in the head with the rubber bullet but tear gas canisters were discharged just before he fired and the round caught me in the side, bursting blood vessels and bruising several ribs. I was very lucky it was not much worse.

I was considering my options when a bus came up Main Avenue and passed between me and the patrol. I made a run for it when the bus blocked out their view. When I looked around, they were coming after me. I ran into the nearest house and made the living room, looking for a telephone. The squad came into the house after me and jumped me. I got a kicking before they dragged me out and placed me in the rear of an Army Pig. A hostile crowd gathered and it was minutes before the vehicle moved down the hill towards Newry. An IRA unit opened up from the high ground and bullets were hitting the vehicle as we approached the Meadow school. The soldiers made me sit in the open doorway while they moved back into the bowels of the pig. I saw it all from the back door, the school yard at the Meadow school and a child at play, dust puffs as the IRA bullets struck the ground around him and a running figure in the distance. The child was hit before the teacher made up the yards. He lifted the child and made a run for the school buildings, bullets knocking up the stones around him. I was taken to the UDR Centre on the Downshire Road and held for a number of hours, then I was released without charge.

I intended to go home but cars turning around on a main road are a warning so I screwed down the window and listened. The beating of a bodhran and shrill shouts from a local estate, figures before the flame of a burning car, fire flicker on frenzy, Doc Martens and weird hairdos shielding the real deal, crunching glass and the night calls of the risen people, the livid wail of a society at war. Joyriders at play in a car park near a gutted community centre, goading the Army near the roundabout, sandbagging the rear window with their mates and bursting through checkpoints, scattering the duck squads to the four winds. The night took on a familiar pattern. Handbrake turns until rubber melts and demolition at dawn, stripped of parts and blowtorched by the hards until the insurance claim was the only thing that remained.

I turn the car and find a safe route out of town. The scene was below me as I climbed the steep hill. A clear night and Carlingford Lough was a firefly in the moonlight, flames in the west ward of the town and night hawks in control of the cramped streets that tumble down to the Clanrye river. Soldiers struggled up a hill but my mind was not on them. The fire trail arches over the cowering houses, searing the darkness before it falls, a sweep of flame on the wasteland and the hards screech in the night. A riot breaks out in the afterglow and the trouble dominoes around the town. A thousand televisions switch off and petrol bombs become a community affair. Carnival time in the west ward and I watched the show for a while. The battle colours wax and wane in the purple sky but the air is cold. The rioters run away from the burning vehicles, bored by the tear gas and the rubber bullets, bent on the chipper and the thumping disco. No sacrifice is unworthy to the young but they do mean things. They hear the street music and they learn the steps and wait for their turn to dance. I start the car and drive home. It was time to bathe my bruises.

My arrest was a distraction, an attempt to intimidate me and a sign of panic. Rightly or wrongly, I sensed that the approach was the right one and I was back in the estate next morning. The statements from eye witnesses were taken by reputable local people in Derrybeg Community Centre over the next few days. There was an important political point to be made. By taking the statements, I, as the local MP was publicly withdrawing my support from the RUC and a political system that failed to convict a single soldier in previous years. I collected the statements when they were ready and delivered them to the RUC. After that, it was a matter of waiting. There was movement in other quarters as well. The RUC informed me that the rest of the foot patrol had made statements to the Military Police, backing up the version of events given by the shooter. It was a colonial throwback, an extra protection for the army when the system failed and a squaddie pulled the trigger without cause. Who is to guard the guards? The funeral of Kevin Heatley was massive, thousands turned out to show their respect and their outrage. The wreath from the residents of Derrybeg contained one word – innocence.

The trial ran its course and Corporal Francis Foxford was jailed for three years for firing an unaimed shot without cause or justification in a trial presided over by Basil Kelly, the Attorney General of Northern Ireland until direct rule. There was no mention of the tape recording in the course of the trial which was very strange to a layman. Foxford never served a day in prison, an Appeal was lodged and he was taken back to England and afterwards acquitted on Appeal. Lord Lowry, the Lord Chief Justice, read the judgement of the court. There was no major issue on the unusual statement taking. He commented on the role of the Royal Military Police and the need to regularise the practice of statement taking but he allowed the statements of Foxford and his comrades to stand. The Appeal was allowed on the following grounds.

That while there was evidence upon which the Defendant could properly be convicted, the conviction should be quashed because:

(i) By alluding in his opening speech to the evidence of witnesses D and me (whose names were on the back of the Indictment and whose evidence was favourable to the accused) and then closing the Crown case without calling them, Crown counsel had indicated to the trial judge that these witnesses were, in the opinion of the Crown, unworthy of belief.

(ii) The Trial Judge treated witnesses D and me, when tendered by the Crown for cross examination, as defence witnesses, and he allowed Crown counsel to cross examine them during re-examination and to attack their veracity although they had not proved hostile.

(iii) To allow a statement made by the accused, which had not been proved in evidence as part of the Crown case, to be put to him in cross examination, constituted a material irregularity.

Twenty other prosecutions of security force members came to trial in the period 1974 to 1994.[1] In the main the accused were charged with murder. Sixteen were acquitted. One was convicted of manslaughter and given a suspended sentence. One was convicted of murder and sentenced to life. He served two years and three months of the sentence. In a case involving co-accused, one was convicted of murder and sentenced to life and served two years and five months in jail and twenty three months in Army custody while a co-accused was convicted of malicious wounding. He was sentenced to seven years in prison and served four. In the last case, co-defendants were convicted of murder and given life sentences. They served six years.

Foxford was the first British soldier to be tried on a serious criminal charge in the Troubles and convicted. It was an opportunity to prove that the system worked for every citizen but the system failed the test. Material irregularities were identified by Lord Lowry so Foxford was acquitted and a young boy was in his grave. Carriage of the case lay with the Crown and mistakes were made in the presentation of the evidence. It begs the question, why were mistakes made and whose fault was it?

I was a layman at the time and I shared the view of the local population, another killing in a local estate and justice had not been done. The killing of Kevin Heatley made a profound impression on me. The ability of the British Army to put themselves above the law and the partial nature of RUC prosecutions were a major concern. The system was incapable of rendering true justice according to law. The judicial system failed Kevin Heatley and the society he lived in. The English common law system was the cornerstone of the Northern Ireland legal system but it was the creation of a society at peace, unburdened by serious political or sectarian dispute. The local legal system was infected, incapable of operating fairly in a society where human and civil rights were continually under siege. It was helpless in the face of discrimination and abuse of power.

The British Army contends, to this day, that Foxford was acquitted on appeal. It does not diminish the fact that he was convicted of the manslaughter of an innocent boy and acquitted on a material irregularity. It was not about right or justice or democracy, it was all about power and the source of it and wrong prevailed in the Derrybeg estate that night. I watched it happen and I hated it but I was powerless to change the legal system at that point in time so I stored the memory away until the time came.

The child Eamon Cunningham was shot in the chin as I was driven past in the army pig but he made a great recovery and I see him often. The teacher who lifted the child was Sean Gallogly, my great friend and my election agent in his time. It was an example of raw courage and humanity from a model teacher and a model man.

There was an election in June 1973 in the run up to inter-party talks about a settlement for the North's crisis scheduled for Sunningdale in England and the SDLP did quite well. We returned a large number of members to the Assembly but I could not shake the feeling I had. I stood in the polling centres in Newry and South Armagh as the voters came in and I knew we were clapping with one hand. The volume was not rising any more. I was in the election headquarters when the returns came in from Crossmaglen and Mullaghbawn and it was not a good story. Depressing really, less than sixty per cent of the minority had bothered to vote in many districts. I saw everything in election campaigns but a half-marked election register in the hands of a polling agent was an awful sight.

It was hard to energise the electorate. There were no factories in South Armagh and few visits from government ministers over the fifty-year period of misrule. There were fly-by-night industrialists in the town of Newry who came and left again when the grants ran out. A man with an English accent in South Armagh was a soldier, not a tourist. There was always a presence on the roads, soldiers with guns and a bad attitude, stopping the public on the way from nonsense to nowhere. Hardly the stuff that drives people out of the house and into a polling station in support of change or the democratic process. The party did well in Armagh. I topped the poll and our three candidates were elected in the constituency. It was an opportunity to celebrate and I did, long after the election was over.

A fist fight on the floor of the Assembly on the eve of the Sunningdale talks between the two strands of Unionist opinion, the pro and anti-power sharing Unionists, deepened the air of gloom. We arrived at the talks without half of the Official Unionist assembly party or any of the DUP who were small in number at the time. The various strands of Republicanism were growing in strength and conviction and the two governments were on our case, hoping that moderation was an antidote to history. There was a full measure of violence in the previous three years and no sign of a slackening. Direct rule was welcome but it left a hole and the gunmen flooded in. The stage was set and we were drinking in the last chance saloon. I was anyway.

I attended Sunningdale in Berkshire as a member of the SDLP delegation in December 1973. There was an agreement to power sharing and a Council of Ireland, very few extras and an absence of solid foundations. The Sunningdale agreement was doomed within a week of the conference. On 4 January 1974 the Ulster Unionist Council passed a motion to reject the Council of Ireland, a key element of the Sunningdale Agreement. Brian Faulkner resigned as leader of the Ulster Unionist Party following a vote of no confidence by the ruling council of the party. Faulkner had a majority in the parliamentary party but that vote was effectively the end of the initiative. On 22 January 1974 anti-agreement Unionists violently occupied ministerial seats in Stormont and had to be forcibly removed. A working group was established to determine which executive functions could usefully be given to the Council of Ireland. The report by the civil servants tasked to consider the implications listed tourism, conservation and certain aspects of animal health as suitable functions. It was a surprise they agreed on anything. Ratification of the agreement was continually delayed.

There was mounting speculation in the media. What names would Gerry Fitt, who would be deputy chief executive, announce to fill the SDLP positions on the power sharing executive? There were six positions and six founder members and that made a neat fit. Nothing is ever as simple. There was the general party to consider and the issue of merit. Nobody ever gave me the hard word, ever put it on the line. There were whispers about a loose cannon and the demon drink but no direct comment. I heard the news on the television along with the rest of the population. I did not accept I had a drink problem and I noted my exclusion in the usual way. I rounded up the usual suspects and dashed for the nearest pub. I was the only founder member of the SDLP who was not included in the power-sharing Executive. I did not deserve a ministerial position because I was a practising alcoholic at the age of twenty-nine. Gerry Fitt made the right decision when he appointed Eddie McGrady.

Argument raged within Unionism about the political and constitutional significance of the Council of Ireland. Unionism saw the Council as a Trojan Horse for Irish unity and the Provisionals saw the agreement as a sell out. There were sweeping gains for the anti - agreement Unionists in the Westminster elections in February 1974 that saw Harold Wilson replace Heath as prime minister. 'Dublin is only a Sunningdale away' was the election slogan of the antis who won eleven out of the twelve seats. Unionism wanted a 'Third Force' (alongside the RUC and UDR) recruited from the Protestant community, an indication of the drift to extremism in our society.

The Ulster Workers Council strike began within hours of the ratification of the Sunningdale Agreement. It had widespread support but it succeeded because electrical power generation lay in the hands of the strikers, who controlled Ballylumford power station. The British government allowed it to happen. Harold Wilson the prime minister decided to sleep walk through the remaining weeks of the Executive. The SDLP voted in the middle of the strike to defer the Council of Ireland until 1977 on the grounds that it would save the power-sharing Executive which meant it was gone. The vote was largely in favour: the votes against were cast by Frank Feely, Seamus Mallon, John O'Hagan and myself. We argued that the deferral encouraged the strikers to increase their efforts and aim at the power-sharing executive itself, which was their principal objective. We were right. The power-sharing executive fell within days. Deferral was a bad mistake. You can ignore the Irish question but one thing is certain, the Irish question will not ignore you.

Sunningdale fluttered and died and the survivors gritted their teeth and battened down the hatches. An SDLP meeting was held in Dungannon, the weekend after the collapse. Leading figures expressed the view that the SDLP was finished as a political force. They had pinned their hopes on power sharing in the North and partnership between North and Sorth and ended up with a bare cupboard. They believed that any hope of Irish unity was gone forever, that the prospect of a minimal Irish dimension in the next two hundred years was virtually non-existent and that there was no brand of unionism present or on the horizon that would be prepared to share power with the SDLP. The political future of the North involved British withdrawal, Civil War and repartition. It was hardly the best time to hold a meeting if they held that view.

I did not share their analysis. The Unionist family did not look in great shape to me. Sunningdale failed because the only parties who bought into the process were the Alliance Party and the SDLP, until the party vote of the Council of Ireland. They were joined in the venture by half the Unionist Party until the Ulster Workers Council strike began. The Provisionals were opposed to the arrangement along with the broad loyalist constituency including the DUP who were opposed for different reasons. The problem was critical mass and the masses were not lining up to defend the new institutions. Call them what you will, loyalist, fascist or 'the people of Ulster' as unionists called themselves, they took to the streets to defend their way of life. You hear it on the radio or in the course of conversation, generally about a politician recently dead. Someone states that the person was ahead of his time and it jars with me. Politicians are supposed to be of their time not ahead of it. Note the slow pace of events in the North. Caution and pragmatism are the watchwords, not the ability to see into the future or idealism for that matter. There stands the broad spectrum of unionism, they could do no other. They were something else as well, they were of their time.

SDLP party policy ceased to be a focus after Sunningdale. There was no need for detailed documents and it was a case of old soup in new plates for a generation. The party proposed quadripartite talks in the late Seventies at an annual conference. From the floor I called it an early letter to Santa Claus. A generation of violence and political stagnation followed 1974, hunger strikes and the rise of the Provisionals, a bitter period for community relations in a bitter community. Politics was the big loser, the tribes reverted to the old pieties and hoped for better times until hope was declared an orphan. I noticed the part that optimism played in politics in the months after the fall of the Executive. There was always an expert, a man with a bag a long way from home, who was speaking to a power player in Dublin or London town who told him that a major new initiative was planned. The thin gruel was fed to us for years as a substitute for progress and some people believed it. Out in the streets, murder was in vogue: a black dog, dripping-fanged and smelter-eyed, growling chaos and dark ages. We were living in dangerous times. The salad days were gone forever.

The SDLP may have been in decline before we founded the party. We emerged from the civil rights movement and took the mantle with us. Nothing wrong with that but there was a price to pay. We left a number of very influential people behind and a substantial part of the movement. Foundation day was the highest point, the following day we were short the civil-righters who stayed away and the people in the minority who scraped attendance at Stormont off the sole of their shoe as if they had stepped on something nasty. It is hard to identify the highest point. We reached a plateau in the Seventies and the Eighties saw the rise of the Provisionals. The SDLP kept politics and ideas in play at a time of great need. We took the ideals of the civil rights movement off the streets and gave them parliamentary form. Democracy is not about special privilege or special pleading or the divine right to rule for fifty years. It is about minority rights and majority rule and the failure of the world to address the iniquity. What the hell does 'widespread acceptance' mean in a divided community? Everybody makes claims after the fact about their performance and history will judge. The SDLP kept democracy alive in the North until everybody got the message.

Chapter Six

I met Anne in Matt Kirwan's pub in Dublin during a night on the town with Paddy Kennedy and Jimmy Boyle from Newry. They were looking for relaxation and I was looking for oblivion. I was supposed to be somewhere else but I cancelled everything in favour of drink. There was a big crowd in Kirwan's and I was floating. I remember Anne talking to me at some stage but I was not hearing very well. My ears were waiting for the sound of ice in a glass. It was a garbled night and I woke with a very sore head and a memory of Kennedy and me and the Garda Special Branch at some odds in a side alley at some stage in the small hours. I had not managed a sober word with Anne but I could not shake the feeling. I drove home about nine o'clock that evening. I stopped in Dundalk at Mark McLaughlin's pub because the night was for drinking. Anne was standing across the street when I locked the car and I was not surprised. The feeling was so strong on the drive down that I knew I was meant to meet her. I apologised for my conduct and we went for a drink in Larkin's in Forkhill. We were never apart again, except for a short period I will come to later. It was amazing that we never met in UCD where she was completing her studies in medicine. Mags McDonald and Beth McCarthy, classmates of Anne and close friends, were well known to me but I never met Anne while I was wasting my time at university.

It was late when we left Larkin's, midsummer light from a crescent moon and very little drink taken. We drove down the road towards Newry, reluctant to let the night end. Cloghogue Carnival on the outskirts of Newry was in full swing, the fortnight of showbands in aid of parish funds that was a feature of the Irish social scene at the time. The dancers were long gone when we stopped at the big marquee beside the railway bridge at Cloghogue. We went into the tent, hummed a tune and danced together in the limpid light. It could have been some Marty Wilde recording but I was older now. I remember the song and the words very clearly, mostly I remember the moment.

> But of all these friends and lovers
> There is no one compares with you
> And these memories lose their meaning
> When I think of love as something new
> Though I know I'll never lose affection
> For people and things that went before
> I know I'll often stop and think about it
> In my life I love you more.

Anne married me on 21 September 1974 in the university church on St Stephens Green in Dublin, four months after the collapse of the power-sharing executive.

She was working as a school doctor in the Armagh area and I was travelling to Belfast, so Newry was a logical place to settle. There was a major problem from the beginning. The early years of marriage are difficult enough but that never impinged on me. It is hard to see the difficulties through a drink haze. Anne was working at the relationship and I was out of control. Making space and making vows were just stops on the road, places where I was more likely to look for a pub than a solution to my problems. I was a full-blown hopeless case, raddled and reckless, unable to get over myself.

I went to parliament regularly and highlighted the local problems but I was lacking a gear. I was no good at busking, the ability to talk around a subject or the ability to talk out a subject and I choked on fudge. There is no particular virtue in this claim. It is impossible to answer any political question directly and the public are wise to the fact. They never knife you for busking. They expect you to highlight political topics not solve them, with the exception of that personal problem that they raised with you on the street. I loved the energy of politics, the feeling of urgency that gripped me when I entered parliament and the energy on the floor of the House. Power lives here and I wanted it.

I carried one positive into the fray. You need to be a performing seal in politics and I qualified on that count. I wanted to star in Croke Park or play guitar with Presley but a mundane career was not cool. I was a centre-court-at-Wimbledon kind of guy in my mind, waving at the crowds on finals day. Life is a Monday afternoon on an outside court in a first round match, two sets down and rain forecast. I had no great gift for publicity and I was in the company of masters. The other SDLP founder members had a fatal attraction for the press and they were worth it. I lacked the self-promotion gene and it is a fatal flaw. There were net benefits to my career along the way. Events stay in my memory, not political intrigue. I am unable to recall the dreary meetings where X said something to Y that washes up in a book sometime. I am influenced by the pattern that events imposed, not the individuals involved. Events influenced me and, in extremis, caused me to change.

I am by nature a dissenter in the political, not the religious sense. I never assume anything and question everything. It is a habit of years. I identify with the aims of the French Revolution and the aspirations of the United Irishmen. I believe in liberty, equality and fraternity and I try to practise these principles. Dissenters are comfortable in the role they play. I realised from an early stage that the alternative view may carry its own reward but it is largely removed from influence and power. I was a political outsider all my life, even in my active period with the SDLP. Never an inner circle sort of guy, never mainstream, never the voice of the mainstream. The party establishment viewed me as moderately good at some things, but erratic. The delegates at conference were keen enough to hear me speak but it was always of the moment. They liked the melody at the time but they never remembered the lyrics when the song was over. Members of the dissenting squad accept their fate. I chose the role I played, not the party.

I found some release in walking and I was well served. I loved the mountains so

I bought the gear and made my way there. Slieve Gullion is perfect hiking territory. The forest drive curves upwards into the mist and I bend my back to the slope, my body searches for normality as the new day conquers old wine. The steam is drawn from me by the time I reach a level section on the way to the summit and the hangover drips from my bones. Dromintee below me amongst the hillocks with the back of the village towards the barracks at Forkhill. It was not a good time for a tour of duty in Forkhill, gateway to the Fews. The watchtowers stand like foxgloves on the heights, piss proud along the drumlins that make up the volcanic ring. The Army built them for their own protection, designed to keep people out, not let democracy in. The British studied the local terrain and commanded the heights, their game plan was the rock of Acropolis or the Tiber marshes. They chose a mountain top because the natives camped on the valley roads. They were safe enough if they remained at base and vulnerable if they broke camp. The sappers cratered the border roads and studded the surface with concrete moulds, pyramidal tank traps airlifted by helicopter and dropped on the debris, dragons teeth ordered up after the generals lost the land war. Jason and the Argonauts swirled about in the mist.

> He sowed the dragon's teeth and from them armed warriors sprang up.. these he set fighting by throwing a stone amongst them..and they killed each other until only five survived..

The moulds lie roughcast on narrow country roads, a barrier to cattle feed at twilight, not extensive barriers like the Median wall between the Tigris and the Euphrates or the Great Wall of China. The wind whispers in the snipe grass on the lower slopes of the mountain.

Breathing hard now, I find a boulder in the mountain heather. Some things are best read on Slieve Gullion for the feel of it. I slump down and pull out a small history and turn the battered pages until I find the place. 'Jesus of Nazareth, King of the Jews, save us from Johnston, King of the Fews.' I steal a glance at the Fews before I begin to read.

> The main and great highway to the north of this Kingdome, from Dundalk to Ardmagh, passes in the fastness of the Feuse, but has a fair surface of carriage width. To the traveller it is not safe, as Tories and Rogues infest the woodes. Here it was that Captain Groves and ten of his men were done to death in the past year. I have plans under hand for a little Barracks, with flankers for a Company of Foot, to guard on that part known as the Black Road.

Always the way of it. English law and Irish tradition, the dialysis of history. The barony of the Fews was unbridled down the centuries and the old coach road from

Dundalk to Armagh was rapparee domain. In the distance the grey string of road over Corramonnon that ran down to the Armagh turnpike. It turned north for Armagh city by way of Newtownhamilton and the Black Bank.

> When love of gain stimulated any man to so desperate a venture as a journey through South Armagh, he first made his will, and piously commended his soul to God. Then, having collected his friends around him, he proceeded under their protection, on horseback, through the dreaded defiles of Armaghbreagh and Blackbank. Even then, he was alarmed by every breath of wind which whistled through the heath, and started with terror when he heard the whirring of grouse wings, or the bleating of vagrant snipe, lest the merciless Tories be upon him... In this state of trepidation, he proceeded, until he arrived at the residence of Johnston of the Fews, who was the terror of robbers and the safeguard of travellers...Johnston preserved the mountainous district of the country from the incursions of Tories and Robbers...Many a traveller whose courage had oozed out at his finger-ends amidst the dreary wastes of Armaghbreagh, felt new spirit invigorating his heart, and new strength nerving his arm, when he saw the smoke of Johnston's house curling in the air. Here, it was usual for the escort to tenderly embrace, with tears in their eyes, and take leave of their friends..

The Lord smiled on Johnston of the Fews. In 1716, he captured and killed two Tories. He spiked the heads of McArdle and Crummy on the gate of Dundalk Jail and collected the reward. He bought the townlands of Drumaltnamuck and Cavan O'Hanlon as it then was and built an inn at Camly near Newtownhamilton. He separated outlaws on the Heading Stone and dumped their bodies in the Tory hole at a bend in the Dorsey River. He evicted the native Irish and settled the town lands with Planter stock. In 1743 the Rector of Creggan wrote to the Lord Lieutenant about the burning of Freeduff Meeting House.

> I hope all their wicked designs will end here, and that examples will be made of those who had a hand in it, for the gentlemen of the country are determined no priest will be suffered in it...We have good reason to hope that this great and good work will prosper and will in the end tend to the downfall of Popery amongst us..

The flight path to the helipad at Forkhill runs over my head and they gather like busy bees in the sky above the base, buzzing and swirling until the time arrives to come or go, almost the busiest heliport in western Europe and the last outpost of the Empire. The birds bomb off the mountain as the chopper struggles along the lee and lurches towards the landing pad. I watch it land in the military barracks and the soldiers exit into the exercise yard. Palestine and Aden are ancient history, the

END OF TERM REPORT

army and the IRA wage war and the people are neutral when it suits and partisan forever. South Armagh is not a court of law. There is no reasonable doubt where the struggle is concerned and the jury is handpicked. Nothing ever changes in the relationship between the army and the people, nothing except the quality of the cloud that smothers the watchtowers on a sharp morning and fleeces down the wind to Mullaghbawn.

The soldiers move out of the fort and the front doors bang on the village street. Men under the bonnets of cars remember urgent business inside the house and children scuttle to a vantage point to watch the action. The hards hold their ground and give the squaddies the long stare, the big come on. Teenage girls watch from the windows and play with their hair. The duck squad walk away from Forkhill and a hard walks over to a public telephone. South Armagh is an information black spot for one army, a live commentary for another. The conversation is brief and the boy emerges quickly. He stands with his fists in his jeans watching the route of the duck squad with an eye on a girl in a window. The soldiers straggle over a ditch, moving directly towards the mountain. They look out for the IRA along the patrol path, wary of the culvert bomb, trying to hobble a ghost, surviving on scraps of slander and serious bias instead of high grade intelligence. The IRA are mineral in clear plastic to the Intelligence services, they can see the IRA but they can't touch them.

I track away from the soldiers in the fields below and take an alternative route to the valley floor. My tendons creak as I start down the goat track through the volcanic rock. Coming down is harder than going up and I groan and remember the night before. I lean back in my stance and step gingerly along the pitted path and look for foot ambushes in the crowded gorse. Blood on the ground, a single gout of dark red on a platter of grass, no sign of struggle or animal remains, no hint of hunter or prey. Nature notes and moves on. The creature left a smear, a bright mark on the land that made him. It would go down with the sun and the night would remove the trace and the platter would be clean in the morning.

There are Famine ruins on a downhill stretch of Slieve Gullion, masked by conifers and mountain ash. The rain shows no mercy. It falls like brimstone on the grass floors and the crumpled casings. Each boulder was a wish and a prayer when young men placed it there, durable shelter from the north wind when a fresh thatch was bedded in and comfort for the waifs. The shelters crumbled into rubble and the dream died. The scattering are welcome here because the land remembers. It waits for the footfall of the throngs who departed in misery. They are spancelled together, the mountain and the land and the small people who combed her hair before the parting. I touch the stone and make remembrance before I tackle the long stretch towards Dromintee.

A day in Newry's Derrybeg estate and I was drunk in charge of a fading politician, bent on a field trip. A local in the estate pointed out the home of a car wrecker after I mentioned a name. There was plenty of sound when I reached the entrance but no answer to my knock. The door swung open under the weight of my shoulder so I tested the remaining hinge and walked in. Cans of congealed paint scattered about the hallway and voices from afar. It was a joy riders' chop shop without the clutter and I was in a no zone: no carpet on the floor, no paint on the walls and no interest in my sudden appearance when I joined the company. There were five men in a room, sitting on tractor tyres and the front seats of cars watching people debate poverty on afternoon TV. They took one look at me when I entered and relaxed because they recognized me, saw me on television once. Television is the new confessional, an axe murderer gives a live interview, admits nine murders and escapes before the law arrives. Someone is sure to approach him if he avoids capture and goes for a walk next day:

Saw you on television last night, you were very good.

I slumped down on a car seat and engaged the men but it was as useful as a second navel. The chop-shop men wanted the Housing Executive to call and replace two tiles that had dropped off the fireplace surround but there was another want in them. I got a distinct feeling that they wanted a closer look at a local tragedy and it took some time for the realisation to sink in. I was in the company of assorted dope-heads and car thieves who felt sorry for me. They sniffed a line of coke and chased the buzz before they left for a while, slaves of the habit and the suppliers and life was good. I left with a cold feeling, they felt good about their lives and they felt pity for me.

Borders are not for the convenience of the locals. They are lines drawn in an arbitrary fashion that block the tribal lanes and trap people in an alien place. Borders are the work of careless people, politicians and diplomats who know about compromise. They are interested in taking as much land as it will hold at the critical time and ignore the consequences for the uprooted. The sundered are another government's problem, cut off from the broader family by a line on a map. Politicians at the centre of power magnify the otherness and Merlyn Rees a Labour secretary of state in the North gave it a name. He called South Armagh 'bandit country', a case of the pot and a black kettle.

I grew up in an independent republic wedged between two states. I am a border cub and there is a massive dislocation in me. Never at the heart of things and never wanting to be, marginalized by the system and suspicious of systems. The body was in the North but the mind was elsewhere, in the South and not in the South as the mood took me. Displaced by events and never settled, disposable when Ireland was divided and disconnected now, like a radio not quite tuned. I was committed but I did not belong, always aware of where we ended and where they began. There was a sense of loss and pain and a need for an explanation, a feeling that a piece is missing, that something dropped off along the way and rolled into the hedge. There is a price to pay for forced separation and forced unity as border people know, Nationalist and Unionist alike. There is a difference between a border line and living. Border people hear two tunes and hum neither. There is otherness in us and a throbbing hurt because we were ignored by two states. We are condemned to a shuttered glimpse of being, falling through the cracks of identity and national pride. Belonging is different from citizenship or identity. Border people are marginal people, where there is a border there is a margin. The border is an occupation, not a crude line on a map.

Unionism was basking in the afterglow of the fall of the power-sharing executive in 1974. The loud celebrations had ended but the raised morale of unionism was impossible to ignore. The Government held an election for a Constitutional Convention in 1975 to fill an obvious political vacuum or in a blind fit of panic. There were rumours in South Armagh that spelt electoral trouble for me on a number of fronts. The Provisionals intended to target me in the election. It was local and it was personal. There were many people who never forgave me for joining the SDLP in view of the family past and I was opposed to the campaign of violence and said so early and often. It was not an attack on the party across the North or on a constituency basis: the target was me. The Provisionals advocated boycott in the run up to the poll and made their preparations.

I was aware of the situation on the ground when I arrived in Crossmaglen on election day, an hour before the close of poll. I travelled on my own because it was my problem and I refused to involve other people. I parked the car in the square and walked the short distance to the polling station. Twenty plus people were present in the gathering gloom and they were in good cheer. There was an absence of election activity, no whizzing cars and election leaflets or busy people caught up in the last minute rush to vote. It was a quiet weekday evening in Crossmaglen and that was very bad news. I passed through the Provisional picket line and entered the polling station. I had two polling agents who stayed all day and showed great courage by their presence but it was time for them to go. I sent them home and waited for the close of poll in the nervous silence of the hall.

I left the polling station when the boxes were sealed. The crowd of picketers in the gateway had grown larger and I moved towards them. The line parted and I went through without difficulty which surprised me. There was no cat-calling and no hostility, just an eerie silence. I was twenty yards away when my name was called and a man walked out of the crowd so I waited for him to join me. He thanked me for organising a prison visit in the recent past and asked me to arrange another one. I told him to ring me in a couple of days in relation to a time and a date. Politics is like that. It seemed an appropriate way to end the evening. The mood was sombre in election headquarters. A number of polling stations in South Armagh had been picketed and reports indicated that the tactic had worked. Less than one hundred people out of 2,700 had voted in Crossmaglen when the polls closed.

I was still hopeful when I arrived at the count. I had had a good result in 1973 and the boxes were still sealed. The votes were not there. My first preference vote was cut in half and I was in a dog fight for the last seat. I was beaten by a margin of 96 votes. Proportional representation is a great system. My elimination ensured the election of my good friend, Hugh News from Lurgan. There were people who regretted my defeat and people who laughed at my difficulties. Such is life, the dogs bark and the caravans move on. The Faulkner Unionists won 5 seats, a massive reduction on the 1973 figure. The UUUC won 46 of the 78 seats and the future was the past. It was a sham fight, a case of no change at Scarva where King James lost every year to King Billy in a rerun of the Battle of the Boyne. A Unionist poster nailed it - bring back the B Specials and let's get back to normality.

Things are rough after an election defeat. There is the numbness of unemployment and a frantic fear about the future, the humiliation of defeat and the public glee it causes and the agony of the first day at the new Parliament. You watch the newly elected arrive for the swearing in ceremony and you are not there. It is a 'poor me' thing and it wounds. The public reaction was immediate. I got invited to a lot of weddings in my political career but very few turned up for the funeral. Not everybody was negative. A good friend told me that the defeat would harden me, it just took time. The political craving was strong as alcohol, a few days and the body is alcohol free and sobriety becomes a mind game. The fix is an arm's length away and you pay for the lethal pleasure. Sometimes it takes a lifetime just like any other addiction. There were times when the rush came, when a big event was on the screen from Stormont or London and that small seductive voice was talking to me about good times and great people. Then I recalled that rainy Monday at Wimbledon and I got back to reality.

The next six months were ego rough, a lot of pain and a mountain of pure bullshit from the loser, a lot of late nights in assorted pubs and dubious company and me with enough talk for four sets of teeth, explaining why I was an important man. The street calls pointed to something different, a satisfaction that I was an ex-MP and there is nothing as X as that. A person stopped me in the street one day and asked me if I used to be Paddy O'Hanlon and it was a killer comment, almost as good as the graffiti saying that Enoch Powell was a count. I wandered about as if I was watching a movie of myself, surrounded by cinema silence, listening to the soundtrack of my rise and fall. It was torture for Anne, never seeing me in daylight and listening to the drunken whinge at night, high and low in the space of an hour. There was no need to think about employment. I was a prime target for the head hunters according to myself. It was only a question of time. I was disintegrating and I refused to mend, my false friend was warming me every night and there was no need to worry, as long as the bottle was half full.

The Northern Ireland Constitutional Convention was a catch-all concept going nowhere. The name was limitation enough but it was a sign of the new reality.

END OF TERM REPORT

The report of the Convention reflected UUUC policy and was ignored by the political world. Seven years of frantic politics and no result, greater divisions than ever before, more armed groups and a rampant paranoia amongst the population. Confusion was rife amongst political parties and there was a lethal stagnation that bred atrocity and counter atrocity.

Anne left me in 1976 and it was hard to blame her. She told me that she had only one life and she refused to spend a chunk of it watching me kill myself. She was working in the Armagh city area so she moved back to Portadown. I missed her and it was a wrench but I would have missed drink more. I had my bottles for company and my freedom to be Jack-the-lad. I was unemployed on the way to unemployable but the crisis escaped me and I refused to discuss the subject. My unfettered drinking started out normally enough, a few pints with the lads and nothing wrong with that. My drinking mates went home on time and the place full of strangers, no money in my pocket and no harm done. A chance to meet new friends who were eager to buy a pint for a famous man. Sad about the election but what goes around, comes around. No money for drink. Would a loan offend you? I know where to find you and the name is sound. Good to have a neck like a jockey's bollocks, good to demean yourself, beg, borrow or steal to put money in the pocket, money for drink. Everybody knew who I was, a guy in the bar on the way to a pit stop, ordering a triple vodka at the window of the snug with another man's money.

Finally, a lucid moment in the madness. I woke in the living room of the house and there was blood everywhere. My clothing was covered in broken glass and the arse was cut off me from lying on a broken bottle. I had no idea how it happened and I was mortified. Drink is dear enough without spilling it carelessly. I tested the dark stain with a finger to see if it was still salvageable. Hard crust on the carpet so I burped my way to the bathroom and looked at the wounds. No artery cut and the injuries were healing nicely. I washed away the blood and treated the wounds and slumped down beside the mess. I was exhausted and flat so I lay there for the day. I fingered the broken glass and mulled over events and asked myself some easy questions. Why does everybody go to the other end of the bar when I enter the door? Why am I alone and unemployed and why did Anne leave me? I took my character apart and left the pieces on the floor to look at. They were not a pretty sight so I turned off the light and fell asleep on the floor, fearful that the pieces would leave me in the night.

I felt better in the morning. It was the result of a day without drink and it seemed to encourage me. I tried a dry run and was sober a fortnight later. The problem was solved. Drink had no dominion over me so I decided to celebrate. I crossed the border and had a couple of quiet pints in a pub in Dundalk and left. Seven evenings later, I had gallons of the stuff in the same place and slept in the car for the night. I failed but I had the cheek to talk about it. Someone told me that I was not a real alcoholic, as if you can be half pregnant or half scarred. It amused me and I told people the story, the few people who cared to listen, and that included the man who came to read the electricity meter. It does not have to be a big thing I said loudly, it has to be something that offends every decent sensibility in a core sort of way, you have to find your own moral gutter. I was an expert on the subject when I was talking about other people, the people who had a drink problem. I was talking myself into a fight by talking about it and I was all talk. It is hard to see ourselves as others see us but it is important to try. A vital part of my drive for sobriety was taking my character apart and holding it up to the pure light. It is a humbling exercise and I was ruthless in the examination. I had a better idea of me when I put the pieces back together and I was never afraid of anything in my life again. It is the same with political belief. There is a vast difference between claiming to be something and being it. People tell you that horse dung is lemons. If you care to believe them, take a sniff and it smells of manure.

I began writing that year 1976. I found myself at a table with a pen in my hand during the lucid moments, working on a novel called *The Vinegar Man*. It was never good enough but it served a purpose. I began to spend more time at home than I did in the pub. It gave me something to do in an empty house during the months I was unemployed. Certain things stay lodged in the memory for life and change the pattern of life and writing stirred the embers for me. It was not Damascus but it was a signpost on a mucky road and it recalled an incident in my football career over a decade before. There were two nights in the year I had trouble sleeping, the night before we played Silverbridge in their backyard and the night after the match. We shared a parish and an obsession with them and we were the best of enemies. Every time I need a reality check I think of Silverbridge. We met them in the bear pit one year and I was playing full back. A high ball dropped into the goal area and I rose to catch it. It was snug in my hands, like a golf ball on a tee, when the Silverbridge full forward hit it with a driver of a fist. The ball crashed against the underside of the crossbar and bounced on the white chalk before the goalkeeper grabbed it. The referee signalled a goal so I chased after him until I was in earshot.

Ref..ref..it bounced on the line,..,it was not a goal..

He never stopped running but he looked around at me with a look that bordered on contempt.

Read the papers tomorrow, sonny..

He ran towards the middle of the park and I stopped running. Read the papers tomorrow: an epiphany moment. We may not like it but we should always know the score.

I deluded myself that night on the floor. I dismantled my ego and laid it out before me but I refused to examine each broken bit. I ignored the mind flashes and the ego assassins that lurked in my head, whispering treason in quiet time, raising the record and the stakes. I was still my own shining leader, above sanction and restraint, impervious to criticism and ridicule. The sad thing was that it was all in my mind and I was alone in an empty room. The whispers kept coming and I was back in Silverbridge looking at the back of a referee. I stayed on the dark side but the voices were coming from the light. A few lines from Shakespeare were drumming in my head – *Henry the Fourth* Part 1:

> I know you all, and will awhile uphold the unyok'd humour of your idleness..

I had a problem with school but I refused to look at it so I stored the quote away for future reference. Always the future, always dreaming, always a laggard. Hal was talking to his courtiers and now he was abroad in my head. The counter case kept coming at me and the writing helped. The day came when I was able to look at myself with one eye open. There were flashes of sanity and I gave them space.

1976 was a leaving time in my life. I left politics behind or politics left me. The people are sovereign and I gave them reasons to look elsewhere, apart with the Provisional pickets. Anne left our home and she was right. Anne left me because she loved me. She was my sanctuary lamp but she was powerless in the face of alcoholism. I lay down with the enemy after she moved out. My mother died of cancer that year at the age of fifty-six. I failed her at school and college and she lived to see me fail again. I was elected to a public job in the area and it should have rung the changes. All I offered was more of the same. I failed her as a child and as a man and she died with the knowledge. Finally, I failed myself as a civil rights campaigner. A foul dictator had power over me and I refused to struggle. I was afraid of failure all my life and now I had failed completely. I failed my wife, my family and my community, my supporters and the constituency. Not many people can count that many failures in a twelve month period but I could. There was no need to search for the moral gutter that I loved to slobber about, the moral gutter was me.

It was some weeks before I packed it in. I had a date in mind for the last drink, not the conventional route to the finish line but it suited me. A touch of Saint Augustine maybe: give me sobriety but not yet. I climbed up the beanstalk and had a scrab at the giant on New Year's Eve 1976 in the home of Patsy McGuigan in Warrenpoint. The giant did all the scrabbing and I was in tatters when Walter Bradley drove me home. It was the last time I took a drink. I went to my first Alcoholics Anonymous meeting in Warrenpoint on 3 January 1977. It was a vital step on my personal voyage. If I ever doubted that I was an alcoholic at any stage in the future, all I had to do was ask myself one question. If you are not an alcoholic, why did you join AA? I had no intention of drinking again but the road to hell is out there and crowded to the point of gridlock.

Everybody has an addictive personality but most people are lucky. They cultivate addictions that are harmless as a rule, like bird-watching or set-dancing or golf. They can be dangerous if taken in large doses but they are unlikely to leave you destitute or dead. Set-dancing might take you to Clare for a weekend but it is unlikely to take you to the outer edge. There were nights I was so drunk I got down on my hands and knees to get under the Egyptian Arch, the railway viaduct in Newry. We all have benefits and burdens in our life, though what some people see as benefits or burdens might be a false picture. I know men and women who kicked alcohol and picked up a gambling rash on the way to sobriety. In the world of addiction that is called a compensatory vice. Every family has a drink secret or a gambling secret, a black sheep or two who sullied the family name. Drinking ran in my family but this is about me. The reason I drank to excess is like a personal fingerprint, unique to the person who holds it. I was searching for something but I was always looking in the wrong place.

I gave up drink for myself and selfishness is a virtue sometimes. If it was about Anne, I would have been away with the first quarrel, out of my head to spite her or to spite me. I needed to stop because of the damage I did to myself and the people around me. It is not about willpower or character or some other virtue and every sober alcoholic has a different answer to the big question. Looking at yourself is the hardest part. Sit six people in a circle and ask them to provide a brief résumé of the other five. You are certain to get a pen picture, flattering or unflattering as the case might be. Ask individuals about themselves and they dry up, become tentative in the extreme. I asked the hard questions and I worked it out just in time. Insight was a crucial factor in my case and that is a gift, not a trait of character.

I remember the story of the crucifixion and the crowd gathered there, Mary and John and the centurion and a number of others who were aware of the true nature of Christ on the cross. What about the vinegar man, the soldier who offered a sponge soaked in vinegar to the dying Christ? Why was he not offered insight, why was he excluded from the knowledge and what became of him? Did he just pack his sponge and go home or did he have a few drinks after the garment rending and find a quiet spot in the garrison to sleep it off? Nobody knows except the vinegar man and he is beyond our reach. I was given insight into my problem and I bless the day but I remember the vinegar man every time I remember the slack-arsed years.

The picketers at the polling stations did not set out to do me a favour but it worked that way. I would not have chosen to leave politics voluntarily. It was high octane stuff and it was killing me, a case of death by inches. If I had won a seat I would have tottered on, unreachable and unchanged. It is said that a gambler looks upon a pile of winnings as a sign that the world loves him. A politician looks upon a pile of ballot papers in the same light. There were elected representatives in the constituency and they knew their job and I was out of work. It was over. The torch had passed and I was not a major player any more. I drifted quietly to the sidelines and learned to value quiet time while I finally came down.

There was no Desert Island Discs moment after the fall, no meeting with a man at the bottom of Leeson Street in Dublin or Chichester Street in Belfast who offered me a job like the voice on the radio. You need an ability to network and a holding pattern in life for that to happen. I was a man with a public record of failure who reversed a well known motto: be nice to the people you meet on the way down because you might meet them again on the way up. In my case I was unable to remember their names. I sought advice from Paddy Kennedy who lost his seat in 1973 and was out of politics completely. He told me straight: you better learn to eat a lot of shit over the next year. I nodded sagely and smiled because I thought he was joking. Out in the streets the laugh was on me. My sobriety was a wonder in the Newry and South Armagh and they were taking bets on me. The smart money was on a second coming in a local bar. O'Hanlon falls a second time.

I made no contact with Anne because it was too early to say. I was solid in my mind about the decision but there were many pressures. Anne rang me up one day and we met in Armagh. We talked for hours, sometimes a heart-to-heart can wreck marriages but it saved mine. A few months had passed and I was still sober so we tried again. We all have our Desert Island Discs moments in life and I had many chances. Some things stand out in my memory but they pale in comparison to the day that Anne came back to me in 1977.

I am a fan of Baudelaire since my youth and I will not deny him at this late stage. The problem was that I read something into his words that I wanted to read. He was a branding iron for me and his words are seared on my brain.

> So that you may not be the martyred
> slaves of time,
> get drunk, get drunk.

I took him at his word and ripped the arse out of everything. I also ignored the following lines of the poem which read:

> One should always be drunk,
> with wine, poetry or virtue as you choose.

I identify with the final lines these days and make choices in my life as they emerge. I wonder what Baudelaire chose in the end?

Chapter Seven

I applied for a lot of teaching jobs after my election defeat but the door was firmly closed. The establishment viewed me as a disruptive influence and I was wallpapering rooms with rejection notes. It must have been me. Colleagues in the party who won seats in 1975 were teaching before me, after the collapse of the Constitutional Convention in 1976. I got a job in a local school with the help of Bernard Crilly and Kevin Campbell and I needed the help. The headmaster in St Joseph's secondary school in Crossmaglen had his doubts but he had an exit strategy. The job was temporary and he needed to fill it and there was a finish line if I failed to shape up. Telling Anne that I was working again was the best part. Archie McMullen gave me a lift and I did not let him down. I remember my time there with pleasure.

Crossmaglen had a national reputation for unrest but the school was an oasis, a place where tradition was strong and respect lived. Teaching and teachers helped me begin the climb back to stability. I began to learn about punctuality, discipline and the need to lower my voice. It gave me an idea what work was like instead of a life without margins. I taught for two years in a temporary capacity and it sorted me out. I had an unwritten agreement with Anne. No bailing out, no financial concessions because I owed a lot of money around the area. I got a lift out each morning with teachers who lived in Newry because I could not afford a car. I paid back everybody that reminded me of a past debt and all the handouts I remembered. I was coming down from two addictions and it was hard time. I was sober and holding but the political drug was still active and it is a habit that is hard to kick.

A telephone call one night helped greatly. Sean Hollywood on the line and on a mission, best man at my wedding and a force of nature, double booked on a night of double rain and asking me to volunteer for a meeting in Hilltown in the Mournes about some minor aspect of civil rights. Anne was home and I was warming by the fire, an alligator sandwich in my hand and a mug of tea beside me. I refused to move and he hit me with the words an ex-politician loves to hear.

> You have to go, Paddy.
> Why is that, Sean?
> You're huge in Hilltown.

The politician was driving out the Hilltown Road before you could say 'junkie'. Had to be done, had to be with my people. It was coming up to eight o'clock so I hurried. The streets were deserted when I parked near the parochial hall. No traffic jam outside the door but Hilltown is a large village and it was walking distance to the hall. Two policemen and a dog and a man sitting in the front row were in position when I entered. The dog looked dangerous so I moved on to the stage and sat down and decided on the next move. Give it a few minutes. My people needed time to gather and I was huge in Hilltown. Fifteen minutes later and nobody darkened the door. I had to decide between the exit and the show before the man in the front row got restless.

He was giving me the big evil from where he sat so I rose to my feet and began to speak. I gave him fifteen minutes of good stuff in the best show business tradition and sat down. The man in the front row was not sympathetic, the kind of guy who sat at home with his feet in the fire keeping himself lukewarm. I was surprised when he stirred himself but it was a frigid night. He banged his hands together a few times to circulate the blood and I made it sound like applause. Movement at the back of the hall. The dog was long gone and the policemen were gathering themselves to go. I was surprised that they were still there. They had barely put pen to paper while I was speaking. I took it badly, must be losing my touch if the police are struggling for a line. I grabbed my notes and jumped off the stage soon after the policemen left. The man in the front row grabbed my arm as I passed.

Where are you going?
Home.
Not if I can help it.
Why?
I am the second speaker.

I got a job in the Youth Service with the Southern Area Board and left St Joseph's in Crossmaglen in 1979. It was a wrench but it was the right move because the youth job was permanent. It was located in Newry so I was able to walk to work. My function was to develop youth services in Barcroft Park and Derrybeg Estate, troubled areas in urban wards where there was strong support for the IRA. The estates were monuments to political indifference and poor design. They were built in the Sixties on the heights above the town, totally exposed to the elements and battery built; human filing cabinets for the people with an absence of recreational facilities, wizened walkways between the housing blocks and poor street lighting, rampant unemployment, nightly riots, army raids and a danger of blood on the streets and in the houses. There was no hope of a youth club because there were no suitable buildings. Anything unoccupied was trashed or burnt to a crisp to stop the army getting comfortable and the Housing Executive had given up the ghost. I was an area youth worker during bad times and it was a difficult job. The word on the street was the long war and the local youth were eager for a piece of the action.

There was a lot of talk in the Sixties about crowd psychology. It passed for conversation on demonstrations and it sounded good. There were endless discussions about what moved people, motivated them, made them act in a particular way. It was the sort of stuff that the long scarves talked about in the students union at the university and forgot on the route to a job promotion. They were big on theory and small on practice and there was a reason: they knew about people but they did not know people. They did not know about petrol bombs and poverty and wee buggers who smashed windows in the local estate for a dare, a great petty tyranny of the modern age. They never considered busted gas meters or the breadwinner home with the wages drunk or the welfare gone to the betting shop while the children circled an empty table. They did not know about silent murderous rage in a shallow walled house on a draughty hill. The long scarves turned down the volume when they got the lecturing job and moved to a safer part of town. They joined the golf club and the bridge club and cultivated a better class of accent and lived their sheltered lives.

I was into leaving in the late Seventies so I left crowd psychology to the wise heads. It was the wise thing to do. We used to canvass the local housing estates at election time and it was a busted flush. The Provisionals were on the rise and the reception was frigid and the post mortem was ever the same, twenty or thirty canvassers on the way back to base complaining about the rise of the Provisionals in working class areas. Would I have voted for SDLP if I lived in those estates? Luckily I was saved from the indecision. I walked the streets for three years and I left them at bedtime for the safer part of town. The tenants would have queued for the chance to put their finger on the button if the offer was made. They lived in bad housing and they wanted it for the rest of the world. No wonder they voted for the Provisionals.

My father died on 31 March 1981. He slipped away at the beginning of the hunger strike, the worst period in the recent history of the North. It poisoned the atmosphere like toxic waste and added to the ocean of hatred. I carry a comment with me like a mantra, something my father said to me in the civil rights days. He said it is dangerous to see the other man's point of view in the North of Ireland because they will accuse you of having no principles. He had no bigotry in him and I am proud of it. I see the other man's point of view and so do the rest of our family. It is his legacy.

An old regret returned to haunt me, unrelated to politics or alcohol, a nagging ambition that never left me and always looked beyond my reach. I lay in the middle of the night, twisting and turning, aware that I was given a chance by Kevin Boyle and turned my back on it. Boyle was a Newry man who lectured in the Law Faculty at Queen's University Belfast in the civil rights years, then became Dean of the Faculty of Law in the National University of Ireland, Galway then professor of Law at Essex University specialising in Human Rights Law. We met regularly at civil rights marches and there was always room for a pint after the event. I told him in the course of a conversation in 1970 that I had an interest in law and that I needed to come to a decision. Kevin was not to know I never studied in my life and the drink was talking at the time. He was unaware that I was just keeping my mouth warm. Kevin took me at my word and rang within weeks. My primary degree qualified me for the vocational legal course at Queen's and he made arrangements for me to register. I signed up for the course but I let him down. I never darkened the door of a lecture room and the moment passed. I had pubs to visit after speeches about dedication and commitment and the role of education in the civil rights movement, high class busking from a man who made a virtue out of bluntness. There was a big difference between can and cant in my case. I never apologised to Kevin for biting the hand but I do it now. I never returned to the subject in the Seventies but I still woke at night with regret on my mind.

1982 and another election called for the month of October. Another attempt to break the deadlock. There was no provision to devolve power until sufficient evidence emerged that it was sustainable. I was pressurised to stand and I did so but my heart was not in it. The deciding factor was that my job was safe. The SDLP and the Provisionals were boycotting the Assembly from the start so I was still employed, whatever the result. October became a huge month for me. I was walking down Monaghan Street in Newry on the election canvass and Gerry O'Neill pulled up beside me, the Armagh Gaelic football manager with a brother called Martin who later managed Glasgow Celtic and Aston Villa. He asked me how I was doing so I told him. I was fed up and looking for a challenge. Gerry gave me the answer. He was registered to do an external Law degree at the University of London and suggested I join him on the course. The registration date for the current year was behind me but it was not a downer. I had eighteen months to the Intermediate examination, the first stage of the course. It was a year of lucky breaks. Anne was a delegate to the central committee of the British Medical Association which met near Malet House in London and she was due to attend a meeting next day. The registration office for the University of London was in Malet House and she made inquiries. I had three days to register for the current course. Anne took the necessary papers back with her and I registered with one day to spare.

There were other days that October, a bitter time and a bitter harvest around the doors. The hunger strike was fresh in the memory and pain poured out of the houses on the canvass in South Armagh. The Provisionals did well. They polled over ten percent of the vote and were the fourth largest party after the election. There were people present on the picket line at the polling stations in 1975 who became new democrats in that election, representatives of the people instead of ghost politicians. I welcomed the change of direction because change is a natural thing. I was changing direction like the Provisionals and I got my second lucky break. I lost by 318 votes to my good friend, Hugh News. Anne was President of the Past Pupils Union of St Louis grammar school in Kilkeel and the dress dance was on the night of the count. We attended the function and enjoyed it immensely. Early the following morning, I opened a text book and began my legal studies.

I gave up active politics when I began the study of law. I was unable to justify the time I was spending on politics so I made the necessary adjustments. Politics is a full-time obsession and I was not prepared to work 24/7 at the political game. I knew it was time to go. There were members of the party who felt that 24/7 was not enough. I pulled out of branch meetings and delegations after that to read about torts and equities. The alternative was sitting at a branch meeting, there to say something rather than something to say, picking holes in the points of a fellow member, reminding them of a man who used to be Paddy O'Hanlon. There were talented people in the constituency and it was their time. I proposed Seamus Mallon for the Westminster seat when the time came in 1983. I always canvassed at election times and signed nomination papers when I was asked, but the political noise died away and I was left to study in silence. There was no place for me in the political world and I was happy where I was. It was quite like the end of my drinking career in a way, a seven day wonder and then I was left alone.

Studying externally is not easy. I was lacking all stimulus and wandering around the Law books in an effort to keep busy. I was putting in the hours but it was hit and hope, a bit like practising a bad golf swing. I was working hard at bad habits and that is a waste of energy. I was not in Belfast or Dublin and I was tied to a day job. There was little chance of a sneak visit to a university hall to intrude on a lecture or speak to Law students and copy their notes. I opened Law books and read them from cover to cover and I had the sinking feeling I was up the left. I vividly remember a case in point. I spent weeks trying to work out when Queens Bench was founded until I realised that Kings Bench has a change of name when the monarch is female. Two minutes and one stupid question in a legal environment would have saved me a mountain of time. There was the inner conflict as well. The mind turns negative when the task is huge so I reeled off the reasons why the effort was wasted. I was thirty-eight years of age, too late to make a mark in the practice of Law and too old. The mind whispered that I would be forty-two before I finished Law and there were some slack years after that. There were mornings and evenings when the urge was overpowering to toss the Law books aside and settle for what I had. I settled for my own reality: I was going to be forty-two anyhow and I was tired of regrets.

Gerry O'Neill had past examination papers and I steadied the ship by Christmas. I had eighteen months to the Intermediate examination and the breaks kept coming. In January 1983, a letter dropped through my letterbox, informing me that I was down to sit the Intermediate examination in the Belfast Institute in early June. It was a mistake and a year too soon but I took it well. I did not point out the error to the authorities or indicate that I was not ready. The examination date was a visual aid every time I opened a Law book. I redoubled my efforts, rising to the dawn chorus to get in the hours of study before I went off to my normal work. The University might realise their mistake and send me a second letter pointing out the error but the mistake was a benefit to me. I was immersed in the Law and determined to succeed so the extra study was a benefit, win or lose in June. I attended a weekend course in Cardiff University in the company of Gerry O'Neill at Easter that year, a crash course for external students sitting the exams, covering the whole syllabus. It was the only steer I got on the pending examination. I noted every emphasis over the weekend, every case mentioned and every topic and I majored on them when I got home, confused and quite depressed at the added confusion. It was an enormous subject and I was scratching at it. I had no learning experience from school to call upon because I passed on all that and passing exams was a harder task than dossing.

There was always the chance that it was a mistake, that the list of names would save me from the ordeal when I arrived at the examination centre on the day. My name jumped out at me from the list when I arrived and I sat the Intermediate in Belfast Institute in a crowded room. I went back to work and waited for the result. I tried not to think about it but it mattered. I made a big effort and time was a huge factor. Saving a year at this stage was gold dust in view of my age. I passed Intermediate and we celebrated in style, afternoon tea in a decent hotel in the area. It was bombed later that year. Gerry O'Neill did not sit the examination. If he had studied for it, he would have passed it. He had business interests that blossomed suddenly and it ruled out study.

I changed jobs between the Intermediate Law exam and Part 1 Final. A sports centre was built by Newry and Mourne Council, an impressive structure that rivalled facilities anywhere on the island at the time. I had a background in sports and practical experience of outdoor pursuits in the Youth Service and I was qualified for the job. I put in an application and was appointed manager of the centre. I commenced work on 1 January 1984. I love sport, no canned laughter or twisted statistics and a break at half time for the obsessed, every fan takes something out of the game and you get to read the papers tomorrow. I had an open brief in the sports centre and I loved it, making space for every sports organisation in a superb facility and helping it grow. I sat Part 1 Final of my Law degree in a room in the Belfast Institute on my own. I was finding a rhythm and the preparation was not as rushed and I felt prepared when I sat down. The supervisor shared her flask of tea with me during the allotted time. I read the questions carefully and divided up the time and I passed the examination. I also enjoyed the tea break. I reviewed my position after the results.

I was missing certain things in my preparation. It was a cultural thing, a certain gloss was lacking because I was not immersed in Law. I had a vocation but it was based on ambition not conviction. I was not a schoolboy who studied the career field until the big moment came after years of academic achievement, a slow dawning and a final decision that law was the right profession. I had no idea if I liked Law and the past was no assistance. The O'Hanlons were coming down with doctors but there were very few lawyers on the family tree, hanging or otherwise. My last visits to court were during the civil rights days when charges relating to illegal marches and other public order offences were put to me. I was sentenced to jail for attending the big civil rights march in Newry after Bloody Sunday and was saved by an amnesty, hardly the conventional route to a career in Law.

The time was approaching when I had to compete with other students and that was a new horizon. They were inured to the Law and the conventions that surrounded it. They were also inured to study. It was not the Sixties and hard work was at the core of university life, not the social life. The students attended without question, they took notes and they imbibed the traditions and the culture that surrounded the course. They prepared well and they looked in the right places for the answers and they attended on examination day and performed. They were adding to the experience of previous years, following a tried and tested formula that worked for them, allied to an insight into the calling. They were shining intelligent but that was not the talent I admired. I was passing on perspiration and recitation and there is a knack in that but the rest of the students had the knack of passing exams.

It was possible to complete the degree in isolation but there was a downside. The practice of Law is a profession and I was strictly amateur. The students had three years advantage on me in the practical sense and every other way that makes sense. They were familiar with courts and Law libraries and the heartbeat of the profession and their practical experience was growing. They knew when to stand up and sit down in a court of Law and how to question a witness and they spoke the jargon. To paraphrase an earlier expression, I knew about Law but I did not know the Law - the traditions and the procedure and the pulse of things. I did not breathe the oxygen of the profession and I getting a bit light headed. I needed to go back indoors to have a chance of competing when we reached the day of practice. I needed to take my final Law examinations at Queen's University to have any chance. I needed the appropriate grades to gain entry to the Institute of Professional Legal Studies and I needed to network, on a professional, practical and personal basis if I was to survive in the legal world.

I made an appointment with the Director of the Institute and he was not helpful so I tried another tack. I asked Queen's University for a meeting with the Education Committee to discuss my application. I was punctual on the appointed day and a three person panel was already seated when I entered the room. David Trimble in the chair, the Unionist politician who following the Good Friday Agreement would be First Minister: not a good beginning. We had not been friends in Stormont and I feared the worst. Mr Trimble indicated that they had read my résumé, that the committee were keen to encourage mature students entering the profession but there was a slight difficulty. I held my breath, waiting for slight to turn to serious in the course of a sentence. He told me that I had four core subjects outstanding and the University required me to do a fifth subject to conform with the requirements of the final year at Queens. I agreed with the conditions and the interview ended soon afterwards. I wrote to thank him for his help and received a reply. David wrote to say that I would not have gained admission to Queen's without the appropriate grades. I was now a student at Queens University in Belfast.

I quit my job with Newry and Mourne Council and became a full-time student. I had some money saved and I travelled to Belfast every day with Newry people who worked in the city. These were the dog days. Employment was a safety net and it had gone and I was abroad in a new environment. The children, as the matures in the class called the students, never made strange. The slagging was good natured and they were keen to help. It reminded me of the time I achieved sobriety. People were always supportive, even the drinking classes. They admire the decision to

END OF TERM REPORT

change and support the effort and it was the same with my new classmates. They showed me the library and the way to build a case and I was networking within the month. They helped me through the down time, the bleak mid-winter when the blues came and the library a maze, half-started and half-finished and struggling with a new system. Legal culture ambushed me and I was confused. The students spoke a foreign language called Law and I needed an interpreter. I put the hours in and got a result at the end of the year and was admitted to the vocational year at the Institute of Professional Legal Studies.

I was called to the Northern Bar in September 1986. We took a drive out the Ards Peninsula after the ceremony, through Greyabbey and down the winding roads to the sea. We took photographs along the coast before dinner in a cosy hotel near the seashore and home after dark. Maybe it was different as I drove back towards Newry and maybe it was my imagination. Anne watched me start a lot of things in the desperate years and Law was no different. Staying power was always the problem. I am sure she crossed her fingers when I opened the first Law book and prayed for a fair wind. I handed her the practice certificate in the cosy silence. She showed me the way and I hope she was proud of me, I felt good about myself for the first time in ages.

There was a six month period with an experienced lawyer before I was allowed to practise and the early years at the Bar were slack. Martin Rodgers was an ideal Master. He has an obvious vocation for the practice of Law and an original mind. He taught me when to stand up and sit down and his patience was endless. I went back to the Institute of Professional Legal Studies in a part-time lecturer capacity after the call to the Bar, back to the classrooms where I studied in the spring. I remember the first day at the Institute vividly, wonderful autumn weather for a new beginning, Law graduates hurrying towards the main door, chattering like starlings at the dawn of a new adventure, and I was gripped by the realisation that I was free. I was qualified and back in the real world again and new challenges lay ahead. I got out of the car and felt a wave of emotion as I approached the front door of the post-graduate Law school. I had a right to be here because I worked hard for the opportunity. My major regret was behind me. A few short years and I was changed forever.

I taught at the Institute for a number of years while my legal practice grew. My aim was to survive the early reverses and make a decent income in time as a senior junior. I harboured no ambition to become a Q.C. The need to make my way at the Bar was a stronger urge than any need for promotion. I knew a little Law and I was prepared to work at it. The early years were tough but I survived and prospered. I have a good deal of common sense that I never used when I was young. It was in mint condition when I removed the wrappings and it was vital at Law. I was among friends, including my enemies if that makes sense, in the Bar Library. Unlike in previous walks of life, you always knew who they were. Getting called to the Bar was a huge benefit for me. It opened me up to new experiences and new challenges and it stabilised my world. I had passed through a lot of phases and a lot of jobs to get there and the experience helped in my new profession. I found that my age was not a disadvantage, particularly in the practice of criminal law. The parents of wayward kids were relieved to meet a barrister who was the same age as themselves, instead of a lawyer the same age as the defendant who gave the impression that he was ducking into the consulting room on his way home from the House of Lords. Magistrates liked it also. They were the same age as I was and shared the same preoccupations, except for the right wingers who were not into sharing. I enjoyed the rhythm and the pace of the life and I learned a good lesson soon after I commenced practice.

I represented before the court a homeless person who was arrested for being drunk in a public place. He appeared before a senior magistrate and was given fourteen days. I was in his chambers the following day and the magistrate mentioned the case to me. I said that the sentence seemed harsh and he shook his head. The sentence was a benefit, the prisoner got clean sheets and the use of a shower for fourteen days and fresh food and clothes, a fortnight of shelter might help him survive the coming winter. It was a surprising answer that was not wedded to Law and it made me think.

The members of the Bar worked in cramped conditions, a room that measured about fourteen metres by four with an upstairs library of a similar size, a tea room and a post room just off the main hall where the tangling took place. Hundreds of barristers worked there. Sooner rather than later, you got to know everybody in the place and everybody had a political opinion. Nobody could be described as shy or retiring so you got used to the hits. I was exposed from the beginning to the meat of it and it suited me. I am blunt by nature but I am never personal and the Bar, in the main, speak in the same vein. The degree of frankness shocked me at first but it was refreshing after a while. You walked into the tea room and it was already in uproar and it remained that way. Five o'clock in the afternoon was a special time, barristers came in from every court in the North and they carried the news with them, not news of cases because the detail remained confidential but the news from the streets. Many people were influential members of all the major parties and that added to the cocktail. I was never out of contact with the political situation after I was called to the Bar because it was all around me, every day of the year.

The Bar is a monastic-like existence, not in the area of prayerful contemplation and restraint, but in the area of discipline. We work in isolation in a crowded room, we read the brief on our own and we go to court. There is a man in a red suit on the bench when we get there, looking like an everyday Santa Claus, who rules on matters of Law. A colleague across from me will take an opposite view of the case and it is my job to make the best case I can for the client. Somebody else decides guilt or innocence, a jury in the main and the judge sometimes. Back to the Bar Library at the end of the day to coffee and friends and spirited chat and, hopefully, a new brief in the pigeon hole. Home by dark and a spell in the study at some stage, the isolation suited me more than I knew.

The practice of Law stopped me getting personal about things. A brief arrives in

END OF TERM REPORT

the pigeon hole and I read the briefing notes, the witness statements and any early reports. It is natural to side with the client after reading the brief, to have sympathy with the circumstances and nature of the crime but that was not my function. You lose perspective if you get personal and you are not paid for it. Personal means you look for strengths in the case file and ignore the weaknesses. I went impersonal very quickly. I weighed the good and the bad aspects of the case and I looked for the bottom line when it was consultation time. There is no point in taking a view of the case at the door of a court when a contest is imminent. It shows a lack of preparation and lowers you in the estimation of a client and the instructing solicitor. Never take the side of the defendant because he will not thank you. Give him the support he requires, a professional view of the prospects in the case. The client makes the decision when the time to decide arrives.

Barristers practising criminal law at the northern Bar bore the brunt of the Troubles. They defended paramilitaries of every political hue, when they came before the local courts charged with very serious crimes, and they did it on a taxi cab basis. There was an obligation at the Bar to take the first brief that came along. The tradition was to accept any brief, irrespective of political background and defend any individual brought before the court, irrespective of class or creed. Everybody in practice had political beliefs and expressed them in the tea room every day but they never shirked their obligation to the profession. They practised Law without favour for the duration of the Troubles despite the divided nature of society. There were huge pressures. The situation was very volatile and accidents happened. There was a personal safety factor, whether it was a high profile case or a standard case of blackmail or hijacking. Barristers were always aware of the stakes involved but they ensured that the legal system did not crumble in the face of massive political pressure. The weight of emergency legislation added to the difficulty but they carried on. The situation was dire for a generation but imagine a situation where the legal system imploded. They did an impartial job at the height of the Troubles and eased the path to peace. Criminal lawyers were not representative of society but they enhanced society, they worked for the general good and retained their political convictions. It was a template for society in the future.

I wrote my first play called *The Resurrection Men* in 1983 and Briege McBride from Dolmen Players in Dundalk came to visit. They were keen to do it and I agreed. The play was about an IRA unit who abducted the body of a policeman and went on the run. Gerry Roddy produced and it ran for a week in the Town Hall in Dundalk. Dolmen performed the play in the Dundalk Amateur Drama International that year and won a special award. Aileen Coughlan gave it a great review in the *Irish Times*. The Abbey Theatre asked me to visit after I sent in a script. I met Christopher Fitzsimon who, I believe, was the literary manager and artistic director of the Abbey at the time. He told me that *The Resurrection Men* lay in the top two percent of possible productions but they were passing on it. He mentioned Frank McGuinness in the course of the conversation and had high hopes for his latest work. *Observe The Sons of Ulster Marching Towards The Somme* was performed in the Peacock Theatre about a year later. Christopher was right. It was a master work and vindicated his high hopes. I was well satisfied. I had managed to hit the crossbar and I valued the experience. If you ever fail to achieve, fail at the highest level. A new motto laced with irony, failing was a habit with me but I was beginning to mould it and shape it, just like other people. There was a strange comfort in the thought. I was other people now.

Donatists was my second play, staged in Newry in 1987 and directed by Nick Phillipou from the Royal Shakespeare Company. It was sponsored by the Arts Council and the cast included the great Sean Hollywood. The Arts centre where the play was performed was named after him, after his sudden death. The *Donatists* were a fourth century Christian sect, founded by Donatus Bishop of Carthage. They opposed any reduction in the reverence paid to martyrs. As I said in the play, they were unlikely to have many converts in the North of Ireland, our martyrs are well remembered. Anne liked *Donatists* more than *The Resurrection Men* but I remain loyal to the latter. *The Resurrection Men* was a rant of a play, a personal howl at the moon and a great release at the time it was written. We all need to open a valve sometime.

I founded Clanrye Community Workshop in 1983 in an attempt to address the rampant youth unemployment in the area. I sought out a number of activists to join me in the venture and ended up with a strong committee. There was a difficulty in the North. The system saw merit in the academic arm of education, it did not seriously consider the vocational. The majority of children had talent in the vocational area rather than the academic and they left the education system with a sense of failure. The workshop was based on the principle that no child should leave education with a negative view of themselves or the system. We took these children and allowed them to sample a number of skills and we watched them reach their potential when they discover the right discipline or medium. Clanrye Community Workshop was consistently in the top two in the North of Ireland after we opened the doors. We had a seventy-five percent success rate in placing our trainees in gainful employment after graduation at a time when the unemployment rate in the area was over twenty percent. I loved the graduation ceremony, watching young people accepting a certificate with pride and confidence and ready to face the world. The venture was very successful and we needed bigger premises so I looked around for a location.

I set my heart on mouldering ruins that I remembered from my schooldays. Abbey Yard was an historic part of the town, the site where Newry was founded and the location of a famous Cistercian monastery founded in the twelfth century. It survived until the Reformation when it was dissolved by Henry Bagenal. We togged out in the science hall on the second floor when we played the Abbey on their own turf. Abbey CBS was located in the buildings in Abbey Yard at that time and the football field lay beyond the archway. The Abbey boys were waiting in the yard, eyes raised to the windows of the science room, ready to form a gauntlet when they caught sight of the blue jersey of St Colman's college. We ran down the narrow tunnel of bodies and they guldered us out on the field. There was no need of a scoreboard on the days when Colman's were losing. There was a fence of corrugated iron around the perimeter of the pitch and the Abbey boys hammered it with their heels every time the home team scored. The noise is still fresh in my memory.

Abbey CBS left the Georgian buildings in time and moved to a purpose built school on the heights above the football field and I went to teach there. The original buildings had gone to rack and ruin, the roofs stripped of lead and the rain falling through, the walls crumbling and a belt of a digger bucket away from a career as a car park. I climbed the hill to the new school and explained my mission to Brother Beausang. He wanted to give the site to me but I was studying law now and free gifts always caused problems. The consideration was £20,000 as I recall. The restoration of the buildings took ages but the result was worth it, a row of buildings in mint condition and the preservation of a vital link in the story of the city of Newry. The locals watched history restored and they have a warm feeling about it. The rebirth of the Georgian houses was a symbol of hope in Newry because their renovation coincided with the first stirring of prosperity in the area for centuries. The rededication of the buildings in 1986 was an ecumenical one, out of kilter for the time but a sign of a better way. The economic fortunes of the town reflect the history of the community workshop as well. The time came when the original aims were redundant in a new sense of the word for there is little unemployment in the area in recent times, even in a recession.

We had a problem when the Abbey buildings were finished. Our legal adviser told us that we could not be landlord and tenant of the Georgian buildings and that Clanrye Community Workshop could not be relocated until we rationalised the relationship. There was a friendly split of the committee into property and training companies and we rang the changes. We formed Clanrye Abbey Developments in 1986, a built environment charity that remains a flagship enterprise for the Department of Economic Development. CAD has been a major provider of charitable assistance for over twenty years to voluntary organisations in Newry and Mourne. Building projects undertaken include the renovation of premises for Gateway, the Samaritans and the Salvation Army; the upgrading of graveyards and stone wall surrounds in Newry for the Catholic Church and the famous St Patrick's Church of Ireland in High Street; community rooms for the Presbyterian Church on Downshire Road and construction work for the Dominican Order. Sean Gallogly is co-director and John O'Hare and Michelle Gallagher look after both of us.

Chapter Eight

The two governments came to terms with the consequences of failure after the 1975 Constitutional Convention, laying the groundwork for more than two decades of direct rule. The task of the Convention when it met was 'to establish the provisions for the government of Northern Ireland likely to command the most widespread support throughout the community'. An interesting pattern emerges if you run down the years from 1976 to 1994 in the context of events and violence, the tit-for-tat nature of things and a society condemned to repeat the mistakes of the past.

These following incidents are in sequence and reflect the tragedy of those years. Ten Protestants are murdered at Kingsmill in south Armagh on 5 January 1976 by Catholic gunmen after five men from the Reavey and O'Dowd families in south Armagh are murdered on 4 January by loyalist gunmen. The La Mon restaurant is bombed by the IRA on 17 February 1978 with the loss of sixteen lives. Eighteen paratroopers die in a bomb at Narrow Water near Warrenpoint and one civilian on the southern side of the border on 27 August 1979. There is a hunger strike in the Maze prison – from 9 March 1981 to 3 October 1981 resulting in ten deaths. Three IRA men are ambushed and killed by the RUC on 11 November 1982 near Lurgan in what nationalists called a 'shoot-to-kill' incident. Seventeen are killed, eleven soldiers and six civilians, in the bombing of the Droppin' Well pub in Ballykelly on 7 December 1982.

Supergrass trials begin in Belfast in 1982. Fourteen UVF men and twenty-two Republicans are convicted on the word of police informers. The New Ireland Forum Report in 1984 suggests three possible solutions for breaking the Northern impasse. Margaret Thatcher rejects the New Ireland Forum proposals. The Anglo-Irish Agreement is signed at Hillsborough in November 1985. John Stalker is removed from his inquiry into the 1982 RUC shoot-to-kill incidents. There are allegations of a cover up by the British Intelligence community. Convictions in the Christopher Black supergrass trials are overturned on appeal in Belfast in 1985.

Eight IRA men and a civilian are killed in an ambush by the SAS at Loughgall on 8 May 1987. Eleven people are killed by the IRA at a Remembrance service in Enniskillen on 8 November 1987. A UDA gunman kills three mourners at an IRA funeral in Belfast on 16 March 1988. Two British undercover soldiers are dragged from a car and killed near Casement Park in Andersonstown on 19 March 1988. The Shankill Road bombing by the IRA on 23 October 1993 kills ten people. Loyalist gunmen kill six Catholics at Greysteel within a week. The Shankill and Greysteel atrocities looked like the prelude to Civil War. Many more people lost their lives during this eighteen year period. I am mindful of the suffering of every bereaved family but it is impossible to list them all. It was a depressing time, a litany of death and bloodshed and a lack of political will.

The peace process was started by the Provisionals in the Eighties. It emerged in the aftermath of the hunger strikes and was made flesh in the document *Towards a Lasting Peace in Ireland*. The local population, including the IRA command, doubted the wisdom of the hunger strikes and the prospects for success. Maggie Thatcher was prime minister of Great Britain and parts of the North and she was widely viewed as incapable of rational thought about Ireland. The hunger strikes caused a shift in the tectonic plates of Northern politics and set a new agenda for the future. The deaths of the men radicalised the minority population and allowed the Provisionals to enter the political arena with every prospect of success. The sheer size of the funerals of the dead men had a huge impact also on the Unionist population who were alarmed and concerned about the future course of events by the fact that men were prepared to die for the principle of political status.

The Provisional leadership began to address key questions, relating to tactics and strategy, an exercise that became more pressing after the 1985 Anglo-Irish Agreement. A determined attempt was made to strike at the heart of the Provisional movement in the late eighties through the deployment of counter-insurgency units, the final attempt by Thatcher to impose a military solution on the North. She failed because it was impossible to subdue South Armagh. The Sorth of Ireland had developed their own strategy for dealing with the IRA. The main preoccupation of the two governments throughout this period was to protect the institutions of the state, North and Sorth of the border.

The Provisionals substituted the Long Peace strategy for the Long War strategy. Attendance at Dáil Éireann if a Sinn Féin TD were elected was the first major signal that a change had come. It came in 1986 and it was not given the recognition it deserved. *Towards A Lasting Peace* was presented in 1992 at the Sinn Féin Ard Fheis as a discussion document and was largely ignored by the media and political parties. I did not ignore it. I viewed it as an interesting departure in every sense of the word. The Provisionals were engaged in the Long Peace and had control of the board by this stage. The debate in the Provisional movement was still about victory and defeat but the emphasis was elusive. Were the leadership talking about victory and defeat in a political sense or in a military sense, that was the question.

The trend emerged in time. The objective was the creation of a pan-Nationalist front and the eventual inclusion of the Provisionals as a minority partner in a Fianna Fáil government where they could push the national agenda at will. The trick was to secure endorsements for the strategy from the power players. Gerry Adams collected political names on the way back from the long war like other people collect pepper pots. They did not collect him or convince him of anything despite the popular fiction. People were glad to see him, including the Irish government, when the time came. The great and the good lined up to welcome them and convinced themselves that they were showing the Provisionals the road to Damascus. They made guest appearances on the long walk, endorsing the strategy, making it stronger. They settled for the warm glow of conviction that they were convincing the Provisionals while the Provisionals were intent on a soft landing.

The pan-nationalist front was sealed in 1994 with a handshake on the steps of government buildings in Dublin. It was one for everybody in the audience and a very solid start by the Provisionals, if the mind was strong and you were a serial optimist but the wall of disbelief in this community is strongly built and added to in every generation. There were too many stand-offs down the centuries, too many false dawns and dark nights, only one God to share in defeat and victory and the acid of folk memory to dim the lustre of a silver lining. It was really a Sunningdale moment, an end of the beginning if you did not mind the wait. It was a superb performance by Adams and McGuinness and the rest of the leadership of the movement. They positioned themselves as peacemakers and made new friends while keeping Provisional supporters happy that the old revolution had not been abandoned. It was very easy on the ear and it helped that history endorsed the move.

The corridors of power are clogged with former militants who are, or were, in charge of a state instead of a bazooka. Look no further than De Valera and Sean Lemass or Menachem Begin who was head of the Jewish Irgun underground movement in Palestine before he served as prime minister of Israel in the late 1970s. Nelson Mandela was still on Robben Island then. The Provisional leadership took note of the words of Yasser Arafat speaking at the United Nations General Assembly in 1974.

> Today I have come bearing an olive branch and a freedom fighter's gun.
> Do not let the olive branch fall from my hand

It was a tenable political response to the situation and they kept the gun in one hand while they worked on other matters. They were harping on about the security situation like the other parties, identifying problems not solutions. They had a point. There would be no agreement until primary problems were settled.

Irish America was one of the problems. There was trouble in the bedrock. Irish America was pulling in different directions. Official Irish America supported any political initiative that helped promote peace but the word on the streets was different. The punters put their hand in their pockets in the bars of Brooklyn and the Bronx in support of armed rebellion. It was an unbroken tradition that stretched from the Fenian Brotherhood to the Provisional IRA. Reality on the streets of New York was different from Irish reality. It was a Hollywood fable that gave you fireworks and fury without a sign of shredded bodies. They never showed you the leakage because they never wanted to walk in the spill. Ireland was *Quiet Man* country in American eyes. The IRA sat at bars in rough tweeds, sucking pipes and coming on like the local gentry, defenders of the people who always did the right thing. The IRA were Robin O'Hood and the tavern walls were on message, a print of a Famine scene and a general view of the parade on St Patrick's Day and framed posters blaring 'England out of Ireland' with the right stain remover. There were no pictures of mangled remains after a street bomb and no word of the civil rights movement. The Irish question was about 'the lads' and reform was for wimps. Pictures from the old country fought for space on the walls of the taverns with the local culture. If Michael Collins had played for the New York Mets, they could have cut down on wall space but Collins was still a divisive figure in the local taverns. To some Irish punters he was dead sound on the Irish question, to other people he was sound dead.

I went to St Louis Missouri for a speaking engagement on 16 November 1985 at the time of the Anglo Irish Agreement. I stayed at the Missouri Athletic Club. I was told by my host Joe McGlynn, the Honorary Irish Consul, that the Irish were not welcome in the club in 1960, the year that John F Kennedy became President. Getting there was the objective, now being there was the thing. I went back to New York after the engagement in Saint Louis and spent a few days in the city. The words of Joe McGlynn were on my mind and I needed more. Visits to the Frick museum and the Metropolitan museum were followed by a political visit. A friend took me down to City Hall. Very few about the building because it was a Saturday and I got a crash course in history. The Irish had huge political influence in New York from Boss Tweed to Jimmy Walker and were safe in the boardrooms when city politics changed. It took the portrait of Jimmy Walker longer to get back on the wall of City Hall than it took the Irish to make the transition from minor to major in the business life of America. It took the Troubles to move Irish America, to look at means and issues, to support the enduring dedication of the Kennedy family.

Washington and street level America were different constituencies with different agendas and there was no unity of purpose, no single message. Official Irish America wanted a political settlement but the street went with the old revolution. It was the way in America and the reason why the Irish vote was not decisive in the corridors of power. Harry Truman said on one occasion in relation to his close association with the Jewish Lobby:

> In all my political experience, I don't ever recall the Arab vote swinging a close election.

That is the reality of American politics. Americans never reach down to pick you up but they never blame you for standing. If you have the numbers, make them work. Irish America has the numbers but you have to know how to use them.

Ireland knew very little about America and less about Irish America when the Troubles began: the reverse was also true. This was partly to do with national guilt about emigration and the failure to address that curse. Emigrants got on a plane and disappeared from sight and sound, in many cases forever. It was different in 1860. Letters came to every parish in Ireland from every state in America carrying news and remittances, firing imagination and ambition and funding chain emigration. There was a slow decline in the level of knowledge after that. Nation building in the Sorth had an impact when peace came in 1923 after the Civil War. The effort to survive the early years of statehood immersed Irish minds and

America was a job market out there in the mist. Some things were not forgotten by the emigrants when they left these shores. They carried the Irish question with them and they kept the memory fresh. Their willingness to support the cause was potent and permanent. They were different and dislocated like the border cubs and their interest never waned down the years.

The Catholic Irish did not leave for the new world with the Presbyterians in the early part of the eighteenth century, although conditions were similar for both religions in Ireland at that time. Catholics who remained endured rack rents, bigotry and famine but it was famine that made them move. Millions of Catholics left these shores in the period between the Great Hunger and the American Civil War. The total population of America was estimated at twenty million in 1860 and the Irish kept coming. The survivors of the Atlantic crossing poured into ports on the east coast of America and adjacent ports in Canada causing major pressures where they landed, particularly in Manhattan. The Irish left the boats and made for the Five Points and the Nativists were out to meet them.

There was a flavour to the time and Dagger John Hughes was the pilot light. Hughes was a young man when he left a tenant farm in Tyrone and boarded the boat for America. He made his way to Emmitsburg in Maryland and tended a seminary garden for a living. He attracted the attention of Mother Mary Seaton who secured his steely piety for the church. He served with humility and debated across America with the Nativists – the American Party who were hostile to Catholics and immigrants - in defence of the Catholic Irish. Dagger John rose through the ranks on the strength of his personality. The newspapers called him 'green lightning', a dazzling flash often followed by thunder. He protected the faith of the young immigrants who crowded into New York when he became archbishop and he did it his way. Dagger John carved his mission on the parishes, headstone large. Schools before churches; daily bread before the nave and the pulpit and an end to the poverty of ignorance. The archbishop demanded moral obedience and made little impression. Morality was a private affair, rarely tested in the schoolroom. He was abrupt and dictatorial and the people loved him because he stood up to the Know Nothings, another name for the Nativists in New York City. He laid the cornerstone of a new cathedral to replace the old Saint Patrick's in 1858, up Fifth Avenue where the quality lived, up in the mid-town area.

The Irish bought the deal that Lincoln offered in the Civil War, a gun and an army blanket and a dice with death, a cut at life if you survived. About one third of the Union Army was native Irish or of Irish extraction and huge numbers of the Confederate soldiers came from the same pool. They distinguished themselves in the war and word of their deeds seeped out despite the best efforts of the Mayflower press to damn their name. First day at Gettysburg on ground chosen by Myles Keogh from Leighlinbridge. Keogh was the right arm of John Buford, the most underrated cavalry general in the war. Keogh almost captured Stonewall Jackson at Port Republic in the Shenandoah Valley when he was a bare eight weeks in America and four weeks on the staff of General James Shields, a Tyrone man who was commanding officer of Robert E Lee in the Mexican war. Shields represented four different states in Congress in his time and challenged Abraham Lincoln to a duel. There is a statue in his honour on Capitol Hill.

Buford had two brigades to hold the Confederate advance until the Union Army got up. The Brigade commanders were Tom Devin, second generation Irish from New York City and William Gamble from Co Fermanagh. Dragoons from every county in Ireland surrounded the campfires along Seminary Ridge as they waited for Robert E Lee. The whole Confederate army was out there in the darkness. The brigades were totally outnumbered so they dug in along the ridge that crossed the marching route of the Confederate soldiers and forced them into a bottleneck. The plan was to hold the ground for as long as possible and fall back to the high ground behind the town of Gettysburg, where the Union Army was massing. The brigades held the ground until the Union army arrived. It was an heroic defence and they got little credit because very little changes in politics over the centuries. Patrick O'Rourke, an Irish immigrant who finished first in his class at West Point, saved the Union line on the second day on Little Round Top and paid with his life. The third day brought Pickett's Charge with the remnants of the Irish Brigade at the stone wall, the centre of the Union line. One battle in a bloody Civil War but a crucial one and little-known Irishmen at the heart of the action. The Know Nothings looked elsewhere for heroes and Custer got the nod from the newsmen. Keogh was unlucky enough to see military service with Custer again. He died with him at the Little Big Horn in 1876.

The Irish were home from the war in 1866. The newspapers were full of Reconstruction and prejudice and carping fear. The Know Nothings called the Irish a living plague that God had visited upon the city, mired in criminality and ignorance, raddled by drink and disease and idle to a man, marked by violence and fornication. They were the dirt beneath the toenails of the people, nearest to the earth and nearest the grave. The Irish endured it all. It was better to have a hand on the ladder in America and a contact in Tammany Hall with a job in his gift than a levelled hovel and the fist of a landlord in your ear in the old country. The Famine strays formed a bridgehead into the new world and Ireland moved over, starting at the bottom when they landed in New York. Everybody had a chance in America but it pays to look the right way.

Ireland was there and Ireland was here and millions saw landfall on the Manhattan shore. Labourers stayed when they landed because there was work for quick learners on the stalks that blocked out the skyline. The Irish provided the bulk of the dock workers, coachmen and draymen, cooks and barbers and waiters. The immigrants needed New York and New York needed the Irish but there were few jobs for tillers and turf cutters on the city streets. No money to purchase mid-western farms so they moved out and lifted the load. They married their own and made room for themselves. Children were born and there was less Gaelic at meal times and a reduced hint of the old country in the young voices. They poured into the mining industry and railroad construction and sacrificed themselves for their children. The parents endured and the children secured, waiting for the moment and making their move. A multitude of other languages flooded into the city, pushing the Irish away from the gutter. There was democracy here and freedom and room to breathe. They shared a street and they shared a country and sometimes it shook until the hinges creaked, but they all found a way, like the builders on Manhattan. The Irish were leaving the Five Points and moving up Fifth Avenue in 1866 but they stayed loyal to Tammany Hall and the election district committee. They took the five points of power with them. Politics because there was strength in numbers and a massive volume of Irish in the city, the church because religion was refuge and domination, identity because it was an eternal engine, work because it was good and memory because it was a goad.

Andrew Johnson was a Southerner who was chosen by Abraham Lincoln as his running mate to balance the Republican Party ticket in his campaign for re-election and became President after the assassination of Lincoln. He was an uneducated anti-black dirt farmer from Tennessee who knew a great truth. Personality and policies were all right but you needed votes to win elections. There was a huge Irish vote in New York City, the swing vote in the congressional mid-term elections that year, so the President cut his cloth accordingly. He identified with the Irish cause, permitting the Fenians to fundraise on the streets of New York. The Civil War trained vast numbers of Irishmen in the use of arms and there was a view amongst a section of the returning soldiers that an invasion of Canada was appropriate, to highlight the Irish cause and politically embarrass England. It was a popular political move amongst the Irish in America.

The Union Jack was flying on buildings in Canada scarcely two hundred miles away from the main centres of Irish population. The Fenian Brotherhood used American soil as a launching pad and President Johnson turned a blind eye to the preparations. Johnson twisted the tail of the British lion again when the administration sold surplus guns and ammunition to the Fenians for the military venture. The association with the Fenians allowed Johnson to settle an old score. Britain had antagonised the Lincoln administration by granting belligerency rights to the Confederacy. British shipyards built and outfitted Confederate privateers that blockaded the ports on the east coast of America and caused untold damage. The Fenians crossed the border into Canada and failed to secure a foothold and the expedition force was captured and returned to America. Johnson failed in his ambitions also, the mid-term elections made little impact on a fading career and he stumbled from pillar to post in his remaining years in office.

The fallout from the Canada affair rumbled on for years in diplomatic circles until normal service was restored by the Washington Treaty of 1871, which settled the differences between the United States and Britain arising out of the American Civil War. A convention arose in Washington, just like Westminster, that the Irish question could not be discussed in depth or promoted by an American president at Anglo-American summits. It was an easy convention to enforce because the Irish question never raised a domestic head of steam in America. Resolutions in support of the Irish cause were passed by Congress every time the Troubles returned to haunt them but the pressure ended on the floor of the Senate or the House. There was no sign of executive displeasure at the antics of successive British governments in Northern Ireland and no rupture of the special relationship. It stood the test of time, allowing George Bush Senior to tell the Irish leaders during the St Patrick's Day celebrations in Washington in 1992, that he was willing to help find a solution but that the United States would not dictate one.

The Democratic primaries were in full spate when Bush's comments were made. The Democratic primary in New York was imminent and Gerry Brown was gaining ground. John Dearie, an Assemblyman from the Bronx - who organised a forum for the discussion of Irish concerns by the Democratic hopefuls during each Presidential campaign - issued the usual invitations. One hopeful, Bill Clinton, was a revelation when he spoke at the forum: well briefed, eloquent, commanding and committed. He promised the appointment of a peace envoy to Northern Ireland and direct Presidential involvement in the search for a solution. He said in passing:

> Sometimes we are reluctant to engage ourselves in a positive way because of our longstanding relationship with Great Britain..

The British government led by John Major protested vehemently at 'Clinton's cynical playing of the green Irish vote'. The Clinton camp was unmoved by the comments and the dispute began to grow legs. The Major government publicly supported Bush Senior's campaign in the light of the comments - in Britain and in America - and led to frosty relations between Clinton and Major after Clinton became President. The policy paper on Ireland, when it emerged in the course of the election campaign, reflected his key remarks on the night. It was an historic shift. At a stroke, Bill Clinton shattered a convention that had endured for one hundred and twenty-six years.

President Clinton did not have long to wait for a test of his Irish policy. Whispers of an IRA ceasefire within months of his election followed by a request for Gerry Adams in January 1994 to consult with American supporters. The visa application was highly controversial and set the media in a tizzy. Clinton had to decide if a gesture was needed. John Major considered a gesture obscene. The Major view was taken seriously by the American establishment; the State Department, the Justice Department, the CIA, the FBI and the Republican Party. Opponents argued that the granting of a visa would fracture the special relationship, unaware that the special relationship was already gone in relation to the Irish Question.

Bill Clinton had the support of Anthony Lake, his National Security adviser, Nancy Soderberg and some others when he decided on a response to the application. He sat in the Oval Office with two sets of papers before him and made a choice. Clinton granted the visa and Gerry Adams came to the United States. Some look at the granting of a visa as the high water mark of the policy. It was a signal act but it was not the principle. Clinton lived up to his election promise, direct Presidential involvement in the search for a solution in defiance of the special relationship. Breaking the convention was the principle, granting the visa was the practice. John Major refused to answer telephone calls from Bill Clinton for a week and the American ambassador in London was summoned to Downing Street for a dressing down. It was certainly a snub for the Major government and they did not like it. The reasons for a breach of the convention were different in the case of each President. Electoral in the case of Johnson and personal in the case of Clinton but the result was the same, a second breach of the convention relating to Ireland in the case of Bill Clinton and another hole in the 'special relationship'.

The Provisionals called a ceasefire in August 1994. The reaction to the news at Whitehall proved that power not people mattered to the Tory party. The ceasefire was an opportunity to make progress but the Tories took it as a sign of weakness by the Provisionals and an endorsement of their own virtue. The ceasefire raised the spectre of victory in right-wing Tory minds. Bottom line, Major was not prepared to encourage the ceasefire because it is not the Tory way. There was a basic dishonesty about the position. They were intent on saving their political skin so they took evasive action to head off the Tory nightmare, the day when they were forced to sit down with gunmen and alienate the Unionists who were keeping the Tory wreck afloat in Westminster. They sat down with gunmen from Kenya and Palestine in the past but that was different: those countries were a continent away. It was impossible to ignore the ceasefire so they stalled the steamer and plotted a course of steady as you drift. Major took a hard-line stance on talks with the Provisionals, insisting that the IRA had not yet made a firm enough commitment to decommission IRA weapons to justify talks with the British Government. The prime minister was really saying that a ceasefire by the IRA was not enough, capitulation was required. Victory and defeat are not the currency of democracy but governments make it so.

Gerry Adams asked Bill Clinton for a second visa to visit America for the purpose of fund-raising. The IRA had been re-designated by the State Department in the aftermath of the ceasefire so the application was not unexpected. Adams indicated a willingness to discuss the decommissioning question with British politicians after a meeting with Clinton and the President granted permission in early March 1995. He also invited Adams to the White House for the Saint Patrick's Day celebrations. Uncanny echoes of 1866 and Fenian fund-raising in New York City when Johnson was President. There were strong objections from the Major government. Patrick Mayhew, the Secretary of State for Northern Ireland, was dispatched to America in March in light of the news. He was sent to contact the old boy network in the State Department, to ensure that America and Britain were on the one page in relation to Northern Ireland.

He produced the so called Washington Three preconditions for Provisional participation in political talks when he was there, cobbled together by an MI5 operative in the NIO bunker in Belfast, after a crisis meeting between Major and the Unionists in lieu of their support for his tottering government. Washington

Three called for a declaration in principle by the IRA of a willingness to disarm, an agreement on the modalities of decommissioning and confidence building measures to show genuineness of intent. Paddy Mayhew was not into confidence building measures himself. The first IRA ceasefire was seven months old at this stage and formal talks between the British Government and the Provisionals had yet to take place. Mayhew had no interest in face time with the Provisional movement and neither had the Tory Government. There was a simple reason for his failure that rhymed with the imperial past. He was a cold warrior in a Europe that was thawing fast. Washington Three was a studied and deliberate move to uncouple the process. Washington Three was the ultimate stalling process and a blow to democracy.

By early September 1995, the two Governments, led by John Major and John Bruton, were proposing a summit meeting to declare a common position on IRA decommissioning. The summit never took place and the British accused Bruton of caving in to Sinn Féin pressure. It was not the case. There were stories circulating in Ireland about bodies in the streets if the summit proceeded and the press assumed that the leaked stories meant that the IRA would go back to war. This was a misreading of the situation. The bodies in question belonged to any Provisional leader who continued the peace strategy after the Tory Government came up with Washington Three. A government summit did take place in due course. The joint statement issued afterwards articulated a hard line position on IRA weapons.

Bill Clinton was due in Belfast on 1 December 1995. He was directly involved in the search for a solution and the special relationship was in limbo. There was pressure on the two governments to produce an initiative to coincide with his arrival. Senator George Mitchell was appointed chairman of an independent assessment of decommissioning by the British on 28 November 1995, with the consent of the Irish government. The governments outlined a twin-track process on the same day with a view to make progress in parallel on decommissioning and all-party negotiations. The appointment of George Mitchell fulfilled a promise to Irish America but Clinton had no illusions about the difficulties ahead. He publicly commented on the appointment of George Mitchell at a state dinner in Dublin. He turned to his friend and said:

> Well, George, like the song says, I got the mine but you got the shaft.

Mitchell must have remembered his words when his nomination as chairman of the all-party peace talks was challenged at the first meeting of the newly elected Peace Forum some months later.

The appointment of Mitchell changed the nature of the special relationship forever. It was a significant departure from the tried and the tarnished and it was a harbinger of progress. There was another aspect to the appointment. The direct intervention of the American president in the search for a solution opened the way for a personal intervention, if a sniff of a settlement ever emerged.

Some progress was made in the following months. Ground rules were agreed by the political parties in Northern Ireland, along with the two governments, regarding participation in talks on the future of the region. They were known as the Mitchell Principles. All parties involved in negotiations had to affirm their commitment to:

a) Democratic and exclusively peaceful means of resolving political issues

b) The disarmament of all paramilitary organisations

c) Agree that such disarmament must be verifiable to the satisfaction of an independent commission

d) Abide by the terms of any agreement reached in all party negotiations and to resort to democratic and exclusively peaceful methods in trying to alter any aspect of that outcome with which they may disagree and

e) Urge that 'punishment' killings and beatings stop and to take effective steps to prevent such actions.

Provisional acceptance of the Principles was heavily criticised by hardline Republicans - inside and outside the organisation and things were in a delicate state.

Mitchell's body on Arms Decommissioning reported on 24 January 1996 and the British government response was dismal. Major announced in the House of Commons that he wanted decommissioning before all party talks, contrary to the joint government statement about the twin-track approach on 25 November 1995. It was a studied snub of the Irish Government. The twin-track approach was unlikely to work in practice but Major rejected it anyhow. It was the final Tory betrayal, of politics, of democracy, of diplomacy and of nerve. John Major caved in to the 1922 Committee and Unionist demands that no talks take place. It came as no surprise. Major was a prisoner of his right wing and he refused to respond to any external stimulus. The Tories needed to test the mettle of the Provisionals and it should have been easy. Face to face talks, followed by inclusive talks, followed by reciprocal progress or abject failure or another period of Jesuitical argument, bona fides tested all round and understandings reached or unravelled. The Tories offered stagnation as a policy and trundled towards their political end with gritted teeth. So much for democracy in practice.

The failure to recognise the ceasefire was a mistake of epic proportions. A grand gesture was needed and the Tories failed the test. Major may have signed the Downing Street Declaration but he was still looking for victory in the northern rubble. The refusal of the British government to meet the Provisionals placed the IRA ceasefire under intolerable pressure. Most of the IRA were very negative about Adams and McGuinness persisting after Washington Three and they were opposed to a continuation of the ceasefire without inclusive talks, if that was the purpose of the exercise. The huge bomb at Canary Wharf on 9 February 1996 ended the first ceasefire after seventeen months. The blast caused two needless deaths and injury to innocent people. The breach of the ceasefire set the mood and the agenda for

This photograph shows Paddy O'Hanlon Snr (father of the author) Dr Rory O'Hanlon (former TD, Minister of Health and Speaker of the Irish Parliament – Paddy's first cousin) and the author – shortly after his election as the youngest MP ever elected to the Stormont Parliament – taken in 1969. (copyright Paddy O'Hanlon Publishing Ltd)

A photograph of the Mullaghabawn squad which won the County Armagh Senior Championship in 1964 with the author second from right in the back row and his brother Gerry second from left in the front row.

END OF TERM REPORT

This photograph is of the UCD Sigerson Trophy (All Ireland Gaelic Football University Cup) winning team in 1965 with the author on the extreme left front row.

These two photographs show the original founding Stormont MPs of the SDLP (L to R – Ivan Cooper, Paddy, Gerry Fitt, Paddy Devlin, John Hume and Austin Currie) (copyright Belfast Telegraph), the first at the 5th Anniversary meeting in 1975 and the second the surviving five at the funeral of Paddy Devlin in 1999. (copyright Irish News)

The first photograph shows the author with John Hume and Austin Currie on the steps of 10 Downing Street at the start of their two day hunger strike in protest at the treatment of detainees in September 1971 (copyright Belfast Telegraph). The second photograph shows the rather dishevelled MPs joined by Westminster MP Bernadette Devlin later in the protest in Downing Street (copyright Getty Images).

END OF TERM REPORT

Early SDLP meeting. This photograph is an early depiction of some of the senior members of the SDLP including the author and his wife Anne (extreme left front row) and Brian Feeney editor of this book (back row 2nd from right) with John and Pat Hume (centre front) and Ivan Cooper (back row 4th from right). Alasdair McDonnell (extreme right front row) and Alban McGinness (to right of author) are still prominent in the party. (copyright Irish News)

END OF TERM REPORT

The author addresses a Civil Rights Rally in Newry Co Down circa 1969
(Copyright Irish Times)

The author and his wife Anne taken outside the Belfast High Court on the occasion of his Call to The Bar (copyright Paddy O'Hanlon Publishing Ltd)

END OF TERM REPORT

Golf was an important part of the author's life after his footballing injury. This picture was taken on his Captain's Night in Warrenpoint Golf Club in 2002 and shows the author with Seamus Mallon former Deputy First Minister, Dr Rory O'Hanlon and his old friend and executor Rory McShane (copyright Paddy O'Hanlon Publishing Ltd)

A photograph taken at the meeting up in New Orleans of the author, his wife Anne and musician Paddy Cole who was a friend for many years and played at the author's funeral (copyright Paddy O'Hanlon Publishing Ltd)

END OF TERM REPORT

The author was very interested in the American Civil War and made a number of visits to the United States to visit battle sites. This photograph was taken at Gettysburg at a memorial to the 82nd New York Infantry – note the shamrock on the memorial. (copyright Paddy O'Hanlon Publishing Ltd)

This photograph was taken at the launch in December 2001 of the Task Force on Policy regarding Emigrants (chaired by the author) which reported to the then-Minister for Foreign Affairs Mr. Brian Cowen, T.D. in 2002. The report was highly influential in prompting a new relationship between Ireland and the Irish abroad. (copyright Irish Times)

END OF TERM REPORT

the rest of the year. Canary Wharf ensured that there was no split in Provisional ranks but there seemed to be a fallback position. Provisional statements reeked of damage limitation rather than the smell of war.

There was another victim of Canary Wharf. 'End the violence' had been the catch cry back in 1994. Call a ceasefire and peace will come. It was a grossly simplistic analysis and some people believed it. They ignored the facts that the ceasefire carried the problem with it and that peace is difficult. Besides, they were talking about two different conditions in the one sentence. A Tory government was in power and a ceasefire looked like surrender to the 'hang them and flog them brigade' in the 1922 Committee. History shows that the Provisionals called a ceasefire and nobody in government talked to them, that the atmosphere turned rancid and a bomb went off at Canary Wharf. The end of violence was a legitimate goal, peace was a completely different ball game. Preconditions like a ceasefire can be arranged but could anybody guarantee peace? Where were the elements of a settlement, the nuts and bolts to secure the ideal and placate my favourite group, the residual constituency of the disaffected? The search for the causes of their disaffection was an end in itself. The breach of the first ceasefire was not a case of back to where we started, it was further back than that.

Elections took place on 30 May 1996 to a Peace Forum. The elections were the formal entry point for the talks due to start on 10 June 1996, featuring an electoral system that ensured representation for loyalist fringe groups like the PUP and the UDP, fronts for the UVF and UDA. The Provisionals were barred from the all-party talks because of the bombing of Canary Wharf and they pressed for a boycott in the run up to the elections. The SDLP refused to join them and the Provisionals participated in the election after a lot of agonising. Talks started between the two Governments and the remaining parties and bogged down quickly on points of order and procedure. The Unionist parties took issue with the appointment of George Mitchell as chairman and his status at the talks. It was decided by the parties that he was an economic envoy rather than a peace envoy, to frustrate Clinton's election commitment. The decision sent a cold political message to the outside world. The talks were suspended in early July, about the only agreement reached in the session.

The summer of 1996 saw the worst civil unrest that the North had experienced for many years. Loyalist rioting and road blocks across the North in the lead up to the Orange march at Drumcree in July caused serious damage. Rioting in Nationalist areas was of similar ferocity after the march was forced through. The Loyalist Volunteer Force was founded in September and the UDA/UVF ceasefires were terminated. It was almost the worst of times politically, not as bad as the early 1970s or the hunger strike of 1981 but it rivalled anything else. There was little talk of peace in the land.

Chapter Nine

I was surprised that Anne was home when I pulled up at the house. Maura Donnelly was with her when I entered. Small talk for a few moments and then the awful news. Words swam out of the soup of my brain, cancer, lump on the breast, high grade tumour, immediate operation and the words were directed at me. I said something stupid and tried to settle but it was beyond me so Maura stayed until I was ready. There is a numbness that comes after the hard word. The brain searches for an escape route. You hope that time can be taken back. It was not to be, the tumour was malignant and there was a need to hurry. Anne was in the Royal Victoria Hospital within days and the tumour was removed. The results showed no sign of spread into the lymph nodes and I allowed myself to hope. There is nothing else to do. It was important to be positive and the first results were good. The seasons of our life changed and a pattern returned to our days after the initial shock.

Months passed. Anne had a pain in her side so she went to Belfast for a check up. A routine examination turned into a terrible discovery, a secondary tumour on the liver. I stumble over the question when she tells me. There is no treatment for a liver tumour that will cure it, just a chance of slower growth and extra time. More talk about the grade of tumour and length of time and I was drowning. Anne gently explaining the next move and me in a far place, refusing to come closer. It was the last time I let her down. We transferred to St Vincent's in Dublin after the diagnosis, under the care of John Crown. Anne had a trip to make before the chemo started.

We travelled the world together in the good times, all over Europe and around the Civil War battlefields in America with friends from the Northern Bar, along with Rory and Theresa O'Hanlon. The battlefield trips were a mixture of history and recreation and we had a regular routine. John Creaney QC met up with me and we chose an area to visit, hired transport and planned an itinerary around the local battle sites and scheduled a visit each morning. The rest of the day was for fun. Creaney and I were talking, before the awful news, about a trip up the Mississippi river on a paddle boat from New Orleans to Natchez, then a flight to Nashville where there is a significant Civil War battlefield site and a night in the Bluebird café.

Anne never saw the Bluebird but she saw New Orleans. Jazz was her thing and she wanted to see Preservation Hall before she died. We went to Preservation Hall two nights after we arrived in the city. A queue round the block moving very slowly, the sweet sound of New Orleans bursting out the windows and falling into the street while we waited. It was a building like the parochial hall in Mullaghbawn when we entered and not much bigger, the home of jazz where the greats made their bones, Armstrong and Jelly Roll and Bechet and countless other legends. Wooden benches in neat rows facing the musicians, everybody seated and no crouchers allowed, constant movement and a two-set rule, the best available talent on the stage and that clipped, Deep South, down home beat. The rows rippled like an anaconda and people moved on. Anne was transported. She ignored the two-set shuffle without a hue and cry and she stayed until it was time. I was so glad she got to Preservation Hall.

We were wandering aimlessly on the last night in New Orleans and Anne disappeared for a while. It happened often when we were abroad and I was not worried. She was always pulling me into places I was reluctant to enter and accepting my thanks afterwards. She did it once in Salzburg during the festival, a sell-out event, and she disappeared in the front door of the Mozarteum. Soon she was talking to a man about late cancellations. Seats in the Gods for a chamber music recital and seats on the stage for the last night. The stage never registered in magnitude and we wore what we could, two blistered blobs in civvies in a sea of formal dress and Anne Murray almost tripping over us on the way to perform to a packed house. A well-known conductor was sitting next to me and we talked about Tom Waits during the interval. He never mentioned my jeans.

Finally Anne was back and in a hurry, she grabbed my arm and pulled me down the street.

There was a crowd near a deli selling po-boy sandwiches and there was the modern day Bard of Armagh with his teeth in one. Tommy Makem played guitar for me one night in The Pavilion in mid-town Manhattan in the mid-Seventies. I always called when I was in town and he invited me up to sing The Boys of Mullaghbawn. We went down to the Village afterwards, to a folk tavern somewhere around Bleeker and Grove, a late night venue for the best talent in the city. Dylan was at a corner table with a number of people. It was a lift to see him. I am a huge Dylan fan and I carry his songbook in my mind. Tommy asked if I wanted to meet him but I left it alone. There was a risk that Dylan was not in and I preferred the memory of his music.

That night in New Orleans Tommy was playing at Flaherty's in the Irish Channel and we went along. He took the stage and the old magic came, a legend in Ireland and still underrated. He stood up to the mike like a centurion and let rip with that classically trained voice, strong and clear as Keady on a fine day. A great concert and a touch of Ireland and it is good to remember, contact with home is important when there is terrible news.

The loyalist ceasefire was announced when we were in New Orleans October 1994. Gusty Spence and the platform party announced the news and we were glad. The people of the North had shared a bitter experience. We had the blood of a generation on our hands without exception because we were there. Prejudice kills as well as inhumanity and the spoken word. There were things that never warmed me, bigotry spoken by an educated voice, the way that minds somersaulted in defence of tribal traditions, the rupture of reason and the massaging of the murder word into something more palatable. The IRA and loyalist ceasefires were a sign that the unspeakable was an option, that after thirty years enough was enough.

I left Anne in Portadown on a Saturday night in August 1996. I was captain of the Barton Shield side at Warrenpoint Golf Club and there were two All-Ireland matches in Kirkiston Castle golf club the following day. Everything was normal and she told me to go, so I spent the night in Newry. I returned to the clubhouse at six o'clock in the evening after a full day on the course. A message from Rory O'Hanlon when I got in. He was called to Portadown during the course of the day and Anne was on her way to St Vincent's Hospital in Dublin. I went directly to the hospital from the golf course. I was not ready when the time came. Her birthday was in July and I had bought her a present. Anne was not impressed so I asked her why. She said that the present she wanted was a grave in Mullaghbawn cemetery. I had not bought a plot because I refused to accept that she was going to die. It was a human response but I was wrong. I rang my brother when I arrived at the hospital and he did not fail me. Gerard rang next morning and told me that he had found a plot beside the mass rock in the graveyard. I was able to tell Anne the news if she asked me, and she did ask. She smiled and patted my hand when I told her. She drifted away over a four day period as I sat there, afraid to move.

Anne died on 8 August 1996, the unkindest thing she ever did to me. The cars did not stop in the street when she left me, the snarl of traffic on the busy road was the loudest sound in the room when I finally reached over and closed her eyes. The rest of the period is a blur. My comrades on the 1964 county championship winning side were formed in a guard of honour when the hearse pulled up at Mullaghbawn church. I took great strength from their presence.

The aftermath of bereavement is shuttered time, slivers of memory of a period when I was so happy I failed to realise it, glimpses of the chasm in my life and the horror of the future without her, the practical problems of living. I refused to think about the hole in my life but the soul searching lasted the length of the day. I was obsessed with getting home. People invited me to dinner or a show, to get me out of myself, but I was watching the clock after an hour and counting the minutes to leaving. People did not realise I was out of myself already and I needed to get in again. I had a need to be in the house. I finished work and rushed home and sat in the sitting room in the winter dark and tried to work out who I was, like a snooker ball bouncing off the cushions, seeking a direction. Anne and I were a couple for twenty-five years and she was gone. I needed to work out what part of me remained. We were not blessed with children and it was a blow but it seemed to make us closer, more dependant, more together. There is a great downside when death comes, no younger voices to break the silence, to clamour away the lagging time, to bring some relief. I came home from work in the early days, opened the door and called her name in the familiar way. The only sound was a ticking clock.

There is no structure to grief. It is not a scale drawing, quantity surveyed and costed, stress levelled and strain tested to confirm that the frame will not crumble in extreme conditions. There is no container made that can hold the outflow because grief is the measure of the world. Society should build a grief tank where they tuck

END OF TERM REPORT

the torn away until the shock has subsided, safe from a torrent of questions and no answers. Most people experience loss at some time in life but we are at a loss to explain it. I recycled it for months, pulping and mashing the fibre until it was wan pap. I believed that there was a bottom to it. I donned an aqualung and tested the depths until the pressure was too much. Death is a natural part of life but I was off message. I was a life crash after Anne died so I morphed in a chair, unable to get past that time. It is the parting that throws us and I was far flung. There was a great silence in my life and I was afraid to break it because the scream would rush in. I tried to rationalise it and it ruptured me. I attempted a holding pattern and nose dived at the same place every day. Finally the words of Jesus on the cross, 'Father, why hast thou forsaken me?' A human cry from the son of God when at the darkest hour.

We are born to suffer, it is part of the package. The strong hoard the warm moments and release them in the big freeze, the weak turn inwards and make noises like a porcupine and show their spines to the world. Are there only five stages of grief, is there a pat progression of denial and anger, that sort of thing. It all seems so remote, so clinical. There may be five stages of denial and ten stages of anger for all we know. There is no central core to grief, how can there be? How do you solve the mystery of the mind? Every bereavement is different. You mix and match and occupy yourself and try not to think too much. Nature places a scab over the wound because healing is of the spirit. Hurting means that you never forget. If you forget the pain, you forget the pleasure and the joy of being, the joy of love and being loved. Eventually, there is a reckoning. I remember a story about a Protestant woman whose husband was shot dead by the IRA and her only child, who served in the UDR, was shot by a lone gunman. She was asked a question by a reporter. Would she not be better to get past the memories? She paused before she replied, 'What do you do if these memories are all you have?'

I should have widened the lens and imagined a life without her, a life where I never knew her or a life after her death. If the right answer is a vote for love and life, why did I turn it into me? There was a rage in me after Anne died, a small rodent with sharp teeth who gnawed at my entrails with red-eyed fury. It was a killer of living things and I gave it murder rights. Everybody gets a knock but the Lord did not knock for me, so I played the small man with a big want at the dead end of a dark street. I counted my prejudices in the quiet hours and lay in wait. Maybe there is no other way. Rage is a lusty emotion and it has a purpose. It is not life but it magnifies living and I chose living in the end.

I never felt like drinking, not even in the darkest hour. Anne would been ashamed of me if I had broken and there has been enough shame in my life. I stayed with the AA programme and I stayed sober. Part of it kick-started me when the pain was raw and I needed to stir myself. I used the same procedure every day. I rose out of bed and said the Serenity prayer, had a shower and brushed my teeth and got on with the rest of the day. You need a social network at these times, a place to go when you stray on the dark side. An autumn evening in the early days and the thoughts flooding in until you are drowning. Warrenpoint Golf Club was always there. I got into the car when the feeling came on and escaped to the club. There was always somebody at a table in the lounge having a cup of coffee. You sit down and talk rubbish for an hour or two, content to escape from the tyranny of silence.

A time came when the heal was on and I settled into the discomfort zone. Grief is a bit like bruising and older people heal more slowly. The ache has subsided and the edges are purple yellow, pain free unless you poke the bruise with a finger. Anne changed me forever and I bless her every day. My current addictions are not self destructive and I manage. The world is colder but I cope the bulk of the time. I miss her sun on my face and there is a great chill when the sun goes down. I know how to cook and I know how a washing machine works, I have learned to pay bills on time and the milk rarely goes sour. I do these things because she trained me well.

Chapter Ten

I returned to the practice of Law within a few weeks of the funeral, in a conspiracy to murder case. I was led by John Orr QC who stayed for the duration. I took notes and talked to the client and his family during the trial. The sound of normality was everywhere, legal argument and cross examination and immersion in detail and straight home afterwards, a review of the evidence and it was time for bed and unquiet rest until the new day dawned. The trial lasted three weeks and I was the better for the experience. John ran the whole case and he put no pressure on me and I remember him when I remember the comradeship of the profession. You need great faith to survive pretty and I was not blessed with that. I survived ugly but I survived. I remember the signposts along the way, the time when shock turns into reality and the slow drag of acceptance. The early months were spent on auto pilot outside work and between the four walls of a room. Reality finally kicked in when I realised that Healer Time is always late. I was growing stronger now and able to take the hit.

There was an air of gloom about the Bar in 1996, a fear for the future. The courts were full of young men and women who had a point to make with a gun or a bomb in their hands and the deaths kept coming. It was a rudderless time, a new Labour government waited in the wings and likely to be in control within months and Major waiting it out. Waiting was the in word and the political system was freeze dried. Waiting was not an option for me. There was a familiar look to the future if it arrived at all. Any prophecy was depressing because it predicted the past. Like this.

An election takes place and the governments and the parties circle each other like weary old pugs: a rope-a-dope thing, clinch and hold and wait for the referee to shout 'Break!'. Nothing new under the sun and the dragon's teeth of policing and prisoners and other issues flush on the road to a breakthrough. There were new contenders on the scene, the Provisionals in strict training and the DUP waiting for the champ to fall. Neither organisation was in any hurry, not their time yet and there was a lot of political pain out there. The dragon's teeth were impassable and there was no need to intrude on private grief. Better to shift and sway and put your faith in a lucky uppercut, or a blind referee, to gave you victory in a tight contest. Years not months to the restoration of a ceasefire and parties content with re- election and the strength of a new mandate from the people, a mandate that was centuries old.

I had my own political demons. Washington Three was partisan and the idea of parallel decommissioning filled me with grave doubt. It seemed unworkable in principle and the Provisionals were likely to stay away as a result. Decommissioning can mean anything if you consider it. A slogan on a whitewashed wall makes the point, 'not a bullet, not an ounce'. I recall some other Provisional slogans: 1973 was supposed to be the year of victory and that did not work out so the date was changed on New Year's Eve and every year was the year of victory after that. It was not a wasted journey for the man with the bucket of whitewash. It was an opportunity to wish all his customers a Happy New Year. And if a start was made on decommissioning, what happens next? The IRA produces an ounce of plastic explosive or a bullet to the decommissioning body and departs. Is this decommissioning of ordnance, is this acting in good faith? Uproar follows and it boils down to a question of fact and degree. It leads to lively political debate but the door is not opened to all party talks.

The Westminster elections were a few months away and there were problems on the horizon if Labour won. Governments take time to settle in after an election and the spooks are always busy. They were likely to use the Tory rap in the circumstances, advise caution and slow everything down, stress the need to revive old networks and allow for the growth of trust. Worthy arguments in the round but short on ballast. Words like revival and growth thrive on early contact, not on late delivery. There was need of an intervention if the log jam was to move. Understandings needed to be reached before the general election took place if the ceasefire was to be restored within weeks of the vote - sooner rather than later - based on inclusive talks and formal contact with the new Labour government within a reasonable time. The alternative was more wasted years and that was a frightening thought.

The new Labour government were not tied to a set position. They supported the Mitchell Principles but that was the starting point for progress in my mind, not the end. Time was of the essence if the political landscape was to be transformed. I felt it was time to make a move, see what was out there, so I made a few calls. I needed to know if formal or informal contacts were in place between the Provisional movement and the Labour Party in view of the pending election. Contact with both organisations was likely to confirm that moves were taking place behind the scenes and I could settle myself but I needed to know. It was a reflex action, a single sally that did not disturb my nuclear winter and likely to take a day. It was also survival. I needed to be busy and it was alternative therapy, I was also aware of my promise to Anne. I arranged a meeting with Eugene Grant and Brian Feeney as a matter of urgency.

Eugene Grant QC was not in party politics but he is very political. He was immersed in the internal politics of the bar in 1996 and was instrumental in the election of the first woman chairperson of the northern Bar Council and the first junior to serve in the position, two firsts for these islands. He was totally trustworthy and had an intuitive grasp of political detail, vital attributes in relation to any future initiative which had to be based on absolute secrecy. Eugene was nominated with me by the Criminal Bar Association to lead a criminal costs campaign on their behalf. It was a small sub-committee because there was a small prospect of success. The sub-committee was unloved and unwanted by the general membership of the Bar and it dealt with a topic that was unlikely to attract public support. We were seeking more money for barristers who practised criminal law. It was a simple case to make. London barristers were earning three times the fee paid to criminal lawyers at the northern Bar for similar work. The key was the development of a matrix of criminal fees that would deliver London rates to local barristers. The dispute over fees attracted the attention of the Bar Council in England and Wales and a great deal of support was forthcoming from the right quarters.

Gareth Williams was chairman of the Bar Council of England and Wales when discussions began. He was Cambridge educated after his upbringing in a Welsh-speaking area of north Wales. He was a QC and Recorder by 1978 and leader of the Wales and Chester circuit. Gareth offered help with the comparatives, the scale fees applying in England and Wales compared to those applying in the North of Ireland in relation to similar work. He was very supportive of the cause and put his chief clerk, Alan Kilby, at our disposal for the duration of our research. Kilby came to Belfast to work on a matrix of fees for the future negotiations and to consult with the Criminal Bar sub-committee. Part of the preparation of the matrix took place at chambers in London, headed up by Gareth Williams. The campaign was a major success. Equivalent fees were eventually paid for similar work in the two jurisdictions.

Dr Brian Feeney was in the SDLP at one time and a political fellow traveller of mine at all times. He was an SDLP representative on Belfast City Council in the dog days when legally held weapons were carried in the chamber. We found ourselves in the same lobby when party votes were taken and we generally lost. We served our purpose and our time and finally moved on. Brian should have been a major political figure but the dice did not fall for him. The SDLP did not love him and they certainly did not promote him. They always had a problem with radicals. He teaches History in the teacher training college on the Falls Road and he writes a column in the *Irish News*. He was famous now, widely regarded as the influential political commentator on the minority side and a figure of substance on the northern landscape. He had another major strength. He had contacts in the Provisional movement as a journalist and in the course of his daily work.

I got together at the end of the summer of 1996 with Feeney and Grant in Law Society House over a pot of tea and discussed the situation. There was broad agreement on the political situation and the need to investigate further. There was a good chance that it was a pointless mission but we let it breathe. It was not a telephone matter. The nature of the proposal needed to be explored in depth and in private and it needed to be face to face. Brian was to make contact with the Provisionals in west Belfast to find out the current state of play and Eugene and I were bound for London. Gareth Williams was an urbane, articulate and witty man, firmly established at the top of his profession but he had another string to his bow. He was Lord Williams of Mostyn when he went to the House of Lords, a member of the Northern Ireland sub-committee of the Labour Party and the Leader of the Labour group in the upper house.

We met in his Chambers and made our pitch and the response was immediate. Gareth was positive about the proposal. He agreed that a second ceasefire was needed very quickly after the election and that inclusive talks were the way forward. Early meetings were needed between the Provisional movement and the new Labour Government if a second ceasefire was to occur. He confirmed that no contact with the Provisionals was in place. He then made a surprising offer. Gareth was happy to meet the Provisionals, anytime and anywhere, and he was ready to come to Belfast. He said that he needed to clear the meeting with Millbank, the nerve centre of the Labour election machine. We asked him to test the ground, confirm his belief that no contacts were in place and we left it at that. There was a danger that serial meetings would get out. There was no virtue in leaking it for political or practical reasons but rogue leakers never count the cost. The Labour Party would deny sanctioning any meeting if the news did break. Gareth would be hung out to dry and the opportunity would be lost.

Gareth was prepared to take the chance and so were we. He promised to come back to us in a couple of days and we left it there. We reported back to Brian Feeney as soon as we got home. He had been in contact with senior members of the Provisionals and was encouraged by the response. His contacts were keen to talk to the Labour Party about topics of joint interest and displayed an unusual sense of urgency in the course of the meeting. They confirmed that no contact was in place with the Labour Party at that time. He contacted them again to report on the meeting with Gareth Williams and told them that Millbank approval was needed.

Millbank vetoed the idea of a meeting with the Provisionals. They said that the Tory press would have a field day if word of the meeting broke. It would have an adverse effect on the election and the answer was no. Gareth came back to us and he was not happy. He confirmed that there were no ongoing contacts in place with the Provisionals. Gareth tried to lighten the gloom. He said that there was a huge willingness to engage within the Labour party and that we had tapped into something. He said the channels were open between Dublin and London and people were talking about new initiatives. Brian went back up the Falls to tell his contacts the bad news and we arranged to meet in the Europa Hotel after he finished. Brian was shaken and stirred when he got back and dejected. The meeting with the Provisionals was short and sharp. They took the Millbank view very badly. They expected a meeting to take place, even though Brian had told they that Millbank approval was needed, and they also took it personally. He had not seen them as annoyed and he was glad when the meeting broke up.

The veto by Millbank was an angle that I never considered but it made sense if you held it up to the cold light of day. It was too big a risk for the Labour party, a hostage to fortune at a nervy time that was likely to cost them votes if it got into the public domain. There was a need to look for positives. I expected an abrupt reply from both sides in familiar language - channels are open, thank you very much. The reaction was surprising, keen interest in movement and a ready response from both parties to our suggestion, not a bad start. The Provisionals were intent on progress, their reaction to the news indicated that politics was working in a cack-handed way. Their anger was an encouragement, although Brian was disconsolate, and the Labour Party were keen to make progress, but not yet. No talks had taken place with Labour about a second ceasefire so a stated view was necessary.

It was clear that the Provisional movement had a keen interest in the proposal so we decided to press on. Williams could not travel to Belfast but discussions continued. There was another way of dealing with the stand-off. I cannot remember if it was an immediate reaction or occurred in the course of the next few days but I put a proposal to Feeney and Grant. I was convinced that we could return to the subject in a less direct way. A meeting was not necessary if the priorities were agreed and flagged up in a public fashion for all to see. It was not a matter of absolutes, it was a matter of getting people to where they wanted to be. The Provisionals wanted certain guarantees if the ceasefire was restored and these guarantees had to be on the record after the Tory betrayal. There was an obligation on the Labour Party to spell out in advance what they would do when they took power. They were making statements in relation to all areas of party policy and they had a policy on the North of Ireland. There was nothing mysterious about the Provisional position that required elaboration. They called a ceasefire in the expectation that the Major government would respond and were made to suffer for it. They needed to know that things would improve under a new government. A public indication to this effect was needed to move the process forward.

A statement by Gareth in the Lords was not likely to grab the attention of the tabloid press because the Troubles were not news in England any longer. Gareth Williams agreed to detail the Labour Party position in the House of Lords, putting it on record, publicly binding the party to a firm course of action if they achieved power. There was no rebuke from Millbank so it was a go. Further shuttle discussion took place and we were happy with progress. It seemed that everybody knew what they had to do. A certain amount of camouflage was needed, a debate about Northern Ireland and a few studied comments in the middle of random remarks. The follow up meeting with Williams did not take long, a few questions and he was on it. It was his speech and his moment, a case of timing and judgement and it was not long in coming. The occasion was a motion on the Northern Ireland Peace Process in the name of Lord Holme of Cheltenham that arose within weeks. It was perfect because the motion was not in the name of the Labour Party. The motion was well aired before Williams rose to his feet. In the course of his remarks in the House of Lords on 21 November 1996, Gareth made the following key points:

i) We must return to the Mitchell Principles

ii) The Mitchell principles were mishandled by the Government

iii) Any suggestion that there should be decommissioning of arms before Sinn Féin is allowed into talks will simply mean that Sinn Féin will not take part in the talks...and we will be back where we were twelve months ago

iv)   He queries the recent contacts between Sinn Féin and the British Government via the agency of John Hume and asked what is going on

v)   He notes the curiously orchestrated coincidence in time between a speech of Martin McGuinness and a speech of the Secretary of State

vi)   He notes the deep feeling in Northern Ireland...the drift of government policy...wait and see...wait for the election...there is a distinct and deep sense of a dynamic lost and energy dissipated

vii)   He supports the restoration of an IRA ceasefire

viii) Believes, and it is only a subjective belief...that there is a sensible prospect of an IRA ceasefire in the not very distant future

ix)   The ceasefire will be tactical...most ceasefires are in those conditions but the fact that your opponent takes a tactical step means that you need to take your own tactical steps not simply ignore it.

x)   If there is a ceasefire, we must not lose the offered opportunity a second time

I was happy with the content. It was a broad brush approach that was inclusive, pragmatic and forward looking. He reversed Major by opting for inclusive all party talks without parallel decommissioning, subject to a second ceasefire. It showed a deep understanding of politics and the way relationships work and there were no snagging notes. He nailed the main issues and created a reference point for future negotiations after the election.

Major responded on 28 November to Provisional overtures, relating to entry into negotiations on the basis of a new ceasefire. The prime minister said that any new ceasefire would be closely scrutinised before deciding whether and when to allow Sinn Féin into talks. The demand for parallel decommissioning remained while talks proceeded. What were the Provisionals trying to achieve through these contacts with the Tory Party, a lame duck Government with six months to run and political survival on its mind? The contacts gave the Tories an opportunity, in the teeth of the election, to appear strong on security. At a local level, it looked like a bit of 'busking' by some leading players in the context of our initiative, an abortive attempt to steal our ground. It still looks that way.

The speech by Gareth Williams in the House of Lords was a significant move forward and the Tory press ignored his comments. Gareth was in Belfast within three days of the speech and we agreed to stay in contact when we met. Eugene Grant was the newly elected chairman of the Bar Council and often in London and things had settled down in west Belfast. Feeney was in contact again and the situation was stable. Nothing happened in the run up to the general election to disturb the mood, no concern from either side that the will to recommence talks on the stated terms would evaporate when Labour came to power.

I met up with Gareth Williams whenever he came to Belfast in the months before the election. I got the impression during our meetings that most things were possible and the impossible was a matter for discussion. His comments made an impact on me at the time. There were reasons to be hopeful. The initiative could have ended with the refusal of the Labour Party of a direct meeting between Gareth Williams and the Provisionals or rejection of a further initiative by the Provisionals, after they expressed their frustration and disappointment to Brian Feeney in a pointed way. Agreement to a signal in the House of Lords was an encouraging start to a new relationship, if a second ceasefire became a reality. There was a readiness on both sides to take risks to move things forward that boded well for the future. Certain commitments had been made on the record so we sat back and waited for the new government.

Blair came to Belfast on 16 May 1997 to make his first big speech as prime minister. It was within days of his election victory and it was an earnest of intent to get involved in the search for a political settlement in the North of Ireland.

29 May 1997 and Clinton was in London to attend a meeting of the Labour Cabinet. Clinton and Blair met the assembled press in the garden of Downing Street. What was said was revealing. They spoke about pulling their respective parties away from the old orthodoxies. Then Blair said:

> We agreed, too, and have for some time, that this is an era that calls for a new generation politics and a new generation leadership...this is a generation that prefers reason to doctrine...that is strong in ideals but indifferent to ideology..

Clinton, for his part, said that peace talks could only succeed if there was an unequivocal ceasefire in word and deed. I was sure of one thing, a second ceasefire would come and it would come soon and Blair and Clinton would still be there.

Prime Minister Blair announced in June 1997 that talks on the future of the North would begin in September 1997, with or without a cessation of violence. It was one of his first initiatives when he came to power. Tony Blair set out the conditions in a speech in the House of Commons, that applied to Sinn Féin for inclusion in the all party talks. Sinn Féin were welcome to join the talks six weeks after the IRA declared a new and unequivocal ceasefire. He offered a timetable for talks, to be completed by May 1998. He told the Commons that decommissioning was not a precondition for negotiation. It was the end of Washington Three. Labour had a huge majority in Parliament and there were consequences for all parties to the talks. The Westminster veto was gone and the power of Fleet Street would be unleashed on the foot draggers, whoever they might be. It was bound to be a white-knuckle ride.

On 19 July the IRA announced a ceasefire, beginning the following day, allowing Sinn Féin to participate in the September talks. It was ten weeks since the general election. It was possible that formal talks between the British government and the parties would take place within five months of Labour returning to power.

It was one thing to include everybody in talks, as of right after the second ceasefire, it was another to get them there. Some might choose to stay away from the talks but everybody got the opportunity to attend. On 29 September 1997, Sinn Féin was invited into the multi-party talks at Stormont by the secretary of state Mo Mowlam who accepted that the second IRA ceasefire was genuine. It was barely five weeks since the IRA declaration on 20 July.

The first meeting between Sinn Féin and the UUP took place on 23 September 1997. The UUP used the negotiating table to accuse Sinn Féin of continued involvement in violence and the British Government of bringing murderers to the table of democracy. They claimed that Sinn Féin had rejected the Mitchell principles of democracy and non-violence that they had signed two weeks previously. The UUP claimed that the Markethill bomb, a bomb that devastated the County Armagh village, was proof of this and they challenged the British and Irish Governments to exclude Sinn Féin from the talks. The UUP then left the meeting without waiting for a reply.

Procedures were agreed at the multi-party talks the following day. The decommissioning issue was sidestepped, so ending Washington Three and the Tory stalling procedure that lasted for three years. Substantive talks at Stormont began on 7 October 1997. Politics settled back into a familiar routine, charge and counter-charge and a frantic search for an empty glasshouse. There was a vast gap in the strategy for peace. Those who attended looked at their opponents across a vast gulf of politics, culture and tradition. They might be around a table but there was no basic agenda and no policies to effect change in the possession of any of the parties. There was no will to move from set traditional positions. The two governments were the only actors with the ability to move them and they had no idea how. They had a second ceasefire and nowhere to go.

Tony Blair shook hands with Gerry Adams for the first time in October 1997, the first British prime minister to meet a Provisional delegation. It was three months since the second ceasefire. It is useful to contrast the performance of the Tory party and the Labour party in the last days of the local cold war. Major resolutely rejected inclusive talks while the Labour Party supported the principle and acted upon it when they gained power. Three meetings for the Provisionals with Tony Blair within six months and a myriad of meetings with his officials; no meetings with Mayhew in the nine months after the first ceasefire and a roadblock created by the NIO to all-party talks in the shape of Washington Three, the last wretched shaking of the rags of imperialism in the last outpost of the empire by a party that no longer practised one nation Toryism.

Chapter Ten

Frank Feely at the door on a cold November night in 1997, on his way home from the all-party talks at Stormont and always welcome at the house. If I had gone to the ends of the earth and never met him again, I would remember him warmly as a teacher and a man. I was in third year in St Colman's when he arrived and he made an instant impact. He was unconventional in teaching methods, dress and habits and he had a rebel cut to him. Feely was fresh out of Galway university and raring to go and our class went along for the buzz. He was a welcome addition to the teaching staff at St Colman's and inspired many pupils to considerable academic success. He taught me English in Junior year and I remember the main prose text, *Autobiography of a Super Tramp* by a writer called W H Davies. I should have paid more attention: twenty years later and Davies was talking about me. Feely left St Colman's College and entered politics in 1973. He was a local legend, a Mayo man who arrived into Newry town and made room for himself. He was elected to parliament within fifteen years of his arrival in the area and had not lost an election since. Feely was a stalwart of the SDLP. He toiled in the vineyard for twenty-five years and never got much credit for it.

It is always a master class with Frank. The game was to work out the point of the visit so I sat down and paid attention. He was unhappy with the inclusive talks at Stormont and spelt it out in graphic detail. One innocuous line added to the primary agenda after two months of talking, war and rumours of war, whispers about repartition and a sustained lack of goodwill on all sides, a lot of skirmishing and heated exchanges since the talks began in September and no sign of peace or a prospect of movement in the near future. Frank was prone to purple speak at times so I watered it down a piece. What I did not water down was his concern. The turgid pace of the talks was a topic in the Bar Library, a source of celebration to some, a cause for depression in others.

It took time for the reason for the visit to emerge. Feely was looking for a constitutional lawyer who was willing to write a party document for a small fee. Nothing is ever what it seems with Feely so I pushed the boat out when he finished. I asked him why he needed a constitutional lawyer. He said that a sense of urgency was injected into the current process by the imminence of talks in the spring and it was necessary for the SDLP to work on a paper, particularly in relation to what was called Strand Two of the talks, the relations between the North and the South. Feely said that the May 1998 deadline was beginning to loom and everybody was getting nervous. I was worried by the reference to a particular strand of the talks which were arranged in three so-called 'Strands'. The problems were mainly in Strand Two, North-Sorth and Strand Three, the relations between Britain and Ireland, but the voting system proposed for the assembly was a major problem and it was a matter for Strand One, the relations between the two communities in the North, and he wasn't talking about that.

I asked about the approach of the Dublin government. He said the Dublin government was very keen that proposals should come from a northern source and that any contribution needed to reflect local touch and feel. There was much talk about a northern solution to a northern problem and a sense that Dublin was frustrated by the stagnant nature of the northern political scene. I noted the change of emphasis. The conversation started with talk of a constitutional lawyer and moved on to the need for detailed proposals. The message was confusing and Frank was always a dab hand at smoke and mirrors. I needed to work out a direction from a flicker of the maps.

There were plenty of barristers who were SDLP members and they should have been able to manage. Were they not involved? Frank said that he was intent on a contribution from me and he called to see if I was interested. I was left in a cold place. I assumed that the party had spent the political down time preparing for the moment but this did not seem to be the case. I was comfortable enough with the news because the scene was familiar to me. I never worked for exams until the music was playing. Why should political parties be any different? There was genuine surprise in the parties at the speed of events and there was precious little ante when the parties needed to ante up. The grey skies were gathering again. Time bought by the swift return to ceasefire mode by the Provisional IRA was likely to be frittered away in the coming months in the ante rooms at Stormont. I told Frank to confirm the funding. He left and I thought no more about it. Political conversations are like that, a beginning, a middle and no end.

There was another Feely visit within a week and he was full of news. There was no funding available and I had to do it myself. It was a pure Feely moment, another flicker of maps but the direction was clearer. The 'It' that I had to do was not defined and it was clear I had to work 'It' out for myself. Funding never existed, it was just Feely getting his feet under my table. The observation was off the wall but it amused me. It was Sean Hollywood and Hilltown again but I was battle hardened at this stage. I had left politics, drifted to the sidelines and was content at the Northern Ireland Bar. The dogs barked and the caravans moved on.

I rapped doors at elections like any other party member and made the usual contributions to party funds but my activities were low key. Politically I was dead if I had the wit to stiffen, consigned to the back pages of the party, a footnote rather than a doormat. I drifted away after the 1982 election and never looked back, loyal to the motto of the fireman - when you are out, stay out. The last thing I expected was a political visit. Why was Frank calling on a man who left public life over twenty years ago? He said that I never lost interest in politics and it was worth a try. My reaction was that there was a move on and the prime target was me. There was no need to rush into anything so I stalled. I promised to give him an answer within days.

I felt a need for instant paranoia. It always happened to me when politics called because I always went down with an adverse effect. Politicians and flattery are a lethal mix, a quick stir and anything is possible. Man becomes superman if the ego is massaged successfully. Anything is possible. I issued a warning to myself. Political graveyards are full of people who fail to follow the pin strategy. A pin has a head on it so that it knows how far it can go. I spent some time working out the direction. Feely was trying to drag me in again and I needed to gain control of the board before I made a decision. I tested a number of theories in the silence of my living room. The package that Frank left behind him needed to be handled with extreme care. It was literally a job for the bomb squad. The visit was deliberate or it was desperate. Alternatively it was just Frank on a lonesome. Writing something was not as simple as yes or no, it was far more complicated than that. What business was it of mine, apart from the business of citizenship? Was the Irish Government involved and what was the level of their interest in a document?

Feely made an offer to me, a clapped-out politician who, as the man in the street reminded me often, used to be Paddy O'Hanlon. No politician turns down a chance to shine so why were party members backing off and leaving the stage to a has-been? Politicians are not sentimental and I love them for it. They hold down the jobs that keep them in the limelight and toss hospital passes to the fall guys. All you need to survive is to know who is above you in the system and who is below you, long after you have forgotten the purpose of the organisation. There was no way that they needed the help of a failed politician unless it was a kamikaze job.

The fall guy is an easy mark because he is willing to take a risk because of ego or loyalty or brass neck. Remember the doggerel. They said it couldn't be done, so he smiled that slow sad smile and said he'd do it. So he tackled that thing that couldn't be done and he couldn't do it. A fall guy works on the basis that he is the first to be asked and that he possesses a secret that needs to be revealed to the world. His weakness is an inflated opinion of himself, a belief that he is a hidden diamond. There was a saving grace in my case. Like a diamond, I needed to be cut to make an exhibition of myself in public and I was sober for years. It is easy to see the moves if the political radar is working but mine was in poor condition and working parts were missing for years. There was a danger that, if I took the bait, the day would dawn and things would unravel and I would end up in the mincer.

That night I was a candidate for fall guy because I was working on two visits from Frank and a scrape of facts, certainly not enough information to put pen to paper. I followed my legal training and dug out the documentation. I got my hands on the SDLP Submissions to the Multi-Party Talks dated October/November 1997, fresh as the presence of Feely on the doorstep. It was a position paper, full of broad picture stuff and thin on detail. In the Supplementary Submission the following comment is made:

> Given the paucity of some parties' submissions on previous agenda items, and the limited nature of discussions to date, it would be inappropriate, if not impossible, to present a detailed paper on this agenda item in each strand.

Maybe I was being unfair to the party, maybe they were not showing their hand at this stage, maybe the detailed proposals were ready and waiting and Feely just wanted another individual donation to the policy pot.

There is a flavour of the talks process in the month of November 1997 in the SDLP documents and I quote from the documents: paucity of submissions and limited discussions to date. It looked like the parties could not agree a suitable place for lunch. The talks were going through the motions as Feely indicated. I was more worried by a sentence later on in the Supplementary Submission.

> The policing and political problems of Northern Ireland are intertwined and interlocked, we cannot solve one without the other, if we fail to solve one, the other is incapable of resolution.

Policing was a political problem, not an exotic plant. There were other topics of equal importance, major causes of conflict that also needed resolution. There were no proposals in the SDLP submissions on how policing might be resolved.

Politicians rarely do policy. They poke at it with a big stick and wait for a reaction. They leave it alone if it sits up and bites them. If it does not bite, they leave it alone because there is no public concern about the problem. The policy void is filled normally by civil servants or special interest groups or lobby groups who often draft motions that appear on the order of business of the parliament. Progressive legislation is won by popular struggle, not by grace and favour from above. Politicians are obsessed about the needs of their constituents and the local community. They have little time to major on anything else. Politicians tend to meet, muddle through and mend their nets in preparation for the next crisis. Politics is the hardest work I ever did and it is an iceberg existence. Most of the work is below the surface and rarely noticed by the public. People judge politicians on what is visible, tending to look at the public side of the job. There is a small public dimension where politicians travel to parliament and insult each other, a bit like the local pub on a Saturday night, but the rest of the job is discounted. Wakes and funerals and a rash of weddings, interminable branch meetings and advice centres and home visits, public receptions of all types and the long and winding road of public relations, TV studios and national radio if you are lucky, mostly the drudge of self promotion, press statements claiming credit for any progressive initiative in the constituency, fatherless or otherwise, and condemnation of any public neglect or public omission or public scandal that arises, competing at election time, with your own party colleagues in the constituency not with the opposition, the sweat of the count and the sour spit of rejection if the light does not fall on you when the leader chooses after the result.

The telephone rings from 7am to 2am each day, seven days a week. The callers never ask how you are but they know what you are, a court of last resort like the other representatives in the constituency, someone to turn to when everything else fails. You rarely get thanked when you get something right but dare you get something wrong. You write letters about everything and most of the replies are negative and you never expect thanks because gratitude is a scarce commodity. The man in the street is more important than the delegation in the room and the sound bite is more important than policy. The other problem about the man in the street is that you can carry him round the town on your back nine times but if you drop him the tenth time you will hear about nothing else.

Most people avoid the job like the plague but politicians run for office, not stand but run, on the basis that they will serve the public interest. I was in politics and I did the same, perish the thought that it was about ego or a failure to examine personal weaknesses or a need for love. Maybe I was just a bad judge of character but I always voted for myself. I admire politicians because they provide the ultimate public service. They are sin eaters for the community, a safety valve for public anger and frequent visitors to the public stocks. They dedicate their lives to a zero sum game and suffer brain damage from breathing hot air.

Parties are ruled by archaic conventions that are largely self defeating. In the main, party rules are about control and not about policy. There are too many fetters on individual members, with the exception of the leader and his or her golden circle who are subject to no control at all. Branch meetings are a penance and a prison. The meeting opens and the mantra begins, a long day's journey into fundraising with a summing up on raffles. There is a short discussion at the end on politics if the chair allows. Politics is an attempt to make a square table round and someone has to try. Most politicians I know try very hard because I witnessed the sacrifices made. I am no longer on the job but, in my heart, I am still part of the union. I have worked at eleven different jobs in my life ranging from a timber yard in Park Royal in London to the Bar Library in Belfast and I consider my time in politics as the hardest work I ever did and I earned the right to speak on the subject.

I was not fettered in my response to Feely because I was outside the system. It was better to be on the outside of politics for the purpose of the exercise because it is easier to achieve results. The governments were not awash with detailed party proposals with a consequent need to judge them on the merits or make fudge with them all. They were gambling on a blank page at the beginning and the hope of contributions, followed by the bones of a settlement at the end. They only needed to get lucky once. There was an opportunity here if the southern government had an interest in a document. I was shackled at the moment a proposal was put to me and I needed to respond. I was unclear about the subject, unsure of the source of the instruction and uncertain of the destination of any document and I had no intention of acting without more. Maybe Frank was puffing it when he mentioned Dublin, maybe it was just an extended ruse to gather ideas and prepare for the inclusive talks.

It was time to put an end to the maybes. The document search had clarified the lack of party policy but there was a need for further clarification. I rang Frank a few days later and asked him to arrange a meeting with SDLP deputy leader Seamus Mallon and a representative of Foreign Affairs in Belfast to see if the paper idea had legs. The request would determine if there was any real interest and I would test the water if a meeting was arranged. Things were simpler if a meeting was not arranged. No show by Foreign Affairs meant no Dublin interest or no interest in a document from me and I was a free agent. It was likely to be the end of the line because politics is like that, a swirl of vague promises and jam tomorrow. There was no chance of a Hilltown trip if I got the wrong answers. I did not have long to wait. The meeting was arranged within days at SDLP headquarters in Belfast and Foreign Affairs would be in attendance. The stakes had risen a notch or two.

I came to a crucial decision in advance of the meeting in Belfast. Any document produced by me was for the Irish government, not for the SDLP. There were a multitude of reasons, political and practical, for the decision. I had to give the SDLP a miss because I knew the routine. Giving the document to the party would place travel limitations on it and I was opposed to that. The outcome of a handover would be that the party executive would see it or not see it. I have the highest regard for all party executives wherever they may be but my days of running the gauntlet were over. Executive members are on the way up or the way down or marking time. They are the gatekeepers, forever vigilant and eternally suspicious. They have spent years raising money or rapping doors at election time and they remember the grind of it. They do not view their role as supportive of a poseur embarking on an adventure of his own, the individual who turns up at a party executive meeting and tries to sell them something. They consider new policy proposals as their private domain and the word of the leader is law. All party executive members come from the same gene pool and they all identify with a saying of Gore Vidal that went something like this: whenever a friend succeeds a little something in me dies. They would have viewed the New Testament as a useful discussion document if they lived in Galilee at the appropriate time and they would have banned the sermon on the Mount at branch meetings. They are least likely to say, 'what a brilliant presentation', or 'that man deserves an easy ride'. Best of all, they are right. Their function is to make it hard, not to make it over. Politics is a blood sport, knock them down and drag them out territory where ego is everything and the individual is used. Things get stolen in committee rooms. There is no property in paper once it is presented and no such thing as intellectual property where politics is concerned. Original ideas have a short shelf life. People remember that they were saying the same thing last week, if they like what they hear. If they were not saying it last week, they are saying it now and will soon be saying it to a friendly journalist over a quiet drink.

There is nothing wrong with this, it is the way that politics works. The document would not have survived intact or it would have been stolen or leaked, put back, put down or referred to the relevant sub-committee dealing with party motions for further consideration or flagellation. Put a press statement in a newspaper if you want to keep things personal, if you want to retain ownership of your thoughts. All party executives throughout the world are the same and I love them for it. I never felt precious about anything I have done in life because I have nothing to be precious about. The document I had a mind to deliver might be good, bad or indifferent but it deserved a fair go, not the butcher's knife that is called the party executive. It would not have survived the ordeal. And if it had survived the trial by fire in perfect shape, what then? It might be adopted as party policy and it might not; more likely sent to quarantine because of the source, later to emerge in a speech by a member of the inner circle or the leadership and lost in the political swirl. The document would not get past the executive so I passed on them. I passed on the leadership for similar reasons. It was the wrong time and the wrong process and there was a grave danger of plunder or leak or a mixture of both.

Say the impossible happened. Imagine that the document survived the party executive and, by some miracle, was cleared by the leadership and adopted. Assume it went forward as SDLP policy to the final peace talks. What portion would survive the first meeting with the UUP? Everybody knows the rules of engagement. The proposals would be the subject of routine negotiation and disagreed. Any document emerging from a party political source is irredeemably tainted. It cannot be accepted by the other parties as a matter of principle. Push comes to shove on the shiny surface and they give up somewhere in the middle. Nothing survives the negotiation table intact, everything dies in time due to a lack of oxygen and nobody shouts negligence. Going down the political party route was pointless. Failure to survive SDLP internal scrutiny or a Sumo wrestle with the UUP was the end of the line for the document along the conventional route. I would take my chances with the Irish government if the opportunity was offered.

Position papers are the standard way to proceed in the event of talks. A party lays out a range of views covering the range of issues on the agenda, consistent with a well tried political formula. The paper will be big on shadow and small on substance and suitably vague on the killer questions. The two papers submitted by the SDLP were proof of the principle. The professional approach to a golfing major is appropriate. It is not possible to win the title in the first round but you can lose it in the first round. Specific policies are dangerous for a party because you might shift position and position papers have no impact on a party like the UUP that has known absolute power. The SDLP lay out a position and Unionism lays out an entrenched position based on how far they had come, not on how much they had to change.

There is no place for sentiment in politics. I had no wish to damage the SDLP in a perfect world but I did not live in one and I was trying to change what was there. If the result was to the advantage of other parties, so be it. The ambition was community advantage not party political advantage. The document was aimed at equality and there were political ramifications if it was a success. Some of them were likely to test the SDLP but it was not a factor that troubled me. Other parties would be tested also, a type of equality of pain. There was one final reason to pass on the SDLP. Any document I produced was certain to contain proposals that were not SDLP policy. The document needed to address the causes of conflict and the proposals would be radical. I was a free agent, the benefit of working outside the political system.

The document needed to be inclusive of both traditions to survive the scrutiny of government, a fusion of unity and union. There was a quid pro quo. Equality was too important to be guaranteed by the government of the day: the goodwill of the government of the day had to be guaranteed by Equality. Any set of proposals had to be directed at the elimination of fear throughout the North and spell the death knell of the arbitrary use of power against any group in our society. There was a tendency in the minority community to claim a monopoly on Equality, in much the same way as a section of Unionism claimed a monopoly on right. People who take partisan stances demonstrate an ability to cry out of one eye. The proposals were best presented, jointly or severally, by the governments to the parties. In that way, the provenance of the proposals was not likely to be a discussion point. The proposals would be judged on the merits and decided on the merits without distraction. The parties would have the final discretion in those circumstances and decided to accept or reject accordingly on the merits. I was happy to go down the government route. The document had no chance if it fell prey to bias, prejudice or sectarianism. I had no wish to write a Loser's Charter.

I was in Belfast for a legal consultation on the day of the meeting in party headquarters. The consultation wound up just before noon and I was free for the rest of the day until the meeting. That was a big bonus: it allowed me to work on an approach to the meeting. I found a quiet place in the Upper Library and settled in. I expected a telephone call saying the meeting was off, that Foreign Affairs was unable to send a representative. I was unsure of my position if the southern government passed on a paper so I did not go there. Lunchtime stretched into mid afternoon and my mind was a blank. There were enough issues to keep the whole population busy for a year so I fell to doodling. I wrote down a rambling list of topics that made depressing reading. There was a hopeless bias in favour of Unionism in the institutions of the state, the police and the legal system, the civil service and the voting system. The detritus of fifty years of non-government was plain to be seen. There was a need for a viable set of institutions and the rationalisation of two positions: the wish of the Catholic population to be part of a United Ireland and the wish of the Unionist population to remain part of the United Kingdom. Earnest stuff and bland as a position paper. I toyed for a while with topics and timescale in a detached way until I gave up abruptly and walked down the stairs. Waiting is always the worst time, familiar demons attack the fault lines and play with the head, better to be at SDLP headquarters on time and let it roll. There was a every chance of a quick meeting. I was short on answers when I drove up the Ormeau Road.

Seamus Mallon MP the SDLP deputy leader, Alex Attwood a Belfast SDLP councillor and Colm Ó Floinn from Foreign Affairs were there when I arrived and we got into it. The meeting was very functional. They mentioned the issues for resolution, the agenda for the multi-party talks and they asked me to address these matters in a document. They also asked me to look at mechanisms for change. I never asked for views on any topic and none was offered. There were no instructions to conform to current thinking or some stated line. I got no indication at the meeting that a separate paper was planned by the SDLP.

I listened carefully to Colm Ó Floinn. If he had indicated that the Irish Government were not interested in the document, I would have refused to take it on. I told those present that the document was for the Irish government, not the SDLP. It was a hard message to bring to party headquarters but it would not have suited in a neutral place either. No objection was raised and I moved on. I indicated that I would deliver two copies on the same day, one to Seamus Mallon on a confidential basis and one to Foreign Affairs. I intended to give copies to Frank Feely and Brian Feeney at the same time. Giving it to one source in private is not sensible. It leaves you vulnerable in any future dealings and short on witnesses. It is impossible to tear a page out of history or resurrect the spoken word. I had no major view on the success of the venture but I was protecting the minor chance of a good result. I needed a situation where named individuals could confirm that the document was mine if any difficulty or conflict arose. It was not a question of trust. I could have settled for that but why bother? It was not a question of inflated ideas about the proposals. The document was likely to end up in an out tray in Iveagh House (the office of the Department of Foreign Affairs in Dublin) but I still took the necessary precautions, in the event that it avoided the out tray. I had the witnesses in relation to time, place and content if the document had any merit. It was better to make a secure arrangement than rue the loss of a set of proposals.

There were no arrangements made for a further meeting, except in relation to the handing over of the document. The glass got cloudy on the way home. I had nothing on paper and no ideas and I was fresh from a meeting where I had promised a delivery. In my mind, it bordered on the reckless. Maybe it was some form of private fantasy, the provenance of the fall guy. My mood soon lifted because the major questions had been answered. I had a clear indication of Dublin interest and the need for proposals that were northern in origin.

In my gut I was ready to write a paper but I was not sure what to write about. I sat down in my living room and reviewed the situation. It was a given that the D'Hondt system of electing ministers to a power-sharing executive would be used and cross-border bodies would be set up if agreement were reached in the talks. D'Hondt is not a perfect system but it had worked well enough elsewhere for decades so I left it. All the roadblocks to peace that had bedevilled the North since the beginning were large of the horizon. What was the use of power sharing if the system of voting in the assembly guaranteed majority rule? What was the use of cross-border bodies if a resolution of the policing problem was not found?

The big test beckoned in April 1998 and the parties were hoping for a mild spring. They were sleepwalking into the future, Micawber like, in the hope that something would turn up. A deal was not possible at this stage because they had nothing to deal and time was not on their side. The date of execution had been announced and the muffled beat of the drums was beginning at the edge of the scaffold and the groundwork was still not done. Despite all this, there were still reasons to hope. There had never been a double ceasefire and the beginning of the first multi-party talks in the history of Northern Ireland and that was a cause of celebration. A large number of parties were sitting down together in the absence of the DUP, a great advance on Sunningdale in terms of participation and party cohesion. Some were not talking directly to each other and that was a difficulty. The DUP were not excluded, they were absent by choice.

Getting the parties to talk directly to each other was another story but that was a problem for ABC – Ahern, Blair and Clinton. Bertie Ahern was the new Taoiseach and he was made of the right stuff, immersed in the Fianna Fáil tradition and pragmatic by nature. His biggest plus point was that he carried very little baggage. I was confident of something else about the small amount of luggage he carried: he knew what was in every bag. Imagine Charlie Haughey and Maggie Thatcher in the same situation. They were as likely to make political progress as China and Taiwan, a political limp maybe but no big leap. Ahern was a noted negotiator. He sat down with the trade unions in bad economic times and came away with respect and he was not a sabre rattler, before or after the recent election. Ahern was the most committed of the three leaders because he needed a result, the Irish Question was banging on his door and telling him to get on the phone.

The British had a special relationship with the Unionist population of Northern Ireland. It had to be special. It existed for centuries and survived fifty plus years of one party discrimination in the North without a hiccup. All British leaders honoured the code of silence on the inequity of it all. Waiting for a British prime minister to shift position on the North is like waiting for the French in Irish history: very little arrives and it generally tosses up in the wrong place after a storm when it does. A new man was in control in Downing Street and the scrutiny was on. The press called him Bambi but I was not so sure. There was a hardness about him behind the clipped speech and the ready smile, a street-wise edge to his tongue and a radical cut to the rhetoric. He talked and the Labour Party believed him.

Some people have charisma and some people have the opposite. The people who have the gift have a huge advantage. Blair had charisma and the people knew it. He came across as a font of knowledge and control, a keeper of secrets. The people knew that he had the secret and he believed them but he never said what the secret was. His enemies knew there was no secret but they were silent because the people would not believe them. Blair carried the secret with him and the people were content. He talked about a 'Third Way' and that was only busking, it was merely a term of convenience. It reminded me of a speech by a government minister in Killiney in Dublin in 1949. He was speaking about another eternal problem, the Arab-Israeli conflict. He ventured the view that the warring factions should settle their differences like good Christians. One of his civil servants approached him after the speech and told him that the Christian quote might not go down well in Damascus and Tel Aviv in view of their religious beliefs. The politician replied that it might not go down well in Damascus or Tel Aviv but it went down well in Killiney. Blair went down well with the Labour faithful and the latte liberals but he was hunting for Moby Dick, the floating vote. He looked like Gregory Peck and he had a harpoon in his hand. Blair was speaking the language of change and the electorate wore it well.

Chapter Eleven

One day shortly after I arrived in Stormont as an MP in 1969 I was at a loose end so I wandered into the Reading Room. I did a tour of the book shelves and the periodicals before I took down the most recent edition of Hansard, the bound report of debates in the House. I turned to the end of the volume, interested to see what was the topic in January 1969, just before the election and my arrival in the House. There was a speech by Basil Kelly, the attorney-general, towards the end of the volume. I got to know Basil Kelly in parliament and afterwards in the practice of Law. I remember him as an outstanding judge in my time at the Bar. His speech is a remarkable exposition of the constitutional position provoked by the public utterances of Bill Craig, a choleric right winger who represented Larne at Stormont. The debate gave the attorney-general a chance to reply. I abbreviate the main points below without injustice to the source.

Basil Kelly said: Stormont is a subordinate law-making body. Its legislative power is limited by the Government of Ireland Act 1920 and various Acts, 1920 to 1962, and the Ireland Act 1949. Its legislation is subject to the paramount authority of the imperial Parliament. Apart from exceptional and reserved matters, the Northern Ireland Parliament is a sovereign parliament. Sovereign, in this context, could be equally applied to the rule-making authority of a golf club. The first essential of a sovereign parliament is that there is no law that the parliament cannot change. By Section 6 of the Government of Ireland Act 1920, the parliament of Northern Ireland has no power to repeal or alter any provision of the Government of Ireland Act, or any Act of the Parliament of the UK enacted after 1921. The local parliament was given power to legislate for the peace, order and good government of Northern Ireland. The local parliament can pass laws on all matters that are transferred and the UK parliament passes laws in reserved and excepted matters. At this date (1969), there is no poaching by the Westminster parliament on the preserves of Stormont.

Westminster has the power to legislate on any transferred matter it chooses by Section 75 of the Government of Ireland Act and, through the parliamentary supremacy of Westminster, the UK parliament can make or unmake any law whatsoever without the authority of Section 75. However strong the force of convention (not to poach on transferred matters) it cannot be stronger than the force of law. Since parliament can set aside its own Acts, it is free to set aside its own conventions. A law is something that is enacted in parliament, a convention is a custom that grows up over the years. A convention has little or no force. The attorney-general asked a question towards the end of his speech:

How further do we maintain or strengthen our status? By self examination or, better still, by objective examination and the exposure of injustices if they are found in us..

Courageous stuff from the attorney-general and a warning amongst a number of warnings in the course of a brilliant speech. The convention that Northern Ireland affairs could not be discussed at Westminster was crumbling in 1969 under the pressure of the civil rights movement: other conventions would follow. The attorney-general asked the vital question but there was no follow up. Objectivity was not possible. Unionism was too far down the line. Direct rule followed in 1972 leaving the supremacy of the Westminster Parliament as the sole criterion. Over half a century the relationship, despite the learned words of Basil Kelly, had been changed by stealth. What had not changed was the location of power. Harold Wilson, quoting a favourite phrase from his 1971 memoir, said that Britain had responsibility without power for Northern Ireland. The comment astonished when I read it and it astonishes me today. That the remark came from a serving British prime minister who was proud of it makes it even more chilling. It represents a form of amnesia that is breathtaking and begs the question. What wonky logic led political Britain to the conclusion that the local parliament held the power and why did Whitehall identify with it, particularly the prime minister of the time? They had the power and they had the responsibility and they refused to exercise it for fifty years. Harold Wilson should have known it was Westminster. The frightening thing is that he did not.

Nothing had changed in a generation after 1972. Direct rule was in operation and Section 75 was in mothballs. Decades had passed and there was still no sign that Whitehall had got the message. The question in autumn 1997 was not what the parties should do, but what the governments would do, jointly and severally. They were in pole position. The British had the power and the responsibility and the Irish government had power and responsibility of their own. The question was, had they the intent? I gambled that the two governments were in agreement in principle on the way forward. They needed help with the dragon's teeth that studded the road before them.

I recall a formal dinner in Stormont, when I was a young MP, held in the great hall and hugely attended. I was seated next to a leading civil servant of the time who asked me my views on the recently appointed Derry City Commission. I answered him by rote. I said I was disappointed that non-elected officials were placed in charge. What we needed was more democracy not less democracy. He smiled and patted me on the shoulder and said:

> There is a problem with that point of view.
> What is it?
> Northern Ireland is not ready for democracy.

Not a bad place to start if you think about the past and examine the clinical evidence in 1997. The first part is easy. Discrimination happened because Unionism was not ready for democracy. They turned the North into a political slum and drew no conclusions from the extent of the squalor. Remember the language of the Troubles. The 'people of Ulster' meant the Unionist people when a Unionist politician spoke. Minority politicians talked as if the majority Catholic vote on the island was the killer point in any debate. Would the minority have behaved differently if the roles were reversed? I think not. It is obvious that no section of our community has a monopoly on virtue and wisdom. It is a tenable argument that if the predominant characteristic of Unionism since the foundation of the state was bigotry, the predominant characteristic of Nationalism was prejudice; opposing sides of the same coin and equally poisonous. It was not a matter of where blame starts or ends, it was a fact of life. The pathology of the problem was brutally clear. The political views of the two sections of the community were mutually exclusive. Anything that caused discomfort to one section of the population had an equal and opposite reaction in the other section. The word majority was used like a political cudgel and Belfast City Council was the litmus test of political goodwill where a large republican movement representation did not warrant an equitable share of the key committees. Words like consensus and compromise were not part of our political vocabulary in 1997. We used democratic terms to define our condition but we were washing our feet with our socks on. We were a politically crippled population in need of help, and that included everybody. Even if agreement was reached, we were still not ready for democracy.

Decisions made as a result of negotiations need to be written down. Too much was taken on trust at key historic moments. Understandings were reached on a wink and a nod and a firm handshake between the participants but good feelings barely survive the trip home and memory is fallible. The northern Senate was supposed to operate by weighted majority vote to redress minority concerns and Proportional Representation was the chosen voting system, but neither arrangement lasted long. There was a consistent exercise of bad will by the Northern authorities. Any future agreement needed to be recorded and endorsed by the parties and registered internationally. Nothing must be taken on trust. The worst of bad ink beats the best of good memory every time.

It was the eve of the bi-centenary of the 1798 United Irishmen rebellion and the radicals were on my mind. I recalled the resolutions passed at the formation meeting in Belfast attended by Wolfe Tone and Thomas Russell.

> That the weight of English influence in the government of this country is so great as to require a cordial union among all the people of Ireland, to maintain that balance which is essential to the preservation of our liberties and to the extension of our commerce...that the sole constitutional mode by which this influence can be opposed is by a complete and radical reform of the people in Parliament..

> To unite the whole people of Ireland, to abolish the memory of all past dissensions and to substitute the common name of Irishman in place of the denominations of Protestant, Catholic and Dissenter.

It was the manifesto of a nation. Tone redefined the Irish people on an inclusive, secular basis. He advocated political rights for Catholics and Dissenters and stressed the importance of numbers, instead of wealth, in the affairs of a nation. His ambition was to change millions of his fellow countrymen from subjects into citizens. A national movement could not have emerged without the American and French revolutions and the year of liberty set in train an enduring struggle. The manifesto based all hope of radical reform on the inclusion of all, irrespective of religion. Nationality was prescribed by the United Men and endorsed by the Catholic Committee through the appointment of Tone as secretary. The appointment was not universally welcomed but it made a political connection between Catholics and Presbyterians and defined nationhood. A Nation Once Again is a Catholic anthem now. Was Davis thinking about Tone and the United Men when he wrote it, about a nation of inclusion, not exclusion? I think he was.

The landed elite in Ireland treated Irishness with contempt so Davis took the elements of identity as practised by the native population and turned them into the new ideal when he emerged on the scene. He raised them up and challenged the colonists to respond. The work of the United Men, and Thomas Davis some decades later, was not the end of the matter. It was necessary to make a similar transition. Nationality and identity will always be works in progress. Identity is broader than ideology and needs room. The ties that bind us, or separate us, must always be tested and tried.

The structures of the political parties were a problem when meaningful negotiations were in prospect. The SDLP has a pyramid structure that worked from the top down, similar to the major parties in the Dáil and at Westminster. There is a consensus on the approach to be taken and the leader can take decisions on the hoof if the situation merits it. Conventional parties are not a collective but they obey the party line and they take the view of the party hierarchy as an act of faith. It was hard to know with the DUP if push came to shove. The structure was democratic in line with the Presbyterian tradition but Ian Paisley seemed to have a veto in private, just like the rest of the party leaders. The Provisionals are Stalinist in structure and instinct and it is a habit they will have to shake. It was likely that they would take their time, go back to the base for ratification if ratification was the verdict.

The Ulster Unionist Party was different. It did not work from the top down and that was a problem. The power of the party leader was the last vote at the Ulster Unionist Council, an eight hundred plus body where all major decisions were vetted and vetting was the favourite sport of the membership. The UUP had strong links with the Orange Order and they worked in similar fashion. The best result of any negotiation was agreement in principle by the Unionist leadership and referral back to the UUC, a cooling off period and major contention when the UUC met. The UUP worked at a slower pace to the other parties, at times in the past it looked like they moved at the pace of the slowest lodge of the Orange Order. They worked from the bottom up, not the top down.

Every political advance, beneficial to the Unionist community or not, has been bitterly opposed by Unionist parties in the course of the Troubles. Why did Unionism oppose the shining principle of one man, one vote for local government elections in Northern Ireland? There were many Protestant families, though not as many as in the Catholic community, where only the father as householder could cast a vote. Why vote against a measure that made a material difference to their lives?

It was the same with housing allocations by local government. The system was obscene. Power was in the hands of Catholic and Protestant councillors with the right to allocate council houses within their communities with a consequent abuse of power and corruption. Why did they vote against the recommended open and transparent system? Why did the Unionist population conclude that there was no benefit for their community in the reform?

Proportional representation met with the same clamour. It is patently obvious to any rational person that the system is effortlessly fairer than the first past the post system in Westminster elections that ensured that no British prime minister in recent memory has ruled with the blessing of a majority of the electorate. The approach of the ordinary Unionist voter was not based on injustice, it was based on fear. We talked about equality and Unionism talked about the price that the Unionist people would have to pay.

This approach was fuelled by a paranoid fear of rule by a vengeful southern state with domination on its mind. The Unionist Government fed the fire in the days of absolute power. They told their supporters who to fear and who to blame and counted the harvest of votes at election time. It was hardly a winning formula in the long term. Ground was lost every time the Unionist leaders said no over the decades of conflict. It was therefore likely that Unionism would oppose change of any sort if talks took place. It had become a traditional route. The other parties dealt in the here and now: the Unionist family was more used to the here and no.

The difference in negotiating style was a major cause for concern to me. There was a danger of talks taking place with frequent breaks for the UUP to consult some more, like a time delay on a TV chat show, while the other parties kicked their heels. Stalling periods become the norm and the means. Parties complained at the length of time it took the UUC to convene and the UUC stretched it out until the original opportunity was lost. It was impossible for the parties to agree a deal in view of the bottom up, top down styles of democracy using conventional negotiating methods. There were also problems because of the number of parties, due to attend, a maximum of eight at the last count plus the two governments. The current impasse was present difficulties multiplied to the power of eight parties. I needed an out-of-position paper, a document that started somewhere else and used other tools of democracy. To achieve equality, it was vital not to start from here.

Negotiating tables relate, in the main, to finite things like trade union disputes. The procedure works to a tried and tested formula and there are few surprises in store. It is basically the lore of the cattle market, the tale that a farmer tells when he gets home after selling a beast. He never gets what he expected to get but then he never expected to get it. A trade union dispute and an ethnic dispute cannot be settled in a similar manner. Trade union disputes involve compromise, ethnic disputes are more fundamental. It is not possible to sit at a negotiation table and heal division or the memory of past dissensions. The power of negotiation diminishes when you move beyond the finite, into areas like identity, citizenship, political belief, folk memory, symbols and the personal colours of freedom.

I will try to give an example. The 1954 Flags and Emblems Act in Northern Ireland was aimed directly at the minority. An individual could be imprisoned for six months for carrying the Irish flag in a public place as an expression of identity and political belief. On a political plane, taking it to a negotiation might have reduced the length of the prison sentence but it could not deal with the colours of the mind. A reduced sentence could be called a compromise but it could never be called a solution. Sometimes democracy gets in the way of progress when democratic tools like negotiation tables are used. In the absence of a realistic prospect of agreement between the parties governments who hold reserved powers must act. They are obliged to solve the problem for the parties and it must be beyond finite. There are things that governments do in isolation from union disputes and cattle markets. They decide upon the rules of discussion and they determine the bottom line. This is vital in the case of reserved powers. Discussion is a better word than engagement. It means discussion with the parties, after a discussion document is prepared laying down the government view backed by the supremacy of parliament. Reserved power means the government holding the power has the final say. Government commitment to a change of policy must be present and the blueprint must be right.

The pace of change has been a factor in Irish politics for centuries. Timing and the pace of change were vital elements in a forward strategy. Parties cannot handle radical change that results in a loss of face. What they can handle is space and the slow trickle of reform. Time was needed for the new proposals to take effect and the shock of change to abate. The shock itself needs to be cushioned and the ground needs to be prepared. Too big a statement of intent would have serious repercussions in the public mind. People need to become progressively aware that change was coming. If the British Government were prepared to accept their responsibilities - the need to be the master in their own house - then all things were possible. It was a British/Irish government concern in the context of strategy but change in the system was a matter for the British Government. If a particular problem was a bone that they threw to a particular political party then everything was impossible. It was not a forlorn hope, the markers of power were in place to effect this result. Proposals were one thing, the culture of government was another.

You need friendly governments to achieve a durable settlement. Hostile is impossible and neutral is not enough. There are major gains in a strong relationship, apart from growing trust and confidence. Friendly governments can take further steps as the relationship builds. Each government can become a guarantor of goodwill, become the first guarantor of one tradition and the second guarantor of the other; the second guarantor of the Unionist tradition in the case of the Irish and the second guarantor of the minority in the case of the British. It was a way of safeguarding the future. There was a need to provide mechanisms for an agreed Ireland by peaceful means. It was necessary to avoid another cold house in the context of an agreed Ireland, where the Unionist population was a similar percentage of the population on the whole island as the minority were in the North. The South needed to be as rights-oriented in relation to Unionism as the British government needed to be in relation to the minority.

It was more houses we needed not cold houses. We are all minorities somewhere in an ethnic patchwork and we should be mindful of the fact that it is solely an accident of geography. Loyalism or republicanism, unionism or nationalism cannot guarantee equality in these places, it must be underpinned by other means. The standards are set by the society we live in. The strategy was to solve existing problems, not create new ones. Leaving out was as important as putting in. It was crucial to ensure that nobody was left behind in the rush. Settling historic problems takes time and a generation is a good place to start. The problems begin before the ink is dry. Folk memory marches into the middle ground and demands a hearing, partial blindness is a virtue if the text is far seeing.

There are degrees of identity and it was a problem for a border cub. There was little sense of an Irish identity amongst Presbyterians in 1798, despite the efforts of William Drennan. A significant portion identified themselves as Presbyterians rather than as Irish or British. We have an equation of Catholic and Irish in the context of identity since at least 1690 as if they are synonymous terms. There was an outburst of Daniel O'Connell in the House of Commons in 1834, within five years of Emancipation. It was pointed out to him that the officials he was opposing were Irishmen and he said:

> They are foreigners to us because they are of a different religion..

Where did that leave Wolfe Tone, or Thomas Davis who was about to make his appearance?

A Belfast street orator in the 1930's said on the stump one day:

> If you took all the Orange sashes and the Green sashes and tied them around a ticket of loaves and tossed the lot in the River Lagan – the sea birds would favour the bread but the gulls would go for the sashes.

The quotation had a liberal slant, it was witty and acute but it was not the whole story. It reflects where we were, not where we needed to be. Both communities have cherished symbols that will forever remain in play and they will have their season. Symbols like flags and emblems are reflections of identity and culture, as I discovered on the football fields around Lurgan. Symbolism is important to a divided population, sometimes more important than material things, but partisan symbols have no place in the rule of law or the process of governance in a divided society and they need to be neutral to achieve a settlement.

There are degrees of sovereignty: the European Union, states' rights and federal rights in America, the South Tyrol experience in Italy and the autonomous regions of Spain. Why not the North of Ireland? Radical change was needed and change causes an adjustment of sovereignty. The issue had to be addressed at the forthcoming talks in 1998. New political arrangements, a new polity, required the consent of the minority and the approval of the South. Changes in Articles 2 and 3 of the Irish Constitution and new provisions in relation to Strands 2 and 3 were necessary if agreement was reached to reflect the new arrangements between Ireland and Britain and the northern political parties. Articles 2 and 3 were a matter for the Irish government so I concentrated on the rest. Everything needed to be the subject of an international treaty. The British, and the majority in the North, needed to agree on the new form of government within the jurisdiction and accept that the minority had a birthright separate from the state, that the present constitutional arrangements were terminable subject to consent and the use of peaceful means, and that certain issues had a political dimension, including the issue of prisoners.

Chapter Twelve

I needed to make a start so I retired to the study and stared at a spot on the wall. It was a big ask and I needed luck in running. I refused to place a bet on myself to finish the race in the quiet of a lonely room. Hours passed and nothing happened. I was tired of staring at options and the extent of the problem was beginning to intrude. My ambition was a series of proposals containing the elements of a solution but therein lay a difficulty. The most complex political situation has a few core issues: the trick is the ability to identify them. There were thousands of issues arising from the northern war and I had to choose. There was no future for the document if I failed to choose well. I spent the rest of the night in a fever of activity, in pursuit of the causes of conflict, drawing up lists of topics and reducing them before adding more.

It was a total lottery in many ways. The final six topics might be light years away from the base elements of division. Six alternative options might also suffer the same fate. I was looking for the proverbial needle and there was very little time. Different influences conditioned the core elements and conditioned the Mechanisms for Change section. After that, there was the overall strategy, the tactical approach to the document as a whole, which included earlier decisions on secrecy, the destination of the document and the avoidance of negotiation tables. There are many influences reflected in the final text. Some are stream of consciousness rather than mainstream items and maybe I am wrong. Maybe they were building blocks and maybe they were cement for there is a great need for jointing when you build a wall. They all had a presence in the final document. I was fairly comfortable with the six elements I finally chose, the cornerstones of my solution.

POLICING

The Royal Ulster Constabulary was tasked with abnormal duties from the outset and developed in a partisan way, defending the constitutional arrangements of 1920, enforcing the Special Powers Act and operating the various special constabularies. Any likelihood of the RUC proving acceptable to the nationalist community was undermined from inception by its role as the muscle of the state. The RUC implemented the programme of a tribe at war in the exclusive domain of the brethren. Unionism always worked on the principle that the traditional policing arrangements could not be discarded, believing that the RUC were an extension of themselves. This view endured because Unionism was always negotiating from a position of supreme strength. Unionists could oppose policing changes with impunity because of their special relationship with the Tory party, who supported the RUC, right or wrong, as fervently as they did themselves. The Labour party imagined themselves powerless in the matter and refused to get involved in the local mess. The departure from conventional methods was reinforced during the recent Troubles by the identification of the local police force with the massive body of emergency legislation added to the statute books during that period. The result was a shut out for Unionism because they were always allowed to put back the day of reckoning on policing. Policing was power, policing was the armed wing of Unionism, policing was a tool of the Unionist government.

No serious policing debate took place between the two communities in the period following partition. Megaphones at ten paces was the normal procedure, followed by the exchange of rival certainties. There was no middle ground. Both communities were in survival mode and there it rested. Polar opposite positions emerged over the decades: disbandment of the RUC in the view of the minority and retention of the status quo in the view of the majority. The latter view survived the passage of time because of the special position of Unionism in the corridors of Westminster. An indication of the approach of Unionism was the appointment of James Flanagan as Chief Constable of the RUC on 1 November 1973, just prior to the Sunningdale talks.

It is important to point out that the Unionist government appointed Flanagan to the post, not the British government. Flanagan was a Catholic from Derry who was a committed Unionist all his life and Unionism assumed that the minority would look upon his appointment as a concession. I am sad to say that some people bought the spin. It was supposed to pass for progress on policing and it was a confidence trick. There was worse to come. Policing was not discussed at Sunningdale because it was considered a taboo subject. The appearance of policing on the agenda would have caused an abrupt end to the talks because of a Unionist walkout at some tipping point. There was no attempt to tackle the underlying problem because certain interests would not have it so and the British government would not make it so. The issue of policing, fundamental to any society and a source of killing hatred in the North, was to be ignored. Negotiations on the matter would have demonstrated the ultimate weakness of democracy in practice because of the polar opposite views of the parties who turned up so the British government allowed the wrong to prevail.

Paragraph 13 of the concluding Sunningdale document, stated that :

> It was broadly accepted that the two parts of Ireland are, to a considerable extent, inter-dependent in the whole field of law and order, and that the problems of political violence and identification with the Police Service cannot be solved without taking account of that fact…the British and Irish Governments will co-operate under the auspices of a Council of Ireland through their respective Police Authorities.

The paragraph contains a major inaccuracy. The RUC was not a police service in 1920 and it was not a police service in 1973. The two governments should have franked a message across the paragraph: introduce power sharing and all should be well, until the next security force outrage. The refusal to address the issue of policing in a meaningful way at Sunningdale was an abject failure of diplomacy.

There was a danger that the future talks between the parties in 1998 were likely to be a case of Sunningdale revisited. Any serious discussion between the parties on policing would concentrate on current structures and ethos and was likely to terminate the whole exercise. It was a mistake to tinker with the existing structures in an attempt to water down the iniquity because it was patently the wrong place to start. Watering down was an act of folly. It did not make sense at any level. Systems fail and there is a patent need for radical overhaul. Why sit the adversaries down across a table for a pointless discussion on policing, in effect to haggle over the flaws?

It was important to ignore the political positions of the parties and decide on what would work. The governments had a duty to settle the problem of policing, not settle political nerves. Policing is not the play thing of political parties from any point of the political spectrum and it is not a matter for a smoke-filled room. One other thing was certain. The policing issue could not be ignored in the context of the talks. I made a number of proposals to get around the roadblock.

It was time to replace the 150 year old colonial model that survived in the northern part of Ireland. It was necessary, in the context of reform, to move away from the constabulary structure and the paramilitary trappings that surrounded it. The new police service had to be decentralised and the military-style structures abandoned. Regionalisation was the key to the puzzle. It had never been seriously considered down the years and I considered that this was the moment to break the colonial bind and convert a police force into a police service. Structures were already in operation throughout Europe, relating to societies at peace, that had stood the test of time and worked along certain basic principles. Successful policing had to be local.

There was merit in a ward-based approach because wards reflected population movement. I took Brian Feeney's advice on this (though he didn't know why I was asking) because he was intimately familiar with local government and policing structures. Policing needed to be based on council electoral areas representing a division. A sub-division could be five wards reflecting the politico/ religious area it served. An established percentage of recruits of the restructured force had to be drawn from each ward if the service was to reflect the complete spectrum of society, in particular the Republican and Loyalist communities. The practice of transferring police from, say, Armagh to Fermanagh was a colonial/ military concept and it was unacceptable. I proposed a Police Liaison Committee for every Council area, representative of the community and an overall Police Authority to complete the transition. I made a number of proposals in relation to ethos: uniforms, symbols, the culture of the force, the police oath, the code of conduct, future training and new disciplinary procedures and sanctions. There was a simple rationale behind the proposals. A police service was an impossible dream without major changes and police would never be able to return to Republican and Loyalist areas without their guns if radical change did not happen.

There was nothing original in the text, with the exception of the ethos proposals for a divided society, and my legal concern about the reach of a local ombudsman in relation to complaints. Quis custodiet ipsos custodes – who will guard the guards themselves? There was an intent on my part to create structures relating to a functioning police service in a society at peace because that was the purpose of the document, not a society at war. The radical thing was promoting these particular proposals, centred on structure, legal sanctions and ethos and placing them centre stage in the search for a solution, pitched against an outside climate where people were intent on disbandment or a return of the B Specials as the favourite options. I submitted the proposals as a solution to the problem of policing. Presenting them as a solution was totally original. Sometimes we miss the bleeding obvious.

CRIMINAL JUSTICE

Policing could not be considered in isolation from the criminal justice system, if the rule of law was to be protected. I took Eugene Grant's advice on this matter because as a practising QC Eugene has an intimate knowledge of the criminal justice system having spent thirty years at the coal face.

Policing and the criminal justice system in any democracy are joined at the hip and they are fused in a one party state. The two systems moved as a unit in the North of Ireland, generally against the minority, aided by a raft of repressive legislation. It was hard to identify the core problem but I will try. Son of Joe Bloggs goes into the city on a Friday night to meet his mates. The telephone rings hours later in the family home. Junior has been arrested and taken to a local hospital for injuries sustained in the course of an incident. Joe Bloggs rushes down to the hospital and discovers that Junior has been badly beaten up. His son tells him that he was not involved in a riot, that he was passing close to the scene of an incident and was attacked by the riot squad. The police claim that he was a ringleader, smashing the windscreens of parked cars and attacking police officers.

The story appears in the local newspapers next day with the usual results, the weary stereotypes of the conflict shouted at the reader from the front pages and ancient prejudices reassert themselves. Another rebellious Paddy or SS RUC was the conclusion, depending on your political point of view. The only certainty was that the stereotypes were reinforced as a result of the incident. The sequence of events has a familiar ring to anybody who lived through the Troubles, a sequence enacted in every town and city in the North on a regular basis. Young men drink and they make trouble, the police arrive and the locals fail the attitude test and the whole street gets sucked in. People get arrested who never lifted a hand and other people get arrested for doing wrong. The contradictory stories of Junior and the RUC play out in the local press until the story runs out of print.

The political row about right and wrong gradually disappears from the front page while the incident is investigated. Joe Bloggs is not playing on a level playing pitch when the investigation begins. The police are the arresting agents, the interviewing agents and the state body charged with preparing the evidence with a view to prosecution. The police have carriage of the case to the door of the courthouse and they conduct the trial if the case comes before the Magistrates Court. They are the instructing agents if the case is heard in the Crown Court because the DPP maintain a token presence at the hearing. The police investigation always took a predictable course. Junior is charged with riotous behaviour or assault or actual bodily harm of a police officer. Junior appears in a Magistrates Court months later and police officers arrive in numbers to give evidence against him and ensure his conviction. Junior is convicted and the sense of wrong, real or imagined, endures. It is a massive power in the hands of any agency and it was gravely misused. Crippling damage is done to relations between the minority and RUC and a deep sense of injustice deepens. The case is further confirmation that bias exists at the heart of the legal system.

Police were prosecuting 40,000 cases a year in the North in the 1990s. They were too close to the flame, the sole authority in charge of the investigative stage and obtrusive in the final hearing. They had absolute power in the streets and in the police station and there was a police record for anybody from any community who failed to adopt the servile position on a lonely road. The legal apparatus of the North seemed to operate like some glorified secret society where a select few knew how the levers worked. Nothing came out of the machine in the interests of justice, everything came out in the interests of the state. The necessary openness and transparency were missing and the consequences were politically disastrous. The key was to break the legal stalemate at a very early stage through the introduction of a referee, an independent agency with the power to intervene in the public interest, to access the police file and consider the initial arrest reports on Joe Bloggs Junior in an objective way. The District Attorney system in the United States and the Procurator Fiscal system in Scotland works on that basis. Why not here?

It was vital to reflect this view in original proposals that envisaged a new criminal justice system for the North containing the necessary element of scrutiny. We needed a separate investigative agency and the police out of the prosecution business completely. There was a need to confine them to a non-political, investigative role. I listed the major flaws in the existing system in the document. Some of the functions of the independent prosecutors are also listed in relation to carriage of the case, investigation, interview and treatment of suspects and the collation of relevant documents. I proposed an independent prosecution service that took carriage of cases from the arrest stage, leaving the police with the investigative role, acting on the instructions of an external agency who advise police on the direction of the investigation. Their function was to review all charges prior to their submission to court and take the decision to prosecute, or not, in all cases. There was a need for a public statement on the matter after the file is read to assuage public concern, a small political grace but a vital one in a divided society where police were accused of bias on an hourly basis. It was a matter of coded language: there is no case to answer or charges will be preferred in due course. It made sense in the political climate of the time. I listed the American system, the European investigating magistrate system and the Procurator Fiscal system in Scotland as possible models and the removal of all prosecutions from police hands.

The public had to be briefed about a new service with new prosecutors armed with a new mission statement in decentralised locations and a new outreach process from day one. The new criminal justice system had to be independent, fair and effective if it was to succeed, confident in operation and engaged with the community it served. There was a need for transparency in relation to overall policy, highlighting the decision-making process and the reasons for decisions. People needed to know what the role was and why and how it was carried it out. There was a need for a regionally based prosecution service, located in the community and accessible to the community it served, part of the community it served. It was vital that a new Criminal Justice System developed in tandem with the development of a new Police service. It would be a horror show if the old and the new systems had to search for the join.

THE JUDICIARY

A Judicial Appointments Commission was long overdue when I was called to the Bar in 1986. There was a bias in favour of Unionism in the appointment of judges and the going was bottomless. Representatives of the minority tradition were sparse on the High Court bench, even though almost half of the northern Bar came from the minority population. The North was in turmoil and there was a need for order in the land but Catholics were not to be trusted except in exceptional cases. It is fair to say that barristers from the minority tradition were reluctant to climb to the bench in some cases because of the security situation, more often because they did not identify with the politics of the status quo which was the politics of exclusion. The manners, speech and culture of the courts harked back to another place and another time and the system reflected a colonial mentality.

The backbone of Unionism in my mind was the police, the legal system and the back corridor where the High Court judges rested, not the Shankill Road. There was a whiff of minor public school and Happy Valley about it, homes in North Down and cosy visits to chums in the evening, Royal Belfast Golf Club with an impressive portrait of the Queen inside the entrance and access to the local yacht clubs for a breath of fresh air. It was possible to see Carrickfergus during the evening walk along Belfast Lough and imagine the Norman castle; square perfection in the distance; memories of small farmers and adventurers from Scotland and England who were granted land by a friendly government and settled and survived and prospered because it is the way of the world.

The Bar Library was on the thaw when I arrived but it was frigid down the back corridor where the High Court judges were located. They were isolated and austere in the main and they had a lot of power in their hands. There were 4,000 judicial and quasi-judicial appointments every year in Northern Ireland. These included

Industrial Tribunals and Supplementary Benefit Tribunals, Land Tribunals and Planning Tribunals and the regular appointment of judges at all levels of the justice system. I proposed a Judicial Appointments Commission to complement the changes in the criminal justice system and the police. The three topics were of a piece and a failure to implement change in one area would be a negative in the roll out of them all. The bench needed to be more representative, in terms of gender, experience and representation. It was a matter of public confidence if the necessary changes came to pass. There was a need for the involvement of lay people in all areas of the system, to supervise a new procedure for appointing members of the judiciary and the tribunals and removing the power from government ministers on the recommendation of senior judges, politicians or senior civil servants. In relation to the courts, I made additional proposals about the name of the service, wigs, the removal of symbols, the court culture and future training.

A pressure group creates a hostage to fortune when their call for a government commission is answered. They abdicate any influence they have when the commission is announced and place the outcome in the hands of government. The usual suspects are lined up to serve on the body, safe men and women and, in the interests of overall security, a proxy for that nice man from the black arts department who lives in the basement of Stormont Castle. You get what you deserve in the end. The result may be light years away from what the pressure group imagined or wanted but it is a long time out of the hands of lay men or women when the final decisions are made. Governments believe in minimal change as a rule and minimum fuss. They decide on an outcome and make sure it happens. If the governments were comfortable with radical change, they would fill the Commission with the right men and women to complete the job and secure the bottom line. It was vital to know the result before you set up a commission. Reform is a slow burn, a matter of easing it out, not pushing it out. New policing measures, and changes in the criminal justice system tend to move at their own pace when rolled out, and the ideal pace was a commission. This allows for reflection and debate, centred on core proposals that had been revealed to the general public. Besides, politicians believe in commissions. Someone else confronts the causes of conflict and draft proposals and they get to criticise the result. The blame goes elsewhere. The government adopts the report proposals and the parade passes by.

VOTING SYSTEMS

The history of democracy is haunted by a paradox. Nobody is entitled to a separate eco-system and a personal state so a bulk solution has to do. There is no consensus on the perfect voting system and that means trouble. Some of the bulk solutions are pretty dismal. No British prime minister has ruled with more than forty-two per cent of the popular vote for decades, so fifty-eight per cent of the population are permanently out of power. The attitude of the British parties is that a few years of absolute power is better than democracy. The drive against democracy in the North of Ireland began after the Civil War when Unionism agreed on a system of voting and the garnering of votes. Sir James Craig got rid of Proportional Representation for a number of reasons, the danger of a split in the Unionist family on a right/left basis and the need to remove the support for the centre that the voting system provided. The protection of the minority was not a priority with Sir James Craig but they were helpful at the time, staying away from the polling stations in droves for decades because of partition. They were still doing it at the birth of the civil rights movement in the sixties. Proportional Representation is the enemy of the extremes and it is the bedrock of democracy so the Unionist prime minister recreated the voting extremes. The first past the post system was perfect for a power hungry party, the alternatives available to the electorate were dramatically reduced and the vote was regimented into the polling stations. Majority rule in Stormont completed the exercise. It placed a lock on power and eroded the will to resist the monolith of Unionism and the system survived until the advent of direct rule.

When I sat down to write the document the idea was local Assembly elections and the election of a three member Panel at the same time, to be elected by a single Northern Ireland constituency under the PR system, a proposal originally mooted in the Framework Document the Irish and British governments jointly presented in February 1995 as a basis for negotiation after the first IRA ceasefire. The Panel was to complement the work of the Assembly. It was envisaged that they would have power to nominate Assembly committee chairmen and deputy chairmen, to scrutinise and, if necessary, block legislation. What it meant in effect was a panel of two Unionists and an outvoted member of the minority. SDLP thinking was a variation on the theme, three European style commissioners fulfilling a similar function. One thing was as plain as Ulster speak. It was still two Unionists and an outvoted member of the minority no matter what you called them.

Majority rule had failed northern society. It was the primary cause of the Troubles. The institutions would fail if the voting system agreed was any form of majority rule and that included weighted majority rule. I believed that progress on any substantive issue that arose within the Assembly was conditional upon a majority vote in favour from within each tradition. The proposal, in my mind, was the key to the whole document and the key to the future because it was the only voting system that made sense. I was certain that the blueprint document could not work without it. A majority within each tradition vote on key issues threatened nobody. It guaranteed that nobody threatened key issues in relation to either tradition.

PRISONERS

In most parts of the world, there is somebody in power and somebody sentenced for political beliefs or interned without trial. Imperial powers invade countries, or colonise countries, and then complain that nearby countries have intervened on behalf of the local population. They imagine that well-cut uniforms and massive gun power hold their own truth. They refuse to label insurgencies as home grown and legitimately based and they refuse to recognise political prisoners. There is a reason for this approach. Recognition increases the moral authority of the insurgents and the terrorist word loses its impact. Resistance to an invading force would become a legitimate act and place the paramilitaries on a solid political footing. The media cranks up and there is a weary ring to the offering, one man's terrorist is another man's freedom fighter and rival newspapers reflect the fact. The situation is further complicated by the claims and counterclaims of the combatants and the random use of vicious violence. The result is constant deterioration, constant review and massive regression as the conflict ebbs and flows and the rival groups in the community get involved. The war lobby calls for more repressive legislation and the government of the day responds, secure in the knowledge that there is terrorism on both sides and you can only face one way - towards the group that avows loyalty to the establishment or the group who call for rebellion. It was not a case of making it better, it was a case of making it survive.

In the local conflict, the government of the day faced the Provisionals and ignored the Loyalist gunmen for years. The system looked both ways. It sent paramilitaries to prison and ignored British army atrocities against innocent civilians, like the massacre on Bloody Sunday, one face looking on and the other face looking away. Prisoners sought recognition for their political beliefs and successive governments called them criminals. The British refused to recognise political status centred upon the decriminalisation of political prisoners, the right to wear ordinary clothing and engage in free association. The result was a litany of lost lives and the horror of the hunger strikes in support of an ideal that radicalised the situation and led to the peace process that was creaking along in 1997. The system frowned on a political dimension to the violence but they found a legal way to recognise it. The Northern Ireland (Emergency Provisions) Act 1991 defined terrorism as the use of terrorism for political ends, which concedes a political dimension. The said Act provided for a new category of prisoner. Designation as a scheduled offence unleashed special legal processes that tailored the legal system to the needs of the state; de-scheduling an offence meant that an offence was stripped of political content. It might have ended the legal argument but the political argument raged on.

The middle classes looked upon the paramilitaries as the enemies of democracy, people with blood on their hands. Any decision to release them was likely to attract moral outrage from sections of the Unionist community and an element of the minority community. The arguments presented by the victims of violence are well known and widely accepted. No matter how long the sentence, a prisoner can still talk to his loved ones, but a dead cherished son or daughter is gone forever. None of us are strangers to grief. We can guess at the trauma the victims of the Troubles have suffered, a life ripped away from the warm embrace of the family forever and sometimes the return of the killer to walk the same village streets. It is almost beyond imagination.

It did not cloud a harsh reality. Any settlement that refused to address the issue of political prisoners was doomed to failure. The prisoners were a political factor in the conflict and the political system needed to respond. They were representative of their particular area drawing in their immediate families, their extended families and their local community and they had a stake in the final outcome. Besides, there was no tangible political goal for the Provisionals or the Loyalists in the context of the 1998 talks if the prisoner issue was not addressed. There was pressure on the other parties to accede if the pieces fell into place. Police, the legal system and judicial appointments were away to commissions if the strategy worked and the long road to normality beckoned. It was not likely that these measures would proceed to completion if the prisoners were left behind. Prisoners were the tipping point for the Provisionals and there was no meaningful prospect of a final agreement unless the issue of prisoners was resolved. There was a cross-community dimension also. It was a sticking point for working class loyalists in general and loyalist paramilitaries in particular. There was one compelling argument in support of prisoner release. The existence of the peace process meant that no side could claim military victory. The purpose of the exercise was an inclusive agreement that left no major problem unresolved.

The timing of the talks was an important aspect of any solution. There were periods when the prisons were at breaking point because of the number of prisoners but 1997 was not that time. This was not the 1970s or the 1980s, the bloody decades that live in the communal memory. The torrent of violence had abated, the first ceasefire and the years leading up to it were evidence of that, and the number of Troubles related prisoners going into jail had abated also. Almost seventy percent of the political prisoners in prison in November 1997 were due to be released within twelve months under the fifty percent remission rule. Another ten percent were due for release within three years. Most of the remainder were due for release within six years. It was the optimum time to address the matter.

I recommended a Sentence Review Commission and the detail is in the blueprint and the name did not change when the Good Friday Agreement was signed. It is important to remember that this was not an amnesty, it was not the case that the gates of the prison would fly open. The Commission was instructed to review each individual sentence and prisoners needed to be identified with organisations that were on unequivocal ceasefire to be eligible for release. There were other sanctions involved. Prisoners were returned to prison in the event of re-offending. It would take some time to complete the process.

BRITISH-IRISH RELATIONS

The failsafe mechanism of the possible settlement was missing. There was no obvious safety net for the bad times when trouble comes or difficulties arose. Good relations reflect friendly governments and things were improving. The intergovernmental conference, the IGC of the 1985 Anglo-Irish Agreement was in operation and was working well. There was constant contact between the two governments on a day-to-day basis. It was common sense in view of our flawed democracy. Two diverse political and cultural views arrived daily at the so-called 'bunker', in fact a group of buildings behind a high fence at a place called Maryfield outside Belfast, and an understanding began to emerge. It was a nexus that had merit without more. Putting it on a statutory basis had a number of advantages. It formalised the relationship between the British and Irish governments in relation to the northern problem and it added permanence to the relationship. It was a mechanism to implement change at all levels, including underwriting and safeguarding of a constitutional settlement so that each community had a first and second guarantor. It had a role in any future constitutional change in the relationship between North and South. The first and second guarantor positions would be reversed by the two Governments to reflect any new political reality arrived at by consent and peaceful means. The status of the body had to be enhanced to achieve this. It was necessary to place the IGC on a statutory basis in a post-agreement era.

I passed outstanding work at the Bar and immersed myself for the duration. The document dictates necessary change rather than suggesting it. It creates precise solutions to the main problems supported by background material and based on the implicit belief that nobody should be afraid of equality. The structure of the document reflects the pressures of the task. Strange numbers in the middle of passages of text, an attempt to squeeze an extra sentence or bullet point into a swollen page on the word processor. There is a loose approach to topics at times. There are many proposals on police discipline and legal affairs in the middle of the proposals on reform of the legal system. New ideas emerged after a text page was full and I had to improvise. I had no time to waste on fancy presentations. I settled for cramped lines and smaller case words in an attempt to squeeze it all in. I needed to make it all fit into a page on the screen because one added line put the numbering out of kilter. I was too occupied to care. There was one overriding principle. 'Isms' had not come up to the mark. Nationalism and Unionism had failed to produce a solution down the centuries so I looked for a way to create equality of esteem between the traditions plus an add on. Do not look for Nationalism or Unionism as the basis of the document, it is grounded on rights, duties and responsibilities, a phrase I first heard Brian Feeney use in a talk he gave at the Tí Chulainn Centre at Mullaghbawn.

The text took three weeks to complete, almost twenty four seven. Most of the document came in a great rush but the detail kept coming until the end. I have no recorded date for the finish because it was not important at the time. There is a reference to a Paul Donnelly in the blueprint and a date given, 13 December 1997, the quotation comes from the *Belfast Telegraph* of that day. It was the last thing I included so I submitted the document soon after this. I squeezed the comment in because I considered the point to be relevant. It disturbed the page numbering and the indexing as is clear from the finished work. I had not the patience to rework the pages into neat packages because I was tired of the game. I had one major concern about the finished work. It came of a piece. Take a couple of proposals out, like police without a new criminal justice system, and it would not work. The result would be lopsided and the opportunity lost. The greatest danger was a complete muddle, a document that was strong in parts yet fatally flawed.

I made no recommendations about decommissioning. I thought about it and moved on because it is connected to confidence. It takes time to determine whether the profits outweigh the losses whether the subject is the first or second ceasefires or a political agreement. Decommissioning is a response to a climate of trust and belief and it was too early in December 1997. I took the view that the release of all prisoners would draw an appropriate response from the Provisionals at a suitable moment down the road.

I arranged to meet Eamon McKee of Foreign Affairs to hand over the document, in the home of Brian Feeney, and in the presence of Brian Feeney. It was my first meeting with Eamon and I met him often afterwards. His people had roots in the Newtownhamilton area and that was an extra bond. He is an outstanding civil servant and a pleasure to know. There was a need for absolute secrecy if the document was adopted. The real prospect of success lay in the protection of the source so that the proposals could be judged on the merits. I ruled the SDLP out on that basis so I ruled myself out as well. The provenance of the document had to be withheld until there was a full-blooded power-sharing executive operating in the North.

Eamon McKee agreed to the condition. I handed a copy over to Seamus Mallon and Frank Feely on a confidential basis and for information purposes only. To their credit, they kept the promise to this day. I was happy with the document as it stood. It had a certainty about it and it ended when it ended. I wrote a document that I thought would solve the problem, not to please people on a political or parochial basis. It was hard to work out what I wanted to do but I will call it. To bring forward policies that help people live with themselves and with other people. I felt that there was a ring of freedom to the ambition. Mostly the document reflected the change in me. I had studied the political situation for a lifetime. I sat the examination when the time came and I was happy with my performance when the test was over. I did not throw the books aside or shirk on effort in an attempt to justify failure. Something had changed in the course of my life and it showed in the blueprint document. Self examination is the beat of life and I try to keep in step.

Chapter Thirteen

I was grateful to Feely for the visit, not because of the proposition but because he forced me to end my nuclear winter. It was over fifteen months since Anne died. The world dragged me along until I was ready to walk again. My big thaw continued, I wrote a political thriller called *The Crossmaglen Dispatch* in the seven weeks following the handover of the document in December 1997 and I struggled the whole way. I have a feel for short stories and plays but the novel form is elusive. The initial part is set in the North of Ireland and the writing was like the local political situation, hard going for a long time and then hard going. The location oppressed the style and the clarity of the piece and inhibited the flow of the narrative. I was glad the main character left the North in pursuit of his obsession. The prose was much better by the time the plane landed in America. The last third of the novel is set in New Orleans and the Mississippi delta and turned into a ripping yarn. The ten weeks were vital for me, sixteen months since her death and I was touching life and spirit again. Reality was dripping into shock and I was coping with the change. I cannot describe the relief I felt.

I was told the fate of the document while I was writing the novel. It was divided up between the Department of the Taoiseach, the Department of Justice and the Department of Foreign Affairs. The Irish Government was running with all of it. I was pleased with the news but I made no material response. I realised there was no guarantee that a single proposal would be invoked and that no promise from any quarter would make it so. The out tray was still visible in my mind and might be utilised at any stage. Phase one was over and the show was still on the road. Phase two depended on Tony Blair and Bertie Ahern with Bill Clinton certain to enter the fray as an impact player if conditions allowed. The major powers of the world generally arrive as a blunt instrument or as a subtle broker. Brokerage was better. It was a proper use of American influence. The lurking doubts remained. Was there anything to fear from the smoke and mirrors men? Was it a joined up venture or a turf war? There were a thousand years of diplomacy at the hand of the British government. What way would the hand move?

The British and Irish governments presented a joint set of proposals, Propositions on Heads of Agreement, to the all-party talks at Stormont when they reconvened on 12 January 1998. The Propositions were presented as a basis for discussion, possibly offering the outline of an acceptable agreement. Outlines are dangerous things. Sometimes the closer you gets, the uglier it gets, but that is a risk that governments take. Frank Feely called with the document on the way home and we dissected it together. It read like a cosy fireside chat amongst friends, a progress report that revealed little progress at first blush. The paper talked about the outcome of the talks, not the content, and it talked to a wider audience about balanced constitutional change and the consent principle, devolution of an assembly, appropriate North/South institutions and implementation bodies.

It kicked on in the last two paragraphs, pushing the agenda out a little, not enough to startle anybody but instructive nonetheless. The last sentence talked about prisoners, security in all its aspects, policing and decommissioning of weapons. It was the first mention of prisoners in the context of a settlement or in the headings for agreement. It was less than a month since I submitted the document and I saw no material sign of input but the tone and the emphasis had changed. It was muted enough stuff on one level but the language was assertive and open and the political lens was wider. Prisoners were mentioned for the first time in print and I wondered. What did 'security in all its aspects' mean to the two governments?

All this was happening against the backdrop of the outside world, murder on the streets and malaise in the meeting rooms in Stormont. It was not an optimistic time. Billy Wright who founded the Loyalist Volunteer Force as a breakaway from the UVF after their 1994 ceasefire was shot dead in the Maze prison in December 1997 and retaliation by his LVF resulted in the deaths of four Catholics by the time the talks reconvened. The Trimble Unionists were still refusing to talk to the Provisionals. The DUP was refusing to participate at all and trying to get the Trimble Unionists to join them on the sidelines. The Provisionals were not happy with the Propositions document and they went to see Tony Blair at Downing Street a week later. They claimed it was a retreat from the 1995 Framework Document but it was an illusion. Significant advances had been made. The Provisionals were in Downing Street along with the British prime minister and Paddy Mayhew was not. The fabled out tray seemed further away after the release of 12 January document.

The package was delivered during the first week in March 1998 from the Anglo-Irish section of Foreign Affairs. I opened it and removed the contents. Strand One: Criminal Justice. A discussion paper by the British government dated 2 March 1998. There was a lot of detail in the document so I will condense it. The opening paragraphs contained an open invitation to the political parties to change the legal system that had operated in Northern Ireland since the foundation of the state. The British government indicated that they would welcome suggested amendments and views on whether it would be useful to develop an agreed definition of the aims of criminal justice and, if so, whether such aims should be enshrined in legislation. So far, so general. It moved on quickly to one of my markers of progress. The discussion paper listed the key criteria under the 1973 Constitution Act for the appointment of judges, including the need for appointments to be open and fair and based on merit. The discussion paper said that options consistent with these principles might include setting up an independent Judicial Appointments Commission accountable to the devolved Executive and with local lay involvement, with responsibility for all but the most senior judicial appointments, such as the Lord Chief Justice and the Court of Appeal. A role was envisaged in the discussion paper for the Irish Government in putting forward views and proposals on the membership of the Commission.

Paragraphs followed on the role and purpose of policing in a criminal justice system and the need for scrutiny of a modern police service. The paper stated that greater external scrutiny could be provided while still preserving independence from political control. One model was to enhance the role of the prosecutor, adopting aspects of the system in Scotland where the Prosecutor Fiscal has special powers. Another option was to enhance judicial involvement in the investigating process by providing for examining magistrates, as is the practice in other European countries. Then another broad statement. The Government would welcome views on whether greater external supervision of the criminal investigation process was desirable and whether any other system provided an appropriate model for consideration. It was revolutionary in some ways, a British government saying that another legal system might be better and offering to explore all options in detail with a view to change.

The paper then turned to the prosecution process in the criminal justice system. It indicated that this could be enhanced by giving the DPP responsibility for all criminal prosecutions, including those currently carried out by the police. This would provide an additional safeguard for the public since there would be an independent review of all investigations before the matter was brought before a court. The Government would welcome views on the proposal. It was an historic paragraph, in my mind, and a crucial concession. It was a move away from tradition, pushing out the boundary of possibility and following the reasoning in the blueprint document.

Paragraph 14 relating to Criminal Justice and the Community is extraordinary by any standards and includes the following

> It should be recognised that there are areas of Northern Ireland where the police in particular have been unable to operate normally for years.

The paragraph refers to punishment shootings and beatings and deplores them, and alternative systems of justice that were currently in operation and deplores them. Finally, the broad statement

> The Government would welcome views on how the criminal justice system can be more responsive to local communities and win greater confidence from all sections of the community..

The government was publicly accepting that police were unable to operate normally and asking how to change this. It accepted the principle of withdrawal of consent by communities living in nationalist areas. It was a very radical paragraph, arriving weeks before the final all-party talks and bang on the button, candid and contrite and refreshingly progressive. The paper was a stunning surprise, like making a record and hearing it playing in a faraway room, in a house that had no taste for your kind of music in the past. You plan it and you go through the phases but you never expect it to happen. The two governments had taken all the main points from my blueprint document and run them back from the British side. I moved on very quickly. My money was down in other areas and the wheel of fortune was still spinning and I wanted it all. The radical might be replaced by the routine in jig time and reduce the criminal justice paper to a goodwill gesture to the minority.

The second document was called Principles for Policing in Northern Ireland and dated 4 March 1998. Paragraph 7:1 stated that any examination from first principles of policing also raised points about the structure and organisation of the Royal Ulster Constabulary. Should it continue to be a unitary service? Should its internal structures be aligned with those of other Northern Ireland public service structures or District Councils? Should it continue to be both a Northern Ireland wide organisation and have elements of regional/local organisation? Should it be more clearly delineated on functional lines: a Traffic and Highways Branch dealing with traffic offences and crimes occurring on roads, a Drugs Branch, a Criminal Investigations Branch dealing with major criminal cases? There was a clear statement in the text that the police were unable to operate normally in nationalist areas.

There followed a number of leading questions that set the limits on future debate and challenged everybody to answer the questions posed. The Secretary of State wanted to hear a wide range of views before the creation of a police service acceptable to both traditions in Northern Ireland and subject to peace in the land. She used the word 'police' in the preface: RUC only appeared at the beginning and the end of the document. There followed another telling passage. The paper warned the parties at 7:1 that the coming debate will be about the first principles of policing in relation to structure and organisation. Recruitment levels were questioned as were the role of symbols and ethos and the nature and extent of operational independence. It was seismic stuff.

The British were prepared to abandon the colonial system of centralised policing, in effect siege policing, that had obtained in Ireland for one hundred and sixty years. There was no direct mention of the paramilitary nature of the force but it was out there. Regionalisation loomed large in the document in the reference to district Councils and other public service structures but the drum was muffled for the moment. The British government was killing centralisation softly in a few short paragraphs on innocuous sheets of paper and they were doing it in public. There was a bit of hedging and trimming but the intent was clear. There was purpose and direction to the documents in areas where the British government held reserved powers and they were saying it in the public domain.

I finished a cup of coffee and went for my daily walk but the discussion papers would not leave me alone. My experience of politics was depressing. I had spent six years as a representative waiting for a flood of reform after a series of meetings with government ministers and came away with a trickle. It was flooding now and I had no wish to contain it. No British Government had ever spoken in such terms before.

The markers laid down in the document were a major step forward. I reneged for a spell, in the course of my weekly attack on the scenic drive on Gullion, in the light of bitter experience. Too much topsy-turvy in our lives. 1968 and the dawn of hope when everything seemed possible and the tragic bloody years that followed; too many negatives, too many times when the surface did not reflect what was happening. It was impossible to sense the invisible and unseen factors that forever shape things. Was this a shifting of the tectonic plates, a sea change in the affairs of the Northern Ireland? Policing reform was a slow drip: the outworking of change would take years to perfect and the people were expecting a train wreck in May. I realised that the negative had no place on this morning. What was ringing in my head was Paragraph 5 of the blueprint document which stated

> We must reassess from first principles the policing requirements of a divided society..

and first principles were at the core of the discussion document. The two papers suggested major change, infinitely better than a cartload of repressive legislation. Dromintee in the distance and I turned in the direction of the Forkhill road. The last section of the walk was downhill but the mountain attacked again. I felt the pressure on my tendons as I eased down the slope. There are always problems on the downhill section.

The words were still on the page when I got home. The sub-heading to the title read – a discussion paper prepared by HMG – and the preface by Mo Mowlam was still there. The policing paper was saying that peace was the lure and normal policing was the aim. The paper asked the questions and challenged the political parties to come up with the answers. The discussion paper was saying that entrenched positions were no good anymore, that change was coming and everybody had to find a new gear. The British Government had changed the terms of debate at a stroke. Policing was a reserved power and they had the call and the call they made was for change, of symbols, structure and ethos. A century and a half was a short while in the history of Ireland and a long time for those who had to endure. Radical police reform was a certainty in the context of a political settlement. It was not discussed at Sunningdale and it was certain to be a key area when Easter week 1998 arrived.

The British government was letting the parties know in advance that they were in a radical mood, prepared to challenge the orthodoxies of both traditions and considering major departures in policy and they were flagging up the direction in advance. The discussion paper outlined the alternatives. Independent commissions were proposed to produce recommendations to inform the Government and the parties, or the Government in consultation with the parties, and take forward the necessary changes identified. It was early March and six weeks took us to early April, the date of all-party talks. There was ample opportunity to respond to the proposals but it came with a warning to the parties who had lived off the scraps of conflict for a generation. Opposition to change and a demand for change needed to be detailed and defended, something that had not been demanded of the parties in the history of the current Troubles. Previously, it was enough to amble in and defend a set comfortable position. The challenge to the political parties was a reality check. Peace was a tantalising prospect in the distance and policing in a peaceful society was the aim. There was nothing in the discussion paper that conflicted with the blueprint I submitted to the Irish government.

The production of the documents from the British side was a dazzling example of diplomacy in action. Production of the document was never an option for the Irish government. Proposals from that quarter had the same resonance with Unionism as a document from the SDLP or the Provisionals or a paper under my name. Besides, the Irish government was sworn to silence about the provenance of the document so the British government was the obvious vehicle. They had power to decide and they had carriage of the matter in the end. The implications were enormous in relation to the future talks. There was obvious co-operation between two friendly governments, otherwise the document would not have crossed the Irish Sea and travelled the whole way to the centre of the policing debate, the criminal justice debate and the judicial appointments debate.

A number of matters were causing problems for the Provisionals during this period. They were unhappy about their expulsion from the talks process for a short period after the IRA had killed two people in February, one a UDA man in retaliation for the UDA killing of Catholics, also the refusal of Unionism to engage with them or accept a comprehensive agenda, a spate of Loyalist killings and the content of the Heads of Agreement document which, in their view, over-promoted a Stormont assembly. It was a good holding position that kept the heartland on message and the back covered, now that the countdown was on. The two governments were in broad agreement and it was important that the Provisionals were in attendance.

Every party knew the mind of the British government on the policing question after 4 March. The broad principles were flagged up in the discussion paper and six weeks set aside for submissions. I was reliably informed that no party responded in detail. On 26 March Senator George Mitchell set a deadline of 9 April 1998 for finding an agreement. It was a major boost. There was no chance of a public statement of this nature if the tribes were at war on policing. The Mitchell script indicated that the talks were on course. I expected some fallout in relation to the content of the discussion papers after publication and the muted response of the parties was an encouraging sign. No histrionics and no walk outs and a final reckoning lay within weeks. It looked like the closing date for a response to the discussion documents was the first day of the deadline talks. I came to realise in the following weeks, that the policing proposals were not contentions, they were needed. The realisation grew with the commencement of the talks. Two days over and no major row about policing reported from inside the talks or in the press. Small skirmishes that faded into nothing on policing, the criminal justice system and the new voting system but no sound of ripping. A deal on prisoners was a code breaker but no word of progress on that.

I had a meeting in Belfast on Holy Thursday that broke up in late afternoon and I needed to feel the heat. I made it back to the car within minutes and it steered itself up the Newtownards Road. I parked in a leafy side street near the Stormont estate and ambled across the busy road to the big gates. The avenue was crowded with sightseers and it was a comfort. A lot of people had the same idea as myself and the game was on. Open house at Stormont and the atmosphere was super-charged. I remember it as a very democratic thing, a big event unfolding and the people turned up for sport. The squirrels playing amongst the trees were taking it rather well but the stress levels were rising further up the avenue. There was an air of carnival rather than chaos about the grounds and some politicians were taking the air or the temperature, hunted or haunted as you choose. The hacks were relay racing, keeping the parties in the picture and Paisley outside with his supporters, loudly objecting. A prayer meeting some distance away and a peace gathering and a man out walking his dog. It was Holy Thursday and things were getting serious. I met a couple of familiar faces so we swapped war stories and our latest health warnings before we parted.

The lights in the main building had an all night burn about them and the smoke-filled rooms were on fire alert. I stepped back into the shadows whenever I saw a politician. I was not there to offer advice or support. My advice was present at the talks and they had a decision to make. Two local politicians knew about the document – Frank Feely and Seamus Mallon – and I left them to it.

> They went to a place called Gethsemane and Jesus said to his disciples – sit here while I pray – he took Peter, James and John along with him, and he began to be deeply distressed and troubled - my soul is overwhelmed with sorrow to the point of death – he said to them – stay here and keep watch –

It was darker in the Stormont garden and the exit beckoned so I stole a last look and walked away. The streets were calm and traffic free as I began the journey back to Newry. Stormont was in the rear mirror as I climbed the rising road, just before the Woodstock Road.

> Then he returned to his disciples and found them sleeping – Simon – he said to Peter – are you asleep – could you not keep watch for one hour?

I crossed the Woodstock Road and Gethsemane disappeared from the rear mirror. I felt guilty as I sped along the Knock bypass but I was happier. I knew that my watch was over, it was time for the politicians to keep vigil.

I was awakened before dawn on Good Friday morning 1998. Frank Feely on the line, telling me that a deal was near and agreement was almost a reality. I dug a little deeper because I expected some reverses, some pieces of bad news. Multi-party talks are a pressure cooker and steam must find a release. Were concessions made in the hurly burly of the action, had the bed cover been turned into a quilt, a mass of patches in place of a single colour? Feely was abnormally specific. There was no slippage from my document in the talks, commissions on Policing, the Criminal Justice System and Judicial Appointments and a Sentence Review Commission to address the issue of prisoners. A Human Rights Commission was to be established and there was a commitment in the text to the incorporation of the European Convention on Human Rights into local law and a Bill of Rights for the North would follow. I pressed him hard on other points of detail. He was vague on the fate of the Intergovernmental Conference but he was adamant that the core proposals of the document survived intact, including the new voting system which was now called 'parallel consent'. Parallel paths, parallel universe, what did it matter what it was called? It was still a majority vote within each tradition on all cross community disputes. Suddenly, the line went dead and Feely was gone.

I was the better for the phone call. Feely kick-started our own particular process and it was appropriate that he was first with the news. I ditched the mobile and stared at the ceiling as the Good Friday Agreement began the first day, a thread of hope in a ragged world. I checked to see if the sun was dancing on the ceiling but it was not Easter morning so I settled for the filtering light and rummaged about in the breaking news. The roll-out was about to begin and the naysayers were already on red alert. The model was facing intense scrutiny from political mechanics who used a sledgehammer as a tinkering tool. How would the Agreement stand up to the pounding that was certain to come?

It was fascination for me, not a deterrent. The new Agreement was not a flutter for the faint hearted. The landing gear was down and the future would decide if it was a soft landing or a crash. Blair did not mention the weight of history when he arrived at the talks. He talked about the hand of history. He was focused on the new day, not the old ways. I sat up in bed and decided that he was right. There were many evasions and much blood under the bridge, there were many lies between us and a new birth was emerging in Belfast, a delicate balance of confidence and trust that needed luck in running; a difficult ask for one person and an Einstein job for two tribes. Individual turmoil is not a matter of one night or one year and it is a longer time span for communities. Political agreement is a major investment, a subsuming of self in a joint venture that might end in bankruptcy. It is a Marco Polo thing, a journey to the edge of the world across many frontiers and the journey was about to begin. It was meltdown or the beginning of knowledge and it was best to take it one day at a time.

Trust is not the work of a political lifetime, it is the work of a century in the damp climate of experience. It is a bit like peeling an onion. It is a trial to remove the outer skin so that work can begin on the layers, never swift and never easy. In the end you hold a needle between your teeth to stem the tears in your eyes. Trusting is an unnatural act in the North and it takes you about as far as you can kick a steamroller. Intimacies fail because nobody knows how to fix things. The trick is knowing the location and detail of the repair manual when the machine breaks down. Mostly in politics, there is no training manual. The ghetto commandments are for guidance purposes only until you break them, and they are silent on love. They are mandatory on the border war and mundane on other matters. Trust not the words and actions of the other sort for they are a fatal snare.

Community criticism for a breach might not be fatal but it is a bugger on street cred. It is better to have the key to the steamroller and move out at your own pace. The dawn chorus was growing in the tree tops and it was a glorious noise. I made a pot of tea and took it out to the patio and settled in. We are a community of empty chairs as a result of the conflict. The past was poverty of spirit and violence and a lot of absent friends and it was hard to look back. A few hardy souls swallow grief raw and the rest of us try to forget. We prefer to take a lead from a tube in the corner of the living room and sometimes we turn on the television. These are the good times and I never expected to live this long. We saw the action live the first time around. I fervently hoped that it was a job for a film studio in the future. The swift calling of the second ceasefire meant that the Good Friday Agreement was delivered within a year of the general election that returned Labour to power.

Things were brighter outside, birds on the wing in the frigid blue spring sky or water-dipping in the bird bath in the garden. Nothing stirred on the local roads, no snarl of traffic to spoil the misty calm of the moment. The end of the beginning was my hope. The road ahead was littered with difficulties but potholes are for filling or avoiding and the infrastructure was sounder than it had ever been. There were referendums to hold and laws to pass before the primary stage was over. The trick was to manage change but it would not be easy. Blair talked on a previous visit to Belfast about a train leaving the station. The parties were now on board and hopefully on the right track. Maybe a plane journey would have been the better choice. Airline staff force the passengers to dump all excess baggage before they step on board the craft and they order them to keep their seat belts fastened for the duration of the trip if it looks like a bumpy ride.

The room was full bright and the sunlight invaded my space. Outside the window life was waiting. Full morning in the garden, blustery and sharp, a light breeze chewing at the buds on the apple trees and chasing the puffs of mist. It was too late to return to bed and I was too energised. Easter competitions at Warrenpoint Golf Club, the start of the golfing year was upon us and I was down to play. A few lucky bounces and I might post a score. Some days it happens like that. Seek out the target in the distance and adopt a solid address position. Keep your head still while you make a good swing and hope for one perfect strike. Try not to look too surprised if it finally happens.

Chapter Fourteen

The governments moved with commendable haste after the Agreement was signed. The Good Friday Agreement was decisively endorsed by referendums, North and South on 22 May 1998. The ink confirming the results was hardly dry before the governments pushed on again, taking a grip on the honeymoon period and setting it to work. The Sentence Review Commission was established by the Northern Ireland (Sentences) Act 1998, which became law in July 1998. It commenced work within weeks and completed the task within two years. The Human Rights Commission commenced work on 1 March 1999. The British / Irish agreement, which replaced the 1985 Anglo-Irish Agreement, came into force on 2 December 1999. The two Governments signed a Supplementary Agreement providing for the establishment of a British/Irish Intergovernmental Conference on the same day. The European Convention on Human Rights was incorporated into law through the Human Rights Act on 2 October 2000. The Commission on Policing was established in 1998 and reported on 9 September 1999. The Police (Northern Ireland) Act 2000 became law on 23 November 2000. The Criminal Justice Review Commission was established in 1998. The Commission reported on 30 March 2000. The Criminal Justice proposals became law in the Justice (Northern Ireland) Act 2002.

Governments have the power to move the agenda in this manner but it is harder to move people. The Agreement was given a fair wind by the population but the politicians were moving slower than the grounding legislation arising out of the event. Caution was the new mantra. The ideologies were mirror images of each other, suspicious of the opposition whom they viewed as reactionary, critical of any refusal to change while refusing to change themselves. Nobody was moving on their own anymore. The parties refused to accept that concession by one side only is akin to clapping with one hand, a case of aimless motion and no applause.

I make reference to the South Tyrol experience in the blueprint document because Brian Feeney mentioned it often and laid out its history and details for me. Some of the South Tyrol was part of the Italian state. Italians call it Trentino-Alto Adige but the population spoke German in the main and they call it Trentin-Südtirol. It had been an area of conflict since Italy annexed it in 1919 and a matter of dispute between the Italian and Austrian governments who were not friendly governments in relation to a solution when the process began about 1969. Each government submitted a set of objectives that they paired off against each other. They created a process based on a calendar of operations and it took a generation to complete. There was an obligation on each side to move in line with the timetable. Step one had to be completed by both before step two was addressed by the other party to the process.

The Irish and British governments had another name for the calendar of operations when the Northern process kicked on. They talked about confidence-building measures when the talking began. In the Northern case, the talking began after the Good Friday Agreement was signed. It was a reversal of the conventional route. Confidence building got off to a slow start. The parties moved into position as required but they failed to move out on time. Below is a timetable of key events in the initial period.

1 July 1998
David Trimble and Seamus Mallon were elected chief minister designate and deputy chief minister designate on the basis of cross-community support, a majority vote within each tradition. David Trimble demanded some IRA decommissioning in advance of the formation of a power-sharing Executive. The demand was a possible veto on progress and not allowed on a constitutional basis. No party had a right of veto over the activities of another party under the terms of the Agreement and there was no cross-community deal about prior decommissioning before the formation of an Executive. Only the Assembly, as a whole, had the right to deem a party unfit for office on a cross-community vote. Everybody reached for the rule book and it was a refreshing change in some ways. People instinctively reached for heavy metal in the past in times of major dispute. There was a downside. Executive formation was the signal to activate other institutions under the terms of the Agreement. Progress came to a halt on all fronts while the parties talked about it and the talking went on for a year.

15 July 1999
Mallon resigns because Trimble will not jointly form an Executive. The *Independent* International *Commission* on *Decommissioning (IICD)*, tasked by the two governments to oversee the decommissioning of IRA arms, tried to find a way that was acceptable to the UUP and the Provisionals.

27 November 1999
The Ulster Unionist Council votes 52%- 44 % to enter Government with Sinn Féin on the proviso that if decommissioning had not occurred by February 2000 Trimble would withdraw. The IRA appointed an interlocutor at this stage to negotiate with the IICD and the Unionists agreed that an Executive could be formed, accepting that actual decommissioning would occur after the formation of the Executive. David Trimble placed a resignation letter on the record, to be activated if there was no decommissioning by February 2000. In effect, the UUP would walk out of the Executive.

29 November 1999
Power-sharing executive elected. The secretary of state triggers the necessary legislation and power is devolved for the first time in 27 years.

It was a turbulent time for David Trimble with repeated votes at the Ulster Unionist Council about current party policy and challenges to his leadership. The secretary of state supported the policing reforms in a House of Commons statement on 19 January 2000. It put further pressure on David Trimble, already grappling with decommissioning. Unionist objections to the police reforms centred on the name change, the badge and the future size of the force. There was little comment on the structural and disciplinary reforms. There were a number of bad calls at the time. Martin McGuinness stated his belief, on a *Spotlight* programme on BBC, that the UUP would not walk out on the power-sharing executive because of a lack of decommissioning. He was wrong.

11 February 2000

The Decommissioning Body announced that it had received no information from the IRA in relation to the start of decommissioning and the power-sharing Executive collapsed.

The confidence of the Provisional movement was blunted by the walkout but nobody walked away and intensive discussions followed.

There was considerable resistance within the legal establishment to proposals contained in the draft version of the Criminal Justice Review report. The old regime was interested in power and control and Diplock courts were a means to that end, a stratagem by which order was maintained at the expense of law. There was a strange parallel in South Armagh. There was also order without law of a more recent vintage in the area and that had a political objective also. The establishment opposition did not have a public face in relation to criminal justice reform but I felt the stirrings in the undergrowth and the cranking up of the old boy network. It was not possible to pin it down because they worked to the best political principle: never hit a man in the mouth if you can hit him on the back of the head. There is a twin benefit to the latter course. The target never sees it coming and never knows who hit him. Resistance did not surprise me because control becomes a habit. There was a short period of uncertainty and uncertainty is bad. I met with Eugene Grant QC to discuss the matter after contact with the alternative old boy network.

The reports that I received indicated that there was a turf war developing between the Northern Ireland Office and the Lord Chancellor's Department in relation to the Judicial Appointments Commission. The Lord Chancellor's Department was running the line that the Judicial Appointments Commission should become a reserved matter, allowing them to choose the time, if at all, when power in relation to Judicial Appointments would be transferred back to a local executive. The Lord Chancellor's Department was intent on amending the draft recommendations of the Review Group to make them more in the image of the English and Welsh legal system. It was vital that an overseeing Commissioner as proposed in the draft Criminal Justice Review report be appointed immediately to secure the interim period pending the devolution of a Department of Justice.

The function of the Judicial Appointments Commissioner was to oversee and monitor the fairness of all aspects of the existing appointments system in Northern Ireland, pending the establishment of a Judicial Appointments Commission and the devolution of Justice to the Northern Ireland Assembly. The Commission was likely to be in gestation for a long time. Progress was slow in relation to the establishment of a stable power-sharing executive which was a precondition for Police and Justice to be returned. There would be no scrutiny of the myriad local appointments if the Lord Chancellor's Department got its way. The failure to appoint a Commissioner would allow the current system to limp on for years in the present flawed state and perpetuate the mistakes of the past. It was not just the Commissioner principle that was in peril, the whole section of the report in relation to Judicial Appointments was in grave danger.

I met Eugene Grant to consider the options. The gutting of a major aspect of the Report and the sidelining of the oversight Commissioner would gravely diminish the impact of the overall Report. We concluded that the cause of legal reform was lost if we stood meekly by and allowed certain elements of the British establishment to walk over us. We decided that Eugene should convene the independent members of the review team and get their agreement to resign or submit a dissenting report, if the Lord Chancellor tampered with the principles of the Criminal Justice Report. By taking the action, it was a no-lose situation.

The independent members agreed to the standoff at a subsequent meeting. The Lord Chancellor's Department was left with two options in circumstances where they interfered with the report: fillet the Review Report and attempt to ride out the political crisis that followed a dissenting report or back down completely. Eugene convened a meeting in the Stormont Hotel in Belfast between the independent members of the Review Commission and the civil servants serving on the Review body, to express his dissatisfaction and to indicate to the civil servants the course of action that the independent members had agreed upon. After the meeting, a civil servant member went to London to discuss the ultimatum with the Lord Chancellor's Department.

No material changes were made to the draft that passed into law as the new legal system in the North. The Lord Chancellor baulked at an international appointment but a Commissioner was appointed. There was a gatekeeper in place who visited the Lord Chief Justice regularly. Work proceeded on the Judicial Appointments Commission during the interim period and we were happy. Eugene Grant and the other independent members of the Criminal Justice Review Commission averted disaster. They were prepared to walk away if the document was gutted or changed. Progress and democracy depends on people who take a stand on principle and see it out without consideration of personal cost. Power and empowerment should form part of the equation that equals democracy. He who places power above empowerment stores democracy in a dangerous place. The Judicial Appointments Commission was established on 15 June 2005 under the Justice (NI) Acts 2002 and 2004.

6 May 2000

The IRA offered to open some arms dumps for inspection. There were confidence-building measures in response. Reductions in troop levels in the North were promised by Secretary of State Peter Mandelson, if the IRA kept its promise on decommissioning, and the Chief Constable indicated that five military installations were to close.

It was a sequencing of events, an indication that certain things would happen if a prior commitment was met like Brian Feeney's Alto Adige/Sud Tyrol model. The following sequence shows how quickly the step by step approach became a pattern.

29 May 2000

Unionists agree a return to Stormont on the basis of arms being dealt with while the Assembly functions.

31 May 2000

The power-sharing executive is restored after the IRA pledge to put guns beyond use.

26 June 2000

IRA dumps are inspected by the Decommissioning Body. They conclude that arms cannot be removed without detection.

28 July 2000

Another seventy-nine qualifying prisoners are released from the Maze Prison by the Sentence Review Commission, bringing the final total in the North to 444.

There is very little movement over the next few months, partly because of reluctance to move, partly because of the looming British general election on 7 June 2001. The DUP and Sinn Féin are the net gainers in that election when the votes are counted.

1 July 2001

Trimble resigns in protest over the IRA failure to decommission.

There are more talks and more failed deadlines and the parties started again. Contact between the parties was improved and they knew each other better than before, not on official speaking terms in some cases but that was just a fiction. The contending parties and personalities knew each other from Belfast City Council and other local authorities. It was impossible to walk on the other side of a corridor in Stormont if you are cheek by jowl with the opposition on a daily basis in the council chamber in Belfast. The process paused for reflection and edged forward again. The alternative was to remain in a state of frost, God's frozen people afraid to come in from the cold. Jumping together, a favourite mantra from the early days, reduces in importance.

23 October 2001
The IRA begin the process of disposing of arms.

6 November 2001
Trimble and the SDLP's Mark Durkan are elected First Minister and Deputy First Minister.

There is comfort in taking a step secure in the belief that an agreed response is pending, that an obligation is there, that the governments are watching. Failure to deliver and a penalty arises, followed by public censure and a predictable reduction in trust. An improvement in personal relations evolved naturally out of the process, tempered by bitter experience on one hand and a dawning reality on the other. It was better to get your share in a cross-community setting than your own way in a tribe. People began listening to each other and began to respond in a constructive way. Listening was an important factor in what happened.

8 April 2002
IRA puts a second portion of its arsenal beyond use.

21 September 2002
David Trimble states that the UUP will withdraw from the power-sharing executive if Republicans do not demonstrate that they have left violence behind for good.

4 October 2002
The Sinn Féin offices at Stormont are raided by the police.

8 October 2002
David Trimble says that he will pull his ministers out of the power-sharing executive if Sinn Féin is not expelled by the Government, that the arrangement was not sustainable following allegations of an IRA spy ring at Stormont

14 October 2002
Secretary of State John Reid announces the suspension of devolution and the return of direct rule by London ministers by midnight.

Two phases of the historic progression were at an end. Phase One related to the relationship between the UUP and the SDLP, which was fraught at times but fairly stable. Phase Two involved the out-workings of the Agreement which centred upon the relationship between the UUP and the Provisional movement. Phase Two got off to a rocky start and kept rocking. The body language between the UUP and the Provisionals was bad from the beginning and the language was worse. Confusion reigned on the obligations of the two parties and press statements made it worse. Contacts between the UUP and the Provisionals were based on a false premise, the belief that a problem can be solved without solving the problem. There was no meeting of minds on decommissioning at any stage so they settled for a cold war because it suited them.

Phase One faded into the background as the dispute between the UUP and the Provisional movement intensified. The UUP were in more difficulty. They were obliged to identify with the steady stream of reform arising from the Agreement, which put a massive strain on the manpower, resources and conviction of the party. They took the heat as the policing changes kicked in at a time when bickering over decommissioning reached Babel proportions and the criticism from the DUP reached a crescendo. The UUP countered that decommissioning was a deal breaker and the ensuing headlines diverted some of the flak away from the policing debate.

The relationship was doomed from the beginning. The Provisionals had a private army outside the door of the Executive committee room and were allowed to leave it there. It invoked an image of earlier times. Unionism had a private army in the days of absolute power and the consequences were disastrous. If you mix democracy and gun power, you end up with a dictatorship and this was a far cry from the aims of the Agreement. The Provisionals harboured the hope that tinkering with decommissioning would lead to a resolution of the remaining difficulties. They refused to move on decommissioning and the Official Unionists finally moved out.

The parties were pushed out into the current of change and politics took a deep breath and moved on. The DUP waited it out and soaked up the steady stream of families and individuals who left Trimble for a stronger brand of Unionism. It is not a matter of blame. Old habits die hard in the face of a fractious future. Some people were using terms like 'too far, too fast' and the public were reacting because folk memory was kicking them on the shins again. There was an alternative view on the street and it was encouraging. People were beginning to go with it despite the stop/start. Stalled talks and a suspended Assembly were no longer a disaster, the politicians moved out of the cabinet room but they loitered in the lobby. The public watched the power-sharing Executive depart with regret and wished it a speedy return after a pause, breathing space and a period of reflection. People were tired of working on reasons why equality was not the answer. It was not my preferred option but there was a side benefit to the closedown at Stormont. The Good Friday Agreement needed to be road tested and suspension of the Assembly was a functional necessity for that to happen.

The suspension of devolution was not a soft landing but it was covered in the Agreement through the creation of the Inter-Governmental Conference. I was confident of the ability of the Conference to handle the extra pressure at a time of political setback but it was useful to see if it did. The results were interesting. The Assembly met for a total of 128 days in the period between November 1999, when the first executive was sworn in, and April 2002. Sittings were reduced to one day a week by the latter date. Twenty-seven pieces of primary legislation were passed during the period. Half were parity bills, legislation given the Royal Assent in London and rubber-stamped by the northern Assembly in order to become the law of the land. Just twelve local bills were passed; three were budgets, two dealt with MLA salaries and expenses and seven were primary legislation bills.

The institutions might not have been at full throttle but the political system was in rude good health. The organs were working properly and the Inter-Governmental Conference was handling the rest. The machinery of government was bearing up well and there was no need to panic. Not much happening but the machine was roadworthy and tooling up for the time when the designated drivers returned. The Good Friday Agreement was moving forward on concept, structure and legislative programme against the backdrop of an irritation of internal opposition that failed to reach critical mass. The suspension of devolution led to a period laced with public statements and private political activity. There were exhaustive talks with the two governments, and between the two governments, sometimes with the other parties but not between Ian Paisley and Gerry Adams. It was back to confidence building measures.

29 March 2003
Gerry Adams says that he can envisage a situation where his party would join the Policing Board. The Assembly elections set for May Day are rescheduled for 29 May.

6 May 2003
The IRA said it was on the verge of a third act of decommissioning weapons. The full implementation of the Good Friday Agreement would provide the context in which the IRA would definitely set aside arms. It would mean calling an army convention.

17 June 2003
David Trimble wins the narrow backing of his party for London/Dublin proposals for breaking the impasse over the Good Friday Agreement. Three MP's, including Jeffrey Donaldson, resign the UUP whip. The Assembly elections are postponed until the autumn of 2003 in the hope of a deal between the UUP and Sinn Féin.

20 September 2003
Eugene Grant rang this morning with the worst news. Gareth Williams had died at the age of sixty-two. I was deeply saddened at his passing. He was our friend, not a political associate. We lost a comrade, politics lost a rising star and democracy lost a disciple. He had an enthusiasm that gave me a pain in the head sometimes and he had no reverse gear. He believed that anything was possible so long as you cleared the diary. His death at a relatively young age was a huge loss to his wife Veena and his family, his friends and to politics. He had convinced me that there was a serious prospect of change within Labour and he was right. The slow pace of progress filled him with impatience and politics can do that to a person. Speed has not a merit in

the political maze. The question is can you get out of the maze?

The second ceasefire in 1997 was a testament to his truth and his integrity and his ability to stay the course. He was not given the public credit he deserved for his efforts in relation to the second ceasefire and that depresses me. Some might say that he was promoted upon the advent of Labour and a bright future beckoned but is it enough? The establishment needs to pay its dues in relation to events and people. They will not feel any better as a result but the public will. People like to know how and why change happens. Gareth Williams is not a footnote of history, he is a window on the future, an early example of the right approach to the Irish problem. He gave us a foothold in the political sense and an insight into Labour thinking in the personal sense. It was rank good luck that we caught Labour in the early phase of government when everything was possible, rather than the later stage where everything is impossible.

21 October 2003

The Northern Ireland elections were scheduled for 26 November 2003. Contacts continued behind the scenes to broker a deal between the UUP and the Provisionals on devolution prior to the election date and a further act of decommissioning by the IRA was set to take place. There were rumours of a deal and the North expected. General De Chastelain the head of the decommissioning body confirmed at a press conference, that the IRA had acted, that the quantity of arms was considerably larger than previous decommissioning. Unionists rejected the act of decommissioning as not being transparent enough. Bertie Ahern had not travelled North for the announcement, an indication that he was not confident of the Unionist reaction. Trimble put the pre-election talks on hold. The Taoiseach was very frustrated in the Dáil the following day. He commented that it was a new day and we had to get on with it. There was much talk about deal making and deal breaking, so many words and so many contacts and no result. The papers were awash with D words like decommissioning, disbandment, demilitarisation and decontamination and C words like closure, clarification, clarity and confidentiality and there was still the bulk of the alphabet to go. Unionists were for something that would remove the veil, the cloak and dagger of it all, if daggers were for decommissioning. A good news story suddenly went bad. Blair confirmed, after further talks, that the election would proceed on 26 November.

In the meantime I had work to do beyond the confines of the North. I agreed to chair the Task Force on Policy regarding Emigrants for the Irish Government in 2002. There is hardly a corner of the world that does not have an Irish population. The experience varies from one country to another and between different sections of the emigrant population in each country, with the result that there is not one Irish community abroad, but many. There are some emigrants who are forced to leave Ireland due to the prevailing economic conditions of the day or because of political or social circumstances, and there are some who leave voluntarily. There are young Irish emigrants who leave the country ill prepared for a life abroad and suffer for the lack of it. There are emigrants who settle in their new homes and those who never settle. There are some who achieve great success in their chosen field and contribute generously to their adopted country and to Ireland and there are those who struggle to survive. There are emigrants who make contact with welfare and support agencies when they arrive in the host country and many who make no contact at all. There are emigrants who are in prison. There are less visible emigrants, elderly as a rule and mainly women. There are people of Irish descent, extending beyond the second generation, who regard themselves as Irish or partly Irish and who have a strong wish to express their Irish identity or get in touch with their Irish identity. There are many who long for the sights and sounds of Ireland on a regular basis and some who switch off. There are emigrants who want to forget about Ireland and emigrants who will never forget. All these people have needs. Even those who want to forget have needs.

I owed it to my aunt and uncles who left these shores and rarely returned. It was a journey of discovery for me. We focused on the countries with major populations of the Irish Abroad in the search for necessary data: England, America and Australia. Almost a million Irish born people live in England, by virtue of the flood of emigration across the Irish Sea that did not abate until the mid Eighties. Thousands of Irish people were part of the 'lump generation' of the Fifties and Sixties, so called because of the construction work system that left many devoid of pension rights or support services when they reached retirement age. There were complex welfare issues relating to the older age groups. A significant section of the Report concentrated on vulnerable and marginalized individuals who had fallen on hard times and the organisations that supported them. I was impressed by the level of commitment offered to the Irish community by the Federation of Irish Societies, who did great things for decades on a shoestring budget.

America was no longer available as a penal colony after the Americans gained their freedom from the British so a new location was needed by Whitehall. Prison ships set sail around 1791, carrying all classes of passengers, including political prisoners, to Australia. About forty thousand men, women and children from Ireland were transported to the colony between 1791 and 1868, the bulk sent for stealing bread and other hunger related activities. Not all emigrants from Ireland were transported. Thousands left for economic reasons but it was involuntary just the same. Irish history is mirrored in the landing records on the other side of the world. The people who went ashore included Ninety-Eight men like Joseph Holt and Michael Dwyer, members of the secret societies involved in agrarian agitation, Young Irelanders like William Smith O'Brien, John Mitchel and Meagher of the Sword and members of the Fenian movement. Ned Kelly looms large in the Australian imagination for gameness along with Peter Lalor and the fight at the Eureka Stockade.

The forty percent of the Australian population who claim Irish ancestry are second generation or more. There will be younger Irish arrivals in the course of the present recession, apart from the backpackers who travel there in their thousands every year. There were significant populations of the Irish Abroad in many other places but it was not possible for the Task Force to visit them all, because of time and logistical constraints. Our trip was very different from the average emigrant experience down the centuries because we got the painless version of it. No boat at a quay in a grey dawn, no American wake or the agony of permanent separation and minimal risk of sudden death on the voyage. I learnt a huge amount about the Irish Abroad and a great deal about myself by walking in their footsteps across the world.

All members of the Task Force made a valuable contribution to the finished work. The Report spurred a major Irish government initiative in relation to the Irish Abroad and reawakened interest in a taboo subject amongst the Irish people. Strong support was given to the Report by the major parties in Dáil Éireann and there has been a rapid increase in aid from the Irish Government in recent years. The 2007 Emigrant Services Grants Summary issued by the Department of Foreign Affairs, who have carriage of the scheme, makes interesting reading on the subject of need. The Irish Abroad Unit awarded a total of €14.165m to organizations in eleven different countries.

The commitment to welfare services remained a priority but there was significant organic growth in other directions. In addition to welfare services, there have been grants to sporting bodies, to music and language bodies, to Feiseanna and Festivals and Forums and to Arts and Heritage bodies. As well as welfare provision in America, grants have been given to the GAA for its North America Development initiative, to the impressive Irish Cultural Centre in Canton, Boston and the Irish Lobby for Immigration Reform. Progressively, the grant aid, offered by the Irish government in response to the Report, reaches out into areas beyond welfare. By promoting Irish history, language, culture and sport and providing opportunities for the Irish Abroad to participate in these activities, we assist the Irish Abroad to maintain and express their Irish identity. Work continues on the need for Irish radio and television contact on a daily basis for the Irish Abroad and on the issue of free travel in Ireland for senior citizens when they visit Ireland.

Other issues begin to impinge as another phase of the project begins, as an examination begins of the range of backup services offered locally to the Irish Abroad. How wide a range of choice do we offer to a second generation Irishman or woman sitting at a computer in Saginaw, Michigan with a strong wish to explore their Irish roots? Can a second generation member of the Irish Abroad access our national archives with ease or are we found wanting when the Irish Abroad search for confirmation and clarity? What would they choose if there was a chance to Google it, Irish history or music, literature or theatre or sport, modern Ireland or traditional Ireland, access to parish records down the centuries or collateral documentation about the leaving? What are the prospects of a positive response to a search?

Most of the national records were destroyed in 1922 in the course of the Civil War including the 1821 census, the first complete census of the whole country. Very little remains of the 1821 returns: two parishes in Fermanagh and three parishes in Cavan, the Barony of Ballybrit in the then Kings County (now Laois) and the parish of Forkhill in South Armagh, including the village of Mullaghbawn. Much useful research has been done by locals and the Irish Abroad who supply pieces of the jigsaw but the broad picture is incomplete. I am aware that there are Irish Genealogical Centres located throughout the island, one to a county, more than one in places like Dublin. In some counties there is no focal point at all.

The aim is to archive the parish records since their inception in the eighteenth and nineteenth centuries, records covering births, marriages and deaths since that time. The same work, I believe, is being carried out in relation to the church records of the Protestant denominations. Work on the project has continued for many years but it is painstaking and under funded. There is an urgent need to finish the work in every county, in all cases in conformity to the same standard. The completed archive will not replace the lost records but it would provide a vast, detailed database to assist in the search for place and roots. We need to fill a huge gap in the Irish story because birth and marriage comes before the leaving and the landing. The same care should be taken to database the history, culture and traditions of the nation where the archives are not readily accessible.

We need to initiate research into the relationship between the Irish and the Irish Abroad and we need to make sense of it, the history of emigration and how it impacts on Ireland today. Following the emigrant trail is a complex affair. The names of passengers were not generally recorded on a ship's manifest. The captain and crew were listed and nobody else. The landing points in the New World assume their own importance because a record of entry is generally available in the host country. It is easy to name the embarkation points, Camp Clinton and Castle Gardens, amongst the earliest landing points for the Irish in New York harbour before Ellis Island, Boston, and Grosse Isle and New Orleans and other ports in America and Canada along with Liverpool in England and the major Australian destinations.

There is a vast chasm of pain and experience separating Ireland and the Irish Abroad and a common bond, an identification and a growing recognition. We need to know their story, the trials that they endured when they left this land and the magnitude of their achievements in the host countries. The key to the future is to join up the dots of their passage, to network, to share information and to plug into the raw energy of the Irish Abroad. It is necessary for the nation to bestow on the distant generations the belated recognition they deserve by telling their story and honouring their achievements. Reconnection with the Irish Abroad should be a key strategy of government in the future, linking the disparate Irish communities on a world-wide basis. We need a communications hub that will reconnect the Irish and the Irish Abroad and we must not charge for the service.

The approach of Irish America to the Irish question during the Troubles was diverse and disparate. There was a section of the population that made it and moved up, a section that grows by the year. They moved out of politics and into business and supported mainstream politicians, on both sides of the aisle in Congress. There was a section of Irish America that took a more muscular approach to the problem, people who supported the Provisionals with their dollars during the recent Troubles and there is the forgotten group, the Presbyterians known as the Scots Irish who mainly left Ireland between 1715 and 1790. English rule prohibited public demonstrations by the dissenting groups in Ireland for fear of insurrection with the exception of religious processions.

To get around the rule people gathered on Saint Patrick's Day, and marched through the streets of Ireland after a religious service. All three sections took the parade with them to America. The Hibernian Society was founded on 17 March, 1812 by thirteen men in Savannah, Georgia. Their number had risen to 44 when they adopted a constitution and a motto a few months later - *non sibi sed aliis* - not for ourselves but for others. They were dedicated to aiding destitute Irish immigrants, largely Catholic. They marched in procession on Saint Patrick's Day the following year to a Presbyterian Church for a service and oration. Not one founding member was a Catholic. It is likely that the founding members fled Ireland after Ninety-Eight, northern men with a link to the United Men and the failed rebellion. The Savannah parade is the second biggest Saint Patrick's Day parade in the world today.

All these groups have a story that needs to be told in the evolving history of the Irish Abroad, three strands with a common past of misery and loss and leaving. They all took passage on a sailboat or a package steamer and they watched Ireland disappear over the curve of the ocean off Cork or Derry or Galway. They all left with a bitter memory of cruelty and injustice and eviction. The story is centuries old but the memory remains in their oral traditions or letters that are yellow with age. Maybe their descendants pause at a piece of traditional music or Irish poetry or a copy of a page from the Book of Kells and search for an elusive memory of another place or another time. There is a need for a three cohort approach, combining, to the maximum extent, official Irish America, main street Irish America and the Ulster Scots tradition because they had the same reasons for leaving Ireland. There is an all-round benefit and a common cause after the Good Friday Agreement.

Chapter Fifteen

There was a tremor of doubt in political quarters in the aftermath of the election results in late November 2003, when the DUP and Sinn Féin emerged as the largest parties within their respective traditions. The DUP were the enemies of the Good Friday Agreement and the sworn enemies of the Provisionals. There was a faltering of belief in the peace process and some Unionist politicians were pronouncing the Agreement dead. Statements about the death of the Good Friday Agreement were derisory. It was alive and well and living in Ireland but some people are fans of make believe. There is a great danger of attention deficit in the wider political community at any given time. Politicians grow frustrated with the pace of change and look around for a new toy in the light of touted rejection of the old one. Even Governments, who take the long view of events, sometimes feel a sliver of uncertainty about the future. It must have looked like the darkest place to politicians, commentators and civil servants alike, not to mention the general public. There was no hope of talks between the polar opposites they said never mind agreement. To me it represented a major progression, it was certainly a major development.

Below is the record of a conversation which took place two days after the election as reported to the Irish Government. The report is the work of the senior Foreign Affairs civil servant who had the conversation with me. It is known within Foreign Affairs as the 2008 Document.

Two Views of the NI Election Result – Brian Feeney and Paddy O'Hanlon

In his regular *Irish News* column yesterday (attached) Brian Feeney presented a very bleak view of the underlying factors which have defined political life in Northern Ireland and would continue to do so – the essential inability and unwillingness of Unionism ever to share power with Republicans and/or Nationalists. In contrast, I spoke yesterday with Paddy O'Hanlon, a founder member of the SDLP and a close friend of Feeney. O'Hanlon was avowedly optimistic and pointed to a radically different set of causative factors that would ultimately and inevitably lead to a durable political rapprochement between unionism and republicanism. That both of these shrewd observers could present such contrasting interpretations is an interesting comment on the divergent responses to the current situation. The following sets out their interpretations in more detail and offers a view as to which might be the most apposite.

Brian Feeney

1.   Feeney, the most influential commentator among northern nationalists, interprets the outcome of the election in the context of Northern Ireland's

history as a unionist state. He argues that the inability to create durable power sharing political institutions is the result of the inherent inability of unionism to share power. Feeney points out that Trimble was in a political minority since 2001 and has had to rely on the PUP to stay, fitfully, in power. His past and current problems have had nothing to do with what the IRA was doing and saying. In fact, he argues, a deal with SF/IRA last October would have "wiped him out in the election". The "mirage" bedazzling the British Government of an SDLP/UUP coalition has now evaporated; its last chance ended when Mark Durkan refused Blair's advice to exclude Sinn Fein in the wake of Stormontgate. Blair knew then that the SDLP was Sinn Fein's prisoner, says Feeney. Not only is there no basis for a partnership administration in the northern assembly, there is no public demand for one, he argues. Unionists will only accept a voting Executive where they can assert their majority status, something inimical to nationalists.

2.   Feeney exhibits the evidence of the newly released 1973 state papers to argue that Unionists had not changed since 1972. Unable to insist on political control, Faulkner was pushed too far to meet nationalist demands, the UUP split and the Sunningdale Agreement collapsed. Feeney writes that consent principles or changing Articles 2 and 3 matters not a wit to Unionists compared to their inability to grant equal status to nationalists. He concludes "They're saying you can't share in running this place if you are not a unionist and there's no indication they'll ever say anything different."

3.   There are many nationalists and more republicans who will nod sagely that Feeney's interpretation is right. It has the compelling power of explaining not just recent events but Northern Ireland's history. Those who spent a few hours over Christmas reading the 1973 papers will be tempted to think that it all sounds so familiar and conclude that nothing has changed in thirty years. The emphatic electoral triumph of Paisley and the humbling of Trimble may seem like the voice of history saying "I told you so". Dissident republicans will think that it is a very good Christmas indeed and content themselves with the notion that it is the Provos and not they who are in history's cul de sac.

Paddy O'Hanlon

4.   Paddy O'Hanlon offered a radically different and positive interpretation of the current situation. He has seen nothing since 1998 that surprised him and nothing that called into question the fundamentals of the Good Friday Agreement. Neither the election result nor its outworking changed this view, though it did effect the timing.

5.   Overall, O'Hanlon stressed the importance of conserving all the elements

of the Agreement which was proving to be a remarkably durable construct. The interim period between now and its full implementation would be taken up with the leaderships of the two ultra-nationalist parties [unionist and republican] preparing their respective followers for the accommodation that lay ahead.

6. In his view, the election was a post -equality one; equality is now deeply embedded in law and would be so in practice over time. In this context, nationalists and unionists were free to opt for the ultra – nationalist versions of what they represented. The election had fast – forwarded what was an inevitable rendezvous anyway. While the GFA was a political accommodation between the SDLP and the UUP, its operation became a complex process of negotiation between the republican movement and the UUP. We are now in the opening chapter of the next inevitable phase – an accommodation between the DUP and the republican movement. *

* Or put another way, the GFA was an agreement between the constitutional orthodoxies of both traditions and its implementation had been about whether Sinn Fein is constitutional enough; the election has only changed the terms of trade.

7. I agreed that there were only two dogs in this fight but wondered about the DUP's willingness to do a deal. He had no doubt that both parties would do business. Sinn Fein had the talent and the hunger for power. The war was over and they were determined to make the Agreement work. The DUP were very similar in terms of talent and political hunger. O'Hanlon believed in the inexorable progress of the peace process and an accommodation between both traditions.

8. O'Hanlon said that he had met a senior Provo in South Armagh recently who said that there were now a lot of politicians in the organisation (who travel often in the company of heavies) and that the time was fast approaching when the leadership would have to tell the "storm troopers" that the war was over. O'Hanlon said that the Sinn Fein leadership probably realised by now that they would have to tackle some of the conservative aspects of their organisation (personnel and activities) sooner rather than later. There was probably too an element of keeping a few baubles for the talks with the DUP. Though that was not to undervalue the immensity of the Adams text last October.

9. O'Hanlon saw much that was comparable to the 1922/23 – 1932 phase of the IRA in the Sorth when it took the guts of ten years to wind down to the point where Fianna Fail could constitute itself in 1926 and take power in 1932. During that time, the IRA had kept its men busy on intelligence gathering

END OF TERM REPORT

and so forth. Many IRA men then had gone off into legitimate professions (or emigrated). In the current situation in the North, some PIRA personnel had gone into illegitimate activities which created its own difficulties (eg hostility to accepting policing and the consequent threat to lucrative black market operations.) Overall, O'Hanlon said a wind-down of a paramilitary organisation was an organic process that took roughly ten years. While the election had pressed the throttle, there were still a few brakes (Provo old habits etc) by 2008 give or take a year, the GFA would be fully established. History might take a surge forward again and reduce this timescale.

10.   O'Hanlon agreed that it was essential to continue the process of reform and accountability set out in the Agreement regarding policing, criminal justice, human rights and so on. (He was concerned that inadequate funding was impeding progress on the criminal justice front. I said we were aware of this and made representations on it in terms of the Luce Review recommendations on inquests.) But essentially this process of reform was on track and he declared himself satisfied, for example, that the substance of the criminal justice reforms had been delivered in the new Justice Bill.

11.   O'Hanlon rebutted the notion of a democratic deficit in Northern Ireland. They had a surfeit of good politicians – councillors, MLAs, MP' and Euro MPs. However, public confidence and interest in politics had been weakened and he saw some danger in voter-turnoff during a period of prolonged stalemate. That said, he did not believe that this would deteriorate into conflict. It was, nonetheless, an issue essentially about timing that should occupy both Sinn Fein and the DUP.

I include the portion of the document that reflects what I said, not the analysis of what I said by the civil servant. There was no dispute in my mind over the primary issue. Brian Feeney was offering a tenable point of view in his newspaper article on 27 November 2003. His column was a wake-up call, a reflection of a real fear that there was nowhere left to go, that the process was in meltdown. It was a welcome reminder to the public in the light of the election result. I was comfortable with my own prediction of a full blooded executive by 2008, one including the DUP and Sinn Féin, and was glad of the opportunity to state it on the record. The election result would have been the same if the power-sharing Executive had been functioning in November 2003. David Trimble had taken too many hits from the Unionist population and the UUP was in decline, just like the SDLP.

There was a need for remedial work. Somebody was always left behind in the North. Local politics for decades was a tag team cycle event where some party was always dropping off the tail of the group. What we needed was a bunch finish. Sunningdale was repeating itself in one vital area and it stood in the way of completion. The all-party talks that led to the Good Friday Agreement were not inclusive, the Provisional movement was half in and the DUP were not in at all, unless you include the particular evening during the talks when they appeared on the front lawn at Stormont.

The excluded party from the talks in November 2003 was the DUP and they excluded themselves. They were not the first organisation to advocate exclusion for future political advantage. The Provisionals put pressure on the SDLP to boycott the 1996 election and luckily the SDLP refused. It is frightening to think about the consequences of a general boycott by the minority at that particular time. There was a need to return to first principles - no local agreement was worth a damn that did not include men and women of every major political persuasion. It was true in 1798 and it was true now. It was a case of unfinished business at the advent of Phase Three.

The fall of the last executive was a year old when the DUP came into their inheritance in November 2003. They had a particular focus that year. They were determined to change the things they could because the bedrock vote was not enough any more. It made the DUP a big player but it never got them over the line in the struggle to beat the UUP in the Unionist popular vote. One thing was a given. There would be no repeat of their experience in the previous election when they stood on doorsteps and listened to voters telling them bad news. Every canvass sheet reported a number of people who wanted to vote for the party but it was a No because the DUP were opposed to power sharing; not every voter but the volume was great enough to make the difference between beating the UUP to pole position in Unionism and standing still in electoral terms.

The DUP was determined not to be caught in that position again, the party had to change tack if they wished to get bragging rights in the Unionist family. Getting ahead of the UUP was the holy grail for the party and they made it happen. It is always good to know where you are going, it is also going to be hard. They fought a different election in 2003, playing down the negative points like no to power sharing and talking up strength and integrity on the question of the Union and their commitment to the terms of the DUP party manifesto. The strategy worked and they swept past the UUP for the first time. They were genuinely enraged that the UUP deviated from their manifesto and did business with Sinn Féin after different talks on different occasions in relation to decommissioning. The manifesto is an article of faith in DUP circles so the party was not likely to follow suit. The DUP would not share power with any party that had a private army outside the door of the cabinet room. Decommissioning and participation on the policing board were the price of power that they had in mind and they were not likely to change.

The Good Friday talks were a defining moment for the Provisionals. It was the end of clandestine meetings with representatives of the NIO spook division, officially or unofficially, and the beginning of serious discourse. Constitutional politics was a new experience for them and it took time to settle in. They were experts at election machines and crowd psychology but they never reached winning before. There were areas that they refused to discuss in depth; taboo subjects like policing. They were reluctant to comment because it would imply recognition of the state so they relied on the disbandment option. Perish the thought that they would share a constructive view on policing with the other parties when their view at the time on policing and the northern state was incendiary. Decommissioning had been sidetracked for the moment and the pressure was off so they waited to be convinced. They arrived with low expectations and ample fears and they came away with enough. They voted for the Good Friday Agreement in due course and supported it solidly afterwards. They were half way towards the finish line after the election in late November 2003 and there was more to come.

There is a danger of repeating the mistakes of the past because the population do not remember the last time. Descriptions of any era are words on a page, chronicles of deeds and misdeeds written by people who were not there or who were generally there for the wrong reasons. The secret was hidden in the past. History is local and history is often family and my instinct was to revert to family history in the search for the future.

The period after the Civil War ended was a period of great confusion and uncertainty. Peace negotiations broke down and the population feared the worst. There was a serious risk of further violence when a general hunger strike by thousands of interned men began in the autumn of 1923. Thousands of Republican prisoners were not released until 1924, a full year after the order to dump arms was given. Ceasefires are always a base camp; there is a steep climb to the summit ahead and conditions may cause the climb to be abandoned. De Valera failed to convince the anti-Treaty IRA and anti-Treaty Sinn Féin to participate in the new democracy. He led his supporters out of the room to form Fianna Fáil and they entered the Dáil in 1927 under the new name. They won 44 seats out of 153 in the June election of that year. The IRA was still active after the split. They seized eleven Garda barracks and killed two Gardai and Kevin O'Higgins was shot dead in 1927. When De Valera took power in 1932, he released all Republican prisoners and lifted the ban on the organisation when he became Taoiseach.

Dumped arms were rarely discussed in the ten year period. Guns are never a sticking point when you lose. There was more pressing business for the new government to attend to and rust was decommissioning weapons in the local bog. The vast majority of the remaining anti-Treatyites followed De Valera into legitimate politics, causing further erosion in paramilitary ranks. Volunteers forgot about politics and returned to the farms and the factories and many emigrated to England and America. Uncle Mick returned to University and finished his medical studies; after that he went to England. My father took up the butcher's trade and concentrated on making a living. Two other uncles, Barney and Peter, returned to Mullaghbawn to work in the family businesses. They were not exceptions to a rule, they were the rule.

There was clear evidence that the wind down takes time after conflict and politics takes time to settle, just like dust. My calculation of the time span was purely mathematical, nine /ten years from dumping arms to government in the case of De Valera, nine/ten years from the Good Friday Agreement took us to 2007/2008. There was no change in human nature in the meantime and the DUP and the Provisionals, two organisations who had never experienced real power, were in pole position. 2008 seemed like a settling year.

Chapter Sixteen

The governments stuck with the programme. The review of the working of the Good Friday Agreement began at Stormont on 3 February 2004. It was a chance for the governments to calm things down, provide some breathing space in the system, take some soundings and give the impression of progress. They were committed to tweaking and fine tuning some aspects of the Agreement, a staple phrase of diplomacy. The use of particular words put a limit on the degree of change anticipated at the talks. The fundamental principles of the Good Friday Agreement remained, enshrined in legislation. The review was an opportunity to test the views of the parties, particularly the DUP, and nobody stayed away.

The DUP spent the weeks after the 2003 November election working on their devolution plan. They attended the initial meeting of the Review and followed up with a visit to Downing Street two days later to discuss their proposals with Tony Blair. On 6 February 2004, they revealed their proposals at a press conference in Belfast. They indicated that the Assembly could be up and running in the short term before the outstanding questions of IRA decommissioning and paramilitary activity were resolved. They further stated that there was no place for Republicans in a power-sharing executive until the IRA was out of business. The statement was viewed within the DUP as a conciliatory gesture and they were very surprised when the Provisionals responded by saying that the proposals sounded like a return to majority rule. The reaction in their own ranks consoled them, very few telephone calls or letters from the general public and minimal unrest in the ranks of the party faithful in relation to the devolution proposals. Martin McGuinness returned to the detail of the proposals some days later. He described the DUP ideas as a shift away from the never-never land politics that they had had inhabited for decades and brought the DUP into the ballpark of Good Friday Agreement politics. End game was the engagement of the DUP and the Provisionals. The last part of the cycle was about to begin and I was hopeful of a bunch finish at last.

It was a great irony that David Trimble pulled his party out of the review on 2 March 2004 in response to an incident when IRA members abducted Bobby Tohill from a Belfast city centre bar and were arrested as they drove him off in a van after beating him with iron bars. Trimble wanted the Review wound up. It was clear that the DUP did not.

I noted the following progression as the months unfolded.

15 May 2004
The Review talks resumed at Stormont.

22 July 2004

Jeffrey Donaldson DUP MP states that Unionists will guarantee the stability of Stormont if Republicans abandon paramilitarism for good.

27 July 2004

The NIO confirm that the British and Irish prime ministers will host a new round of political talks. The venue is later revealed as Leeds Castle in Kent.

16 September 2004

Leeds Castle. The parties are there with the two Governments. The DUP wanted the IRA put out of business for good. They wanted a transparent act of arms decommissioning and a list detailing the amount and type of weapons destroyed. The Provisionals needed full-blooded power sharing, the full implementation of the Good Friday Agreement and demilitarisation. After that, there was the Police Board to be sorted. Optimistic noises on the way into the three day event and muted noises on the way out. Nothing stands still in politics and there was an equality of agony amongst the parties who were still not speaking. A deal by Christmas was hinted at by participants as they left. It was two years since the last power-sharing executive collapsed at Stormont.

4 October 2004

Paisley meets with the Taoiseach in Dublin.

29 November 2004

Gerry Adams meets with Hugh Orde, Chief Constable of the PSNI at Downing Street.

Concentrated talks take place in an attempt to restore devolution by Christmas and the talks finally fail. The grounds of disagreement were reduced in the frenzy of activity. The major obstacle was the question of photographs of decommissioning and trust in relation to a further act of decommissioning. The DUP were demanding that any future act of decommissioning be photographed and the Provisionals were resisting this. In an article in *An Phoblacht* dated 16 December 2004, Sinn Féin's Mitchel McLaughlin criticised the two governments for raising the question of photographs and demanded face to face talks with the DUP.

The governments displayed a vast amount of tolerance during routine meetings with the Provisionals after the Good Friday Agreement. There was a lot of humouring to be done. The Provisionals had control of the board. They were at the height of their influence and Gerry Adams was the most popular leader in the country. Provisional delegations tended to arrive with a new wish list in their hand and the governments gave way every time. The governments added the latest list to the demand pile and ignored breaches of the ceasefire reported since the last visit because it suited everybody except the Unionists. It was a predictable response by the governments because the wind was behind the risen people, a one way street and the Provisionals were running down it. The wish list got longer in time and still no serious response on decommissioning. It is hard to blame the Provisionals in the circumstances. They were pushing an open door so they pushed their own agenda. It was the right strategy. They were entitled to kick on until they got a refusal.

There was a fever in the streets and a new taste for the politics of attrition. The new mood swept through the Catholic strongholds in the North. There was a new shine to the Provisional shield and a growing confidence in the virtue of the armed struggle. A tide of green rhetoric covered the land, swamping every counter argument and making way for the super patriots, new democrats with an old rap for a new Ireland. I noticed the change in mood in Newry while I made the best of my way home. I survived the sneering years, the cheap abuse that goes with the tag of winner in the time of victory. There were a lot of professional Irishmen around who were eager to tell me what a patriot looked like and he never looked like me. I had one consolation: most patriots I know never speak well of the living.

The Provisional formula was palatable to the minority in the North because of old wrongs. It was a case of kick a man when he is down because you might never get another chance. The mood in the South was different in a time of affluence. There was a superficial attachment to the old ways but the Republic was beyond it now. The middle classes bought shed loads of books about the armed struggle and scattered them on coffee tables for effect but their attitude to the North had not changed. The southern position was similar to the Unionist position for fifty years. Political and cultural concerns diminish in importance when you have power in the land, there is no need to work at them if you are a citizen. The minority were over-committed culturally and politically at that point in time. There was no shared identity of purpose any more, just a shared interest in a settlement and that meant concessions.

The governments turned a blind eye to robberies, punishment beatings and the killing of drug dealers. They indulged the Provisional movement for a depressingly long period, running into years, and put off the evil day when the hard questions needed to be put. It was almost a Sisyphus process, the two governments pushed the old rock up the hill and the Provisionals pushed it down again with the help of another wish list. The process suffered because there was too much nitpicking and special pleading, bogging it down and threatening to destroy it.

20 December 2004
An armed gang steal £26.5 million from the Northern Bank in Belfast city centre. The IRA deny responsibility.

The Provisionals were still in control of the peace process until the Northern Bank was robbed but it was open season after that. A whodunit began with the first news of the robbery and the IRA were mentioned often. There was only one certainty, the robbery was not carried out by Martians. The police, North and Sorth, put the hammer down in earnest and reported within weeks. Millions of pounds recovered at a house in Cork and another million from searches in Louth, Meath, Kerry, Dublin and Westmeath. There was too much money to hide so a man started a bonfire in Passage West in Cork. The evidence pointed towards the IRA but the investigation was at an early stage.

At Leader's Questions in Dáil Éireann on 26 January 2005, the Taoiseach commented in detail for the first time and I am indebted to Brian Feeney for drawing my attention to this answer. Bertie Ahern said:

> However, there seems to be a sinister view that one can, on the one hand, continue the development of democratic politics of a kind and, on the other, it is all right to engage in criminality. There was a view that, for some time, this was tolerated to move the process forward. However, ten years on, we cannot afford to do that. What offended me, and the reason I have taken a tough line on this, was the idea that a comprehensive agreement could be negotiated on the basis of trust and confidence while this kind of criminality went on. It is not a question of the size of the bank raid, and it was a big bank raid. I did not show anger regarding earlier events, for example, the raid on the Makro store in Dunmurry last Easter where a million pounds of goods were stolen and the staff were tied up by armed men. The Independent Monitoring Commission blamed the IRA for that. We in this house took that coolly enough. In October two million pounds worth of cigarettes were stolen from the Gallagher warehouse in north Belfast when a gang held up employees. The PSNI said that the Provisional IRA was responsible for that. The Provisional IRA is also believed to be responsible for the abduction and robbery of a Strabane bank branch on 26 September. What I find really offensive, and again I say it here in the House with members of Sinn Féin present because I did not go around with a megaphone over Christmas, is that there was an ability to turn off the punishment beatings while negotiations were in progress but as soon as the negotiations failed there was a string of them – they are again a nightly occurrence. I will give Sinn Féin full marks for discipline, but not for anything else.

There is an epic quality to the passage. It summed up the nature of the peace process; the small defeats, the secret humiliations, the lack of generosity of spirit on the journey towards the light, the deadly drag of it all. The hurt and weariness leaks off the page and attacks the spirit. It reeks of bad times, the moment when the will wavers and the gloom sets in. It is also a glorious snapshot in time.

It was a bad month for Bertie Ahern and people of goodwill on these island. He was like the player on a football team who failed to score at all in a match, who was asked to comment on the result. He said they were lucky to get nil. Ahern was hurt and he was not happy about it. He made the sacrifices and the compromises and he got whitewashed for his pains. Life sucks us under on occasions and we struggle to resurface but Ahern was different. He was Taoiseach and he had the rod of power in his hand. He was a man of effortless patience but he had to act. It is certain that the passage reflects the core of his message to Gerry Adams when they met the previous day, for the first time since the robbery. It was a frank and brutal meeting. Before it broke up, the Irish government told the Provisional leadership to come back when they had something useful to say. It was the tipping point in the relationship between the southern state and the Provisional movement. The Irish Government stopped off the merry go round and called a halt to the pan-Nationalist front. The Taoiseach delivered another message at the same time. Criminality was at the epicentre of the political debate and showed no sign of moving.

I ignore the whodunit aspect of the robbery because it is irrelevant. The fallout from the robbery was the key factor, not the identity of the individuals or the organisation involved. The fallout was seismic and the terms of engagement were changed forever by the event. Political disasters often have an equal and opposite effect to the imagined reaction. It happens frequently in politics despite what people think. Politicians shift position in an ink storm, often to good effect. The net effect of the robbery was an impetus in the search for a durable deal between the protagonists. You make peace with your enemies, not your friends and it depends how much you want it. The process jumped forward substantially as a result of the event. The DUP had a lucky escape, a UUP moment in the eyes of the public. They nearly signed up to a deal and it was the wrong deal. They went back to the manifesto and waited out the Provisionals on decommissioning and the Policing Board. There was a peace process after the Northern Bank job but the Provisionals no longer controlled it and they had only themselves to blame.

30 January 2005

The Provisionals spent the time after the Northern Bank robbery on damage limitation and worse happened. Robert McCartney was killed by a number of men in a Markets bar in Belfast, known IRA men when the facts emerged. The pressure on the organisation was dramatically increased by the strength and ferocity of the public campaign mounted by McCartney's sisters in the aftermath of the death of their brother. The IRA offered to shoot those responsible. Three men were eventually expelled from the IRA, a barren gesture that failed to convince anybody. The murder of Robert McCartney reinforced the view in the public mind that there was one law for the public and another for the private army. The DUP had withdrawn to barge-pole distance and the peace process was in crisis. Three men later faced trial in June 2008. The trial judge dismissed the charges against the defendants because of doubts about the identification evidence and the flawed nature of other testimony.

The McCartney girls may never get justice for their brother but they have one enduring consolation. They mounted a campaign that ended the debate on policing in our society and the Provisional concept of justice. They showed why the rule of law is important, proper investigative and legal procedures followed by a day in court if there is a case to answer in place of public fear and a conspiracy of silence, and why the alternative is unacceptable in the public mind. Justice is not served by a gang of men in balaclavas, armed with firearms and baseball bats or the feral hatred of a mob. It is not found on a dark street in the Markets area of Belfast or on the floor of a lonely shed in South Armagh.

5 May 2005
A British general election took place. The DUP manifesto stressed that the party wanted devolution but it also wanted a final settlement. The key in the eyes of the DUP, in order to work with Republicans was the disbandment of the IRA. Only parties committed to peaceful means should be part of the democratic institutions. The UUP also expressed a commitment to a devolved assembly under the terms of the Good Friday Agreement. The DUP manifesto was an interesting document. No censure of Provisional activity in a particular sense, just an outline of the price of power sharing. The DUP was not walking away.

19 May 2005
Ian Paisley met Tony Blair and told him that a new beginning was needed because the Good Friday Agreement was dead. Bertie Ahern replied on 20 May 2005 after a meeting of the British/Irish Council on the Isle of Man where the comments were discussed. Ahern rejected the remarks. He said:

> The Agreement was reviewed for the bulk of 2004 and was accepted by the DUP and the other political parties in Northern Ireland before the aborted power-sharing deal last December...it must not be renegotiated again...the basis for moving forward is the Good Friday Agreement... altering the Agreement now was not a possibility..

The DUP accepted the Good Friday Agreement after the review procedure with minor concessions for electing the first minister and the deputy first minister and in the workings of the Assembly. The legislation programme, arising out of the Agreement was almost complete, with the exception of the Judicial Appointments Commission which followed shortly. The future political infrastructure was secure. People, who talked and sometimes still talk about the Agreement being dead, have serious problems with reality. They are refuted every time they vote on a cross-community basis in the Assembly or meet a member of the PSNI on a crowded street.

28 July 2005
The IRA ordered an end to the armed conflict. All IRA units were ordered to

dump arms. The IRA committed itself to exclusively peaceful means. Nobody was throwing their cloth caps in the air because it was a response to pressure. The Provisionals always prided themselves on the ability to control change and they were confounded by it in the end.

1 August 2005

Peter Hain, the Secretary of State, announces a two-year plan for demilitarisation. It included a reduction of 5,500 in Army strength over the period and a repeal of counter-terrorist legislation. Army posts were closed and police stations de-fortified.

26 September 2005

IRA puts all weapons beyond use in the presence of a representative group of clergymen.

Perfect sequencing, necessary housekeeping and the rebuilding of trust that evaporated after the Northern Bank robbery. It was not a time for formal talks because the wounds were too fresh. The governments filled the space, just like they filled it with the Good Friday Agreement review after the 2003 elections.

There was a maturity about the confidence-building measures. The sequences highlighted here down the years prove that there was a lot of tic-tacking going on between the governments and the Provisionals and the DUP and a clear pattern of cause and effect. Very few face-to-face meetings on an official basis but the apron of a council meeting, after the chairman calls a halt to proceedings, is a perfect time to do business.

4 April 2006

The British and Irish governments produce their blueprint on devolution. Assembly members are given until 24 November 2006 to set up a power-sharing executive and the Assembly is recalled in May to that end. Salaries would stop if the members failed to meet the November deadline. The British and Irish governments indicated that they would work on partnership arrangements to implement the Good Friday Agreement.

The two governments sent a message to the DUP and Sinn Féin. Do business or we abolish the Assembly and run the North together. The alternative to doing business for the DUP was more Dublin rule. It was the political message of the last thirty plus years. Saying no was not a fruitful political exercise. The use of the word by the DUP now meant more 'Dublin Rule'.

17 October 2006

The DUP insist that a pledge of support for policing and law and order is in place before Ian Paisley and Martin McGuinness become the shadow First Minister and shadow deputy First Minister on 24 November.

28 December 2006
Gerry Adams indicates that he will put forward a motion to a special party conference on policing.

28 January 2007
Sinn Féin vote to support the police. Over 90% of the delegates vote in favour.

13 February 2007
The last British Army watchtower in South Armagh is dismantled and the guard post at Crossmaglen police station is removed.

27 March 2007
Paisley and Adams speak for the first time, so much for face-to-face negotiations. The process worked as it should without direct meetings. There was no hint of a joint session throughout the process and the absence of hate figures from view when important decisions were made had a positive effect. Agree a set of principles first, talk later and meet when the loose strings are tied up. Sometimes it is better not to meet, to negotiate at arm's length. It removes the risk of shaking hands in public. It also avoids dragging out the old negotiation table when sequencing is the best way forward.

8 May 2007
Direct rule ends after five years. Power sharing is restored.

Power sharing was restored on my birthday. I was sixty-three years of age. I watched the ceremony on television and wished them well. The Troubles stalked me the length of my adult years and I was glad to see the back of them. The new formation had a chance; no private armies outside the door and the ordnance of war decommissioned. I captain golf teams at Warrenpoint Golf Club and we use a phrase after a messy win. ' It wasn't pretty but the business was done.' It was also inevitable as I said in the '2008 document'. Paragraph nine of the document refers to a surge forward in history as a positive force. 21 December 2004 was such a date. There was no alternative for the DUP and the Provisionals. The governments were waiting in the wings and they had the last call, pointing up the alternatives, an historic compromise between the DUP and the Provisionals or an enhanced relationship between Whitehall and Dublin. A great talent in life is knowing when to let go.

The DUP and the Provisionals did the patriotic thing. They took the vast bulk of their supporters home from the long war. Nobody is entirely wrong in any conflict and there are always those who refuse to bend. Nobody should doubt the achievement of Paisley and Adams and McGuinness and Robinson. They crossed the river and their support was virtually intact when they reached the distant bank, that is their distinct contribution to a settlement.

There is always another election in the North and there were big questions out there and no answers. What were the parties to say when they rapped doors and the voters asked about the future? Were they likely to say

> The solution is obvious but we have decided to ignore it...better to choose another generation of no-win conflict and forget about jobs...we used to have friends in both governments and now we have no friends at all... just a functional relationship with two governments who are working on partnership arrangements for the future that will exclude us from decision making..

That sales pitch was unlikely to impress the electorate because people are strange that way. They prefer economic prosperity and food on the table to a rerun of the Troubles, if they are given a choice. Complete decommissioning and a presence on the Policing Board was the price of power sharing and the Provisionals anted up. The price for the DUP was either the Provisionals in government or the birth of a new relationship between Dublin and London. The DUP and the Provisionals are the major influences in the government of the North and the sky has not fallen in.

November 18 2008
Peter Robinson and Martin McGuinness confirm the resumption of meetings of the power-sharing executive and the devolution of Policing and Justice responsibilities. No date is specified for the latter event.

A perfect end to the peace process and the last piece of the Good Friday Agreement will be in place soon. The two governments stood back and let the DUP and Sinn Féin work it out for themselves. It is a mantra for the future.

Chapter Seventeen

The two governments developed a huge expertise in the area of conflict management in the course of the last ten years but reality is diminished in the abstract. We can only engage in conflict resolution if we truly understand how we got here. The governments were energised and prepared to take risks, to change the habit of centuries and engage. The British government came to terms with political status for prisoners, the efficacy of meeting paramilitaries on ceasefire, the need to widen the terms of debate and the exercise of faded imperial power in the last colony. The Irish government closed the book of wrong and negotiated as a government, sovereign and free. The American government was a supportive presence, on hand and engaged, not off hand and disengaged.

Economic prosperity in the Sorth was a huge bonus. It transformed the image of the Republic from a priest-ridden peasant economy into a different creature, confident and forward looking and conscious of status. No more the confessional state, the forelock-touching controlled environment that I recall from my youth where the church held sway, where a belt of the crozier cured all tendencies, like rebelling against the church. There were other positive factors on the way to the outcome, the immensity of the civil rights movement and the foundation of the SDLP near the end of street activism, the patience of the two governments in the aftermath of the Agreement, the commitment of the UUP leadership and the bulk of the loyalist paramilitaries to the Good Friday Agreement, the long way home after the long war in the case of the Provisionals and the DUP.

There are a lot of cares if you run a nation, public pressures and party pressures and the gauntlet of the tabloid press, the dangers of every day that dawns and the great fear that comes with the morning. The crude tumbrel of events, destiny in a handcart and it comes in layered form. It is always the simple things that topple leaders. We were lucky in the North of Ireland. Fate left us in the care of two leaders who made time, too much time their constituents said on occasions. Politics is hard to quantify and so is the life of an individual. Sooner or later we hold a mirror up to ourselves and try to see. What do we count when we try to quantify our lives at the end of a given year? What do we put in the plus column? What do politicians ponder over, the number of constituency cases, the number of TV appearances, the public good that, hand on heart, you can claim made a difference? It is one thing to become the leader, another thing to be a leader. Most people who hold high office have the opportunity to effect fundamental change and never do. Risk taking is dangerous, it is better to engage in more of the same and throw money at a few focus group findings.

The two leaders elected in the summer of 1997 Ahern and Blair, could have played it safe, clung to the old pieties and mimed it. They risked it all on a big play in the first year of their watch and they made it work with the help of Bill Clinton.

Co-operating with the British is frowned upon by professional Irishmen, the people who have a note somewhere signed by Dermot McMurrough's woman saying that they were not part of the original sell out. Bertie Ahern avoided the traditional route in his dealings with the British and went for the deal. He dismantled the old mentality, ignored the hiss of folk memory that corroded the positive in us and made a deal impossible. He led us into a new relationship with the English and anchored us there. The imperial call must have rung loudly in the ears of Tony Blair in Whitehall, a partisan growl about old pieties and white wogs and recent memories of absolute rule in Ireland. Why change something just because it was wrong? Old habits die hard, just like the stench of superiority in high places.

Ahern and Blair deserve great credit for their work in the North. They engaged across the totality of issues and left the baggage of history outside the door. There were many years when the North was in the minus column for Blair and Ahern and there was nobody else to blame. There was no new leader who needed time to read himself in, because they were in it together for ten long years. They spent endless hours on the northern brief when it was a dead weight in their work loads and they came through. The door of government buildings was always open to the men and women who were trying to make sense of the chaos. It was mission impossible and it worked in the end. They are entitled to the gratitude of two nations.

The special relationship with Britain was revived by Bill Clinton when Tony Blair arrived in Downing Street but the relationship has changed in relation to Irish affairs. There is a new understanding, a new awareness of external influences and external relationships and an acceptance by Whitehall that there was an American dimension to the problem. There was a further boost for the new reality. The Bush administration stayed with the Northern Ireland policy laid down by Bill Clinton and was helpful in the resolution of residual problems like decommissioning, the attitude of the Provisionals to the police and the decision of the DUP to come in from the cold. The special relationship now offers support for the political arrangements at Stormont after the restoration of a power-sharing administration in May 2007. It is a major change in a time of major change and very welcome.

There were many years of obfuscation and bloody mindedness provoked by mistrust and hatred on the part of the parties who made the biggest moves. The Provisional movement and the DUP changed more than the other parties and they have a story to tell about how they got from there to here.

I await a major contribution from the Provisionals on the nature of conflict and the road home, the walk on the dark side that changed to the point that the movement takes a non-violent path and talks of a peaceful future. Who can speak about violence and the eventual path to reconciliation and peace better than the Provisional movement? Have they not a contribution to make on the subject of conflict resolution? The same applies to the DUP, a party that reflected the hard face of Unionism for so many years, growing in the use of power and power sharing, a party who once talked about the people of Ulster as if they were all Protestant.

My memories of the Troubles are slivers of recall about community and hardship and an avalanche of grief and bloodshed, rather than political meetings. I am glad that children under sixteen have no real memory of the Troubles at all. There are heartening stories of ecumenism particularly in the sporting field, camogie teams training under lights at Linfield FC, the Antrim hurling team training at Ballymena RFC, St Bridget's Primary School using the grounds of Belfast Harlequins RFC and rugby and soccer at Croke Park. We need new progressions to secure the peace. We have to talk about tolerance, understanding and atonement. A bit more silence from time to time would also be helpful. We need to mainstream reconciliation and the rule of law in our society and work on anger management.

It might be fun. We have not tried these things before on a community-wide basis. The Big Negative consumed our people for eons, North and Sorth, and the situation never changed. Centuries of chaos, so much national pain, so much futility. Ireland has a forward gear for the first time and people are beginning to express themselves, putting something back. It is a time for positive footprints, not carbon ones. It would be criminal not to grab the chance with both hands, now that a great burden has been lifted. We are free to express ourselves for the benefit of all the people. Start a business or a sports club or an ecumenical group, take out that secret passion and dust it down, support a charity somewhere or do a mature degree as you choose.

There is no end to the journey, or should that be the new adventure? Soon we will grow used to each other and everyday concerns will enfold us. I am out of the prophecy business, I am comfortable in the present and the future will emerge as it should. There are net gains already, folk memory is beginning to fade as goodwill grows. It reminds me of ivy. If there is a wall of prejudice or bigotry available, folk memory will climb up it, but no wall, no ivy. Folk memory will diminish with the decades for most people but for some it will never pass, a few people will hoard it like a miser until the call comes. Many people are predicting what the new Ireland will look like but I consider that a mistake. A debate is beginning on the subject in an era of profound change, of relationships between the groups who share the island, of the fortunes of those who live here, of the political language used and the definitions made. The lack of a full-blooded power-sharing executive held up the debate on an Agreed Ireland. Nationhood and identity loom large in any future discussion and there is a crying need for space to let the concept grow. We have no benchmark to judge success or failure in the search for an Agreed Ireland and there is no timescale. It is what it is, the people have embarked on an adventure of our own.

I insisted that the provenance of the 1997 blueprint should be kept secret until a full-blooded power-sharing executive was embedded. An early leak would have been an unforced error and would have caused political complications. It was also a matter of personal convenience. Anne hated fuss and so do I. The leaking of the document would have sucked me back into the political vortex and I was happy at my work. I do gregarious and I pass myself in craic but we all find our own peace. I forecasted a full-blooded executive would be in operation in 2008 and it arrived six months early. Silence is no longer the requirement and I put pen to paper now because I felt the time is right. The political situation is transformed and all the major provisions have been enshrined in the law of the land so I am free to speak. My memory is still sound and I still have teeth to get into it, mortality is deep in the equation and I have a need to give witness. I write this account because history must not be blind. There is a gap in the jigsaw and it needs filling. The people have a right to know the sequence of events and the players involved at every stage.

I finished the first draft of this book on Good Friday morning, 2008. There was nothing deliberate about it. I was editing and I ran out of pages at eleven o'clock. The Agreement was ten years old, a reporter on the radio was talking about recent difficulties and the slow pace of progress. I muttered in the direction of the radio after the reporter had spoken because I found the comments irritating. History is not a speed thing. Two hundred years is a cold in the life of a country, ten years is a cough in time. Getting to the sunny end of a centuries old problem in ten years seems like a miracle to me. The Agreement rolled out when it could, it took the strain at times and moved forward or sideways at a pinch and it is still alive today and kicking on.

I contacted Brian Feeney when I decided to write End of Term Report. One of the outcomes was a social outing because it had been too long. We met in the Fat Buddah restaurant on the Lisburn Road in Belfast along with his wife Patricia and two friends of ours John and Maureen McConnell for a meal. I know that Anne was with us because we dined together regularly in the bad times. In the course of the evening Brian told me that he had told a senior Provisional, one of the contacts in the second ceasefire affair, that the political prisoner proposals would be on the agenda at the Holy Week talks. He never told me that before. It would have reduced my worry count in Good Friday week but it also consoled me. Brian was stitching it into the record and stitching up the wounds. It was good to know that the caravan always moves on. Feeney ran himself into bad health in support of our strategy in the early part of 1998. He is alive and well and living in Belfast and is as big an enigma as ever.

I call this narrative the End of Term Report and it is a deliberate choice. I retired last year. The Bar had been very good to me and for me, but it is time to move on. I am 64 years old and I would hate, if God leaves me alive for a few more years, to look back and say I wish I did that. There are things I want to do and I might have time to do them. Tennyson said it best in *Ulysses*.

> We are not now that strength which in old days
> Moved heaven and earth; that which we are, we are;
> One equal temper of heroic hearts,
> Made weak by time and fate, but strong in will
> To strive, to seek, to find, and not to yield.

He speaks for my generation. Baroque music is the new rock and roll and I walk slowly in case I pull a muscle.

There is a great silence sometimes, a time of night when the traffic calms, the dogs in the neighbourhood stop barking at ghosts and the world subsides. There is peace in silence and I ingest it until a car horn sounds somewhere and the world rushes in again. The wind picks up and whispers amongst the roof tiles and I lean back from the desk in my study and wonder. The sound of running water can be heard in Mullaghbawn graveyard where my ancestors sleep. The river roars when it is in flood and whispers in dry time, a bit like life. The linnets sing in the evergreens near the mass rock and Slieve Gullion towers above me in a blue haze. The area echoed to the sound of battle but that was during the bad times. Sometimes you could hear the people hating above the bark of the guns. The weapons are silent now and the people expect. The bleeding had to stop before the healing can begin. I have tried to keep my promise and I fail sometimes.

The rugby match against England in Croke Park was an ultimate experience. Packed stadium and bulling atmosphere and I finally felt the hand of history, nervous about the reaction of the crowd to the white shirts and thrilled to be present. England came to Lansdowne Road at the height of the Troubles, the other home countries stayed away. Memories of my father and my Uncle Mick and the Cairo Squad and Bloody Sunday 1920 and I wait with bated breath. The largest crowd ever convened to watch a rugby match in Ireland and an opportunity to confront the past through the torn curtain of Irish history.

The crowd stands and greets the two teams and the first reaction comes, warm as a favourite muffler on a February afternoon and I dare to hope. Perfect silence for God Save The Queen and huge applause afterwards, a tingle on the neck at the first bars of *Amhran na bhFiann* and a clog of emotion, tears and lusty singing and a blessed release. The applause at the end seemed to last forever, rolling like a spring tide over one of the great stadiums of the world, taking away the burden of history and the blight of prejudice. Beating England was a bonus but the applause was the memory, laving and absolving us, washing our sins away and making us better for the feeling. Some days cannot hold any more.

My relationship with Anne defines me, not the Good Friday Agreement. The blueprint document is part of my life but it is not my life and I will not allow the rest of it to be a reflection on that time or turned into a meditation on politics. Anne was my sanctuary lamp and I miss her glow. I refuse to think about the gulf in my life because it would destroy me, suffice to say that nobody deserves the joy she brought me. We had heaven and earth and then heaven left me. I needed space and several diseases before I forget the devastation. The savage truth is that I must not forget; if I forget the pain I forget the pleasure of her presence. The same is true, in a broader community sense, of the Good Friday Agreement.

I will go in search of Anne when it is my season. The finite mind cannot encompass the infinite and I will die wondering. The problem with wise years is simple. There are more questions than answers and I realise that I know almost nothing. What I do know is there is no shame in defeat or failure. The great sin is not trying. I did not ask for the northern gig but I did not shirk the challenge when the time came. The Irish Question did not ignore me and I got to see the show.

THE DOCUMENT

Administration of Justice,

Human Rights, Policing

and

Mechanisms For Change.

Administration of Justice,

Human Rights, Policing

and

Mechanisms For Change.

Administration of Justice.

1. The basic Principles of Criminal Law have stood the test of time but it is necessary to adjust the Procedures and Practice of the Trial and Appellate Process to ensure greater Protection of Human Rights. There is widespread community concern at the perceived intimacy between investigation and prosecution in this society; between the Royal Ulster Constabulary and the Department of Public Prosecution. There appears to be a relationship that damages both agencies.

   The main concerns include the following:

   - Public Disquiet about existing structures and relationships.
   - Lack of effective judicial supervision of the pre-trial phase of the criminal process.
   - Lack of satisfactory and just arrangements for providing scientific evidence.
   - The absence of independent assessment of the nature and quality of information, furnished by separate investigative agencies, in determining the offences to be charged.
   - Inadequate, slipshod and easily disregarded Rules of Practice, in giving the defence relevant information that could be material. For example, the existence of a witness who could support an alibi.
   - The DPP prosecute in name only. There is a need for an Independent Prosecution Service to conduct criminal trials. The DPP see their role as an independent decision to prosecute and nothing more. The inevitable absence of the DPP officer in charge at the vast bulk of serious criminal cases means that the police officer in charge conducts the prosecution and advises counsel. The said police officer is often a witness in the case. A junior clerk is generally, the only DPP presence at hearing. What is left is a police prosecution in the name of the DPP.
   - The restrictions imposed by Law on effective judicial intervention where there are grounds to believe there has been a miscarriage of justice.

2. In France, the preparation for trial is a judicial responsibility from the moment of arrest; sometimes earlier. The judicial power is concerned with the investigation and enquiries needed to discover the truth. This change in procedure would provide a valuable judicial function and necessary protection of the suspect. The whole pre-trial procedure would be under the judicial arm of the state. While the French system is flawed - the *juge*

d'instruction is a junior judge at the beginning or end of his career - it is a system that can be moulded to local needs.

3. The Scottish Procurator Fiscal puts the onus of supervision of the whole pre-trial period on the Crown Prosecution Service. The system seems to work well. The Procurator Fiscal has control of the prosecution at, and after charge, and the Office has power to discontinue a case. However, no Nationalist would welcome the prospect of putting supervision in the hands of the existing Department of Public Prosecutions. In the light of our experience; who is to guard the guards?

   Another possibility is the District Attorney structure in the United States.

4. I propose the creation of the Office of the Criminal Justice Commissioner.

   The Criminal Justice Commissioner would have a duty:

   • To satisfy himself/herself that a confession is genuine.
   • To indicate the investigations and enquiries to be made in the preparation of a case.
   • Ensure that the defence is kept fully informed of all relevant matters.

5. Defence lawyers would have the right to:

   • Apply to the Criminal Justice Commissioner for an Order in matters arising during the preparation for trial. There should be a Summons for Directions and the accused could seek disclosure of information, including reports of scientific or other investigations in the possession of the judicial authority or at the prosecution's disposal.
   • Make a separate trial application.
   • Make an application to delete prejudicial material etc.

6. The Criminal Justice system is sound in principle but it must adapt in apparatus and procedure to a changing world. Judicial supervision of the pre-trial period would give the defence the opportunity, information and resources to obtain justice. Acute damage can be inflicted between arrest and charge; the period when the accused is held and interrogated by the police. There is need for supervision by an authority other than the police.

7. The functions of a Criminal Justice Commissioner re investigation will be:

   • Independent monitoring and reviewing of the decisions of police officers in relation to detention, interview and treatment of suspects.

- A supervisory jurisdiction over police interviews, which would ensure greater compliance with PACE; in tandem with audio and video recordings.
- The responsible collation of documents. This would facilitate and ensure proper and adequate disclosure. The efficacy of disclosure of unused material is contingent upon general knowledge of the existence of material, particularly where such material is in the care, custody or control of a third party. Certain investigative agencies control documentation:

- The Royal Ulster Constabulary.
- Social Services.
- Hospitals.
- Forensic Science laboratories.
- Other Agencies; depending upon the type of case.
- An investigative jurisdiction at the time of arrest which would assist in relation to:

  - * Determining possible innocence as opposed to a
  - * Process to secure a conviction.

- Guarantee the independence of Forensic Medical Officers. Present contact between police officers and Forensic Medical Officers and other forensic witnesses is open to abuse. There is a tendency for police officers to seek confirmation of evidence, as opposed to seeking independent analysis of evidence.
- Review progress in criminal proceedings and discontinue the said proceedings in certain circumstances. The number of cases withdrawn following lengthy periods of remand in custody, gives rise to present concerns. There is a need for the Scottish 110 day rule in this jurisdiction.
- Be accessible to the victims of crime, in appropriat circumstances, in relation to the carriage of their case.
- Be responsible for statutory consents to prosecution in all cases.
- Prevent continued interviewing of suspects by police officers:
  - a) Against whom a suspect has made a complaint.
  - b) Who makes a complaint of assault against a suspect.

The present situation is unhelpful, bearing in mind the provisions of the Criminal Evidence Order.

- Supervise the procedure whereby an allegation of child sexual abuse is investigated. No proper supervision of the investigation takes place at present. Preparation of video recordings, where the Children's (Evidence) Order 1995 is to be invoked, should be under the supervision of the Criminal Justice Commissioner. More particularly, having regard to the disclosure duty, imposed by the said Order.
- Have direct input into the investigative process where members of the security forces are suspected of an offence. This would raise a greater degree of public confidence.
- Supervise the investigative process. This will act as a safeguard in relation to the intelligence gathering aspect of many investigations, particularly drug-related offences, and ensure proper and impartial prosecutions.
- Ensure the attendance of the suspect's solicitor. There is concern amongst the general public that the police often fail to ensure the availability of the first choice solicitor. There is concern about the deferral of legal access in many cases.
- Review prison disciplinary decisions. The institution of the Criminal Justice Commissioner will reduce the number of Order 53 challenges, by providing a mechanism for the redress of operational wrongs, and free Supreme Court judicial resources.
- Choose the Panel from which the Police Doctor is summoned. There is public concern about the objectivity, or otherwise, of the present incumbents. The present system is open to abuse. The new Panel to operate on rota.

8. There is a need an Independent Forensic Service. The present system encourages duplication of evidence and recurrent, pointless expense.

9. Police disciplinary matters

The Criminal Justice Commissioner will have the powers to:
- Suspend an Officer
- Take evidence on oath or order disclosure

where he/she is satisfied that there is a case to answer in relation to the detention, treatment and interrogation of suspects or conduct unbecoming a police officer during the course of his general duties.

10. The Independent Commission for Police Complaints recognised that, if a key element in accountability is a satisfactory system for the handling of complaints, it failed to meet the test. The ICPC repeatedly sought Government agreement for a number of specific measures, which the Commission felt were necessary to enhance Commission credibility. The creation of a Police Ombudsman, under the terms of the new Police Bill which will get a Second Reading this week (December 1997), has rendered the Commission obsolete, but the specific measures they sought are worthy of note.

They contended that:

* the ICPC, rather than the Chief Constable, should be able to direct that a complaint be recorded where a dispute exists on what constitutes a complaint;

* That the ICPC should be able to call itself in; to initiate investigations in the public interest where it considers grave or exceptional circumstances exist, and where no complaint has been made. This is currently a power enjoyed by the Secretary of State, PANI [Police Authority of Northern Ireland] and the Chief Constable. The ICPC point out that only seven non-complaint matters have been referred to it since 1988.

11. I propose:
   - That the Criminal Justice Commissioner be given power to direct that a complaint be recorded.
   - That the Criminal Justice Commissioner have power to call himself in.
   - That a Criminal Justice Commissioner, serving in another region, would hear any matter arising out of a situation where the Criminal Justice Commissioner has called himself in.

12. Complaints to be arbitrated on the civil standard of proof. At present, police officers are formally disciplined or dismissed if it is proven beyond a reasonable doubt that they have contravened their Code of Discipline. Other public servants are judged on the civil standard. The lower standard of proof must apply in Police Disciplinary Hearings. Conduct unbecoming a police officer to be the criterion.

13. The Police Ombudsman proposal is old soup in a new plate.

Paul Donnelly, the present Chairman of the Independent Commission for Police Complaints, said in the Belfast Telegraph on 13 December 1997:

We freely acknowledge that the present system for management of complaints has many shortcomings and drawbacks..policing everywhere needs to move away from command and control regimes and towards a learning and service improvement ethos.

Questions must be asked arising out of these comments. Why were the stated shortcomings not remedied - in view of persistent allegations of police investigating police - in view of the 25 year currency of the allegations and why was the ICPC request for specific measures ignored by the relevant authorities?

14. Each Criminal Justice Commissioner will have supervision of a Region of the North of Ireland.

    There should be Nine Regions: two Belfast Regions, seven other Regions.

    The Regions to be based on Westminster Constituencies.

15. The proposed Regions are:

    - West Belfast/North Belfast
    - Lagan Valley/Upper Bann
    - South Belfast/East Belfast
    - Foyle/ West Tyrone
    - Mid Ulster/Fermanagh and South Tyrone
    - Strangford/North Down
    - South Antrim/East Antrim
    - East Derry/North Antrim
    - Newry and Armagh/South Down

16. The Regional Criminal Justice Commissioner would:

    - Be responsible to a Central Criminal Justice Commission and
    - Reflect the ethos of the prevailing tradition in their particular Region.

17. General Proposal

    * A body of Judicial Officers responsible for independently monitoring and reviewing, *inter alia:*

* Decisions of police officers relative to extension of detention, treatment of suspects and conduct of interviews.

* Decisions of the DPP relative to the initiation, termination and conduct of proceedings, and in addition:

* Determining pre-trial motions in the period between committal and arraignment relative to disclosure - primary and third party - and such other issues as may be appropriate in any reformed system of criminal procedure.

* Reviewing prison disciplinary decisions and thus reducing the burden on the High Court whilst ensuring an independent review of the merits of the decision of the Governor and the Board of Visitors.

18. The Criminal Justice Commissioners to be Appointed by the Inter-Governmental Conference.

Policing

1. Policing cannot be negotiated in the abstract. A sequence needs to emerge if we are to resolve our complex problems. There must be a:

   • Permanent cessation of politically motivated violence.

   • Political settlement that attracts cross-community commitment.

2. Policing cannot be considered in isolation. The matter can only be resolved against the backdrop of the Criminal Justice system and the historic contradictions that prejudice attitudes towards the police in our divided society. The objective must be a Police Service that commands the support of both traditions.

3. Support implies people from mainstream Nationalist and Unionist areas joining a Police Service with a sense of pride not guilt, and without censure from their community. It means serving and protecting that community as an indigenous part of it, and in turn being protected by the community; it means the active involvement of Nationalists, as well as Unionists, in policing in a way which has not been possible since Northern Ireland was created. For Nationalists it is the granting of allegiance - for the first time - to a system of policing with which they can identify, politically and ideologically.

4. A Police Service, operating on the basis of consensus, is one of the hallmarks of a properly functioning civil society. That consensus can only be achieved through political debate within the peace process. It is essential that the political talks address, not only how we govern ourselves with the consent of all sections of the community, but also how we police our society, enforce our laws, protect the individual and maintain community stability.

5. We must reassess from first principles the policing requirements of a divided society, enjoying the beginnings of peace. We must fundamentally reappraise how we deliver a Police Service, considering ethos, structures, accountability, and the legal framework within which it operates. Through political discussion, dialogue and negotiation, we must agree a system of policing which commands the support, involvement and Allegiance of all of the people of the North of Ireland.

6. The RUC developed in an abnormal way. From the outset, they were tasked with abnormal policing duties, defending the constitutional arrangement of 1920, implementing the Special Powers Act and operating the various Special Constabularies; the agenda of a tribe at war. Any likelihood of the RUC proving acceptable across both communities was undermined from inception by their role in implementing the Special Powers legislation. That trend has been reinforced over the past 25 years by the association of the police with the large body of emergency legislation which has been added to the statute books in that time. They were not a civilian Police Service in 1920 and they are not a civilian Police Service now.

7. The Sunningdale Agreement 1973, at Paragraph 13, recognised that :

   • It was broadly accepted that the two parts of Ireland are, to a considerable extent, Inter-dependent in the whole field of Law and Order, and that the problems of political violence and Identification with the Police Service cannot be solved without taking account of that fact…the British and Irish Governments will co-operate under the auspices of a Council of Ireland through their respective Police Authorities.

8. The Opsahl Commission June 1993 concluded: Unless genuine representatives of the Nationalist community are given an executive role in policing, Nationalists cannot take responsibility for it. It is unreasonable to expect a Police Force, made up largely of members of one community, to be acceptable to the other community in a divided society like Northern Ireland. The Commission believes that Nationalist support for, and

significant recruitment to, the RUC will only take place in the context of new Political Structures for the Region; in which Power and Authority go hand in hand with Responsibility.

9. Proposed Changes

- The new name to be The North of Ireland Police Service or named after the Region served. 'Royal' was introduced after the suppression of the Fenian rising in 1867; Ulster is what Unionists call the North and Constabulary is old fashioned and paramilitarist.

- The force to be de - centralised. It is presently based on the colonial model, brought in about 1830 with a national HQ in Dublin. In the nineteenth century, it was accepted that a centralised national force did not serve the public. The Dublin Metropolitan Police force was established. It was civilian and based on the London Met. The DMP was set up because the centralised RIC was an armed, paramilitary colonial force, unsuitable for dealing with normal policing. Dublin Castle decided a locally recruited force was necessary for rising urban crime rates. They also established separate forces in Derry and Belfast for the same reason. As communal strife developed in Belfast and Derry, the separate police forces were abolished in 1864 and 1870 and the RIC took over again. Decentralisation and regionalism are recurrent topics. Over a century ago, people in the administration realised that a unified, colonial system was unsuitable so they reflected the English towns structure. It was not attempted in the countryside, because of widespread agitation. Dismantling the Headquarters mentality of the RUC is not unprecedented. Policing has changed repeatedly over the generations and will continue to change.

- Policing must be local. There would be an established percentage from each ward who will police that ward. Extensive redundancies would take place over an eighteen month period, as many as 4,000 with 20/30 years service. This would cost £300 million. There is already pension provision for men with twenty years service. It would not all be a fresh call on the Exchequer. After six months satisfactory service, reservists would be eligible as established police officers. Other reservists, full and part time, would then take their place.

- Policing must reflect the spectrum of society. We need to stand down all full time and part time RUC reservists and recruit a new reserve to reflect the Loyalist and Republican communities, and put a bit of cash into impoverished Catholic areas. Former reservists could apply.

- The new decentralised service would be based on Council Electoral Areas. English forces are based on County Councils and Metropolitan

Councils. Each Council would be a Division, commanded by a Chief Superintendent with Sub Divisions based on Wards. Re - districting in Northern Ireland over the last twenty years has been beneficial. It reflects the population divide accurately. More than 50% of Wards in the North are over 90% Catholic or 90% Protestant; the rest are heading that way. In large areas like Belfast with 4,000 voters to a ward, a Sub Division would cover five wards. An Inspector should be responsible for each Ward.

In rural areas with Wards as low as 500 voters, there would have to be geographical considerations, but the objective is that a Sub Division should reflect the politico/religious complexion of the Area it serves. Wards should not be combined to produce Sub Divisions made up of potentially conflicting communities. West Belfast, Derry and South Armagh present few problems in this regard. North Belfast and East Tyrone are difficult to resolve.

10

- Councils should have Community Police Liaison Committees. Based on wards and made up, inter alia, of councillors, community workers, teachers, clergy and police. The Chair should not be a police officer. They should have functions similar to Watch Committees. There should be a Council-wide Liaison Committee - like Council Police Authorities in England. Police Liaison Committees have a vital community function. They are presently a catspaw of the RUC and removed from the concept of accountable policing. The relevance of these bodies, at present, is summed up in a remark attributed to the then Chairman of the Police Authority:

If they are a talking shop where nothing much happens, then one has to ask why they exist.

Quoted by David Weitzer, Northern Ireland Police Liaison Committees, 1992 Complaints Machinery.

- The Merits of the Ward based Approach.

  I. Wards change every ten years and reflect population movement.

  II. It prevents police Areas becoming fossilised.

  III. Wards are the basis for allocating money from the DOE, IFI and Other agencies.

  IV. If people in a Ward - Ardoyne, Legoniel, Crossmaglen, Shankill, Poleglass or Rathcoole - feel they are in control of the police, you can make progress. The notion of transferring police from Fermanagh to Armagh or Belfast, and vice versa, is a colonial/

military concept and unacceptable. If police won't live in tough areas, a consequence of good salaries, then reservists should live in tough areas.

- There is a need for a Regional Police Operational Structure.

I propose seven Rural Divisions and two Belfast Divisions, which will underpin the concept of bringing policing closer to the community.

The proposed Divisions are:
- West Belfast/North Belfast
- Lagan Valley/Upper Bann
- South Belfast/East Belfast
- Foyle/ West Tyrone
- Mid Ulster/Fermanagh and South Tyrone
- Strangford/North Down
- South Antrim/East Antrim
- East Derry/North Antrim
- Newry and Armagh/South Down

11

- There will be Assistant Chief Constables in Belfast and Derry. There would be 3 Regional Crime Squads based on combinations of Westminster Constituencies with Assistant Chief Constables in command. One would have to be a Catholic. Chief Constable and Deputy Chief Constable would alternate between the dominant traditions. Policing in a dual ethos community needs a multifaceted approach, totally lacking in our society since 1920. We need to learn from other experiences. Liverpool and the Brownsville Projects in Brooklyn are examples of high crime areas, coupled with intense hostility to the police. They deserve study.

- Without reform of this type, policing is impossible. If change does not come despite a political settlement and peace, police will never get in without their guns to Loyalist and Republican areas of Northern Ireland.

- The North of Ireland Police Liaison Authority should be drawn, on the basis of proportionality from the Regional Police Liaison Committees. Decisions, by consensus, ratified by a majority within each tradition.

- There must be a Staff Commission, to vet appointments above the rank of Inspector. Membership to reflect equality of allegiance.

Ethos

1. Uniform.
A Change of Uniform could help in creating a sense of a new departure; a new identification with a newly structured Police Service.

2. Symbols.
Symbols, insignia and emblems must be representative of both Traditions, or neither. The Police fly the union flag over Police barracks in Northern Ireland following the practice adopted in relation to Government Buildings. Police Barracks are not Government Buildings. They belong to the Police Authority. The union flag is displayed on 15/20 days per year - including 12 July. The practice must be ended.

3. Culture.
It is important to restate again a finding of the Hunt Report [1969].

Policing in a free Society depends on a wide measure of public approval and consent. This has never been obtained in the long term by military or paramilitary means

Any future Northern Ireland Police Service should be civilian in character and free from paramilitary trappings.

4. Police Oath.
This should be recast in a form acceptable to both communities, reflecting a will:

> To serve Justice and the Public, according to Law.

5. Code of Conduct.
The version promulgated in 1985 is essentially focused on matters of professional Policing Ethics. It needs to revised to take due account of the special circumstances of a divided society.

6. Training.
Training will play a crucial role in the construction of a new Police Service for the North of Ireland. Current training courses must be overhauled to ensure appropriate treatment of the traditions, history and culture of the Nationalist community. Training in basic human rights issues and in the requirement of policing a peaceful society, without recourse to emergency measures or extraordinary powers, will be essential.

7. Secret Societies
It will be illegal for Government officials, Police Officers, Judges or Civil Servants to be members of any secret society.

Human Rights

14

Human Rights

1. The English Common Law tradition provides the corner stone of our Judicial System. It is the product of a community at peace, the creation of a society unburdened by anarchic, sectarian squabbles. The Common Law system falters in a community where Human Rights throughout the community are continually under siege. The existing Judicial Review Procedure is inappropriate in dealing with discrimination and abuse of political power.

These matters can be resolved:

- Through the incorporation of:

   The European Convention on Human Rights

   The United Nations Declaration of Human Rights

   The introduction of a Bill of Rights for Northern Ireland.

2. The European Convention on Human Rights provides minimum standards in the field of individual rights and the United Nations Declaration on Human Rights has a community rights focus. A local Bill of Rights would assert the fundamental rights and liberties available to every citizen of the North of Ireland, regardless of race, gender or religion.
A Bill of Rights would guarantee freedom of conscience and religion, freedom of speech, freedom of the press and freedom of peaceful assembly and association. It would protect citizens against cruel or degrading punishment and secure the right to trial by jury for serious crime. A local Bill of Rights would guarantee equal treatment under the Law to all persons.

3. These Rights are too important to be guaranteed by the goodwill of the Government of the day. The goodwill of the Government must be guaranteed by an equality agenda for the North of Ireland.

4. The major drawback to these proposals is the time factor involved. It will take a considerable period to frame the appropriate Bill of Rights for Northern Ireland. We do not have that time.

5. I recommend that:

- The European Convention on Human Rights is Incorporated into local Law
- With a Schedule attached, which will Include:
    * The United Nations Declaration of Human Rights.
    * The Convention against Torture.
    * The Council of Europe Principles of Administrative Law.

6. I propose:

The creation of a Constitutional Court
    * This would be a British/Irish Structure.
    * Judges sitting to be nominated by the Irish and British Governments.
    * Judges of the Constitutional Court should not come from the present Supreme Court of Northern Ireland.

7. Proceedings can be Initiated:

    * Through Direct Petition by an Applicant
    * Referral by a Judge in any pending proceedings.

The relevant Human Rights Legislation must be interpreted through Constitutional Court support for the maintenance of, and if possible, enhancement of, the existing right of petition to the European Court of Human Rights.

8. It would be necessary to create a Commission for Human Rights.

- The Commission for Human Rights would be responsible for monitoring, enforcement of, and training in, Human Rights ethos and culture. The Commission would be responsible for
- Issuing a statement of compatibility with existing Human Rights legislation in relation to any Bill introduced in this jurisdiction, irrespective of source.
- Refer new Human Rights Legislation for inclusion on the said attached Schedule

16
Judicial Appointments

1. I propose a Judicial Appointments and Training Commission to take over work currently under the control of the Courts Service. This body will be:

   - Independent of the Lord Chancellor's Department and

   - Answerable to the Inter-Governmental Conference, whom it will advise on all aspects of Judicial Appointments and Training.

     * Commission members will be appointed from suitably qualified lawyers, academics and lay people with suitable experience.

     * The Commission will have oversight of the advertisement of all judicial posts, the selection procedures and training functions.

     * The Commission will be committed to the highest judicial standards and ensure that judges are appointed on merit.

     * The judicial selection process must be open, fair and accessible to all.

     * The Commission will develop a strong, equal opportunities policy and encourage all groups currently under-represented in the ranks of the judiciary to apply for appointment.

2. I propose that the current practice of the Court Service in appointing Deputy County Court Judges should be discontinued in principle as an institutional earnest of judicial impartiality. The Standing Advisory Commission on Human Rights have seriously questioned the current use of Deputy Judges in any circumstances. I am concerned about:

   - The wide variation in awards made by Deputy Judges.

   - The frequency with which a solicitor involved in a case sits as a Deputy Judge, unaware that own firm cases have been listed.

   - The Court Service has made no attempt to eradicate this serious anomaly. They seem more concerned about clearing the backlog.

   - The frequency with which barristers sit in cases where a Government department, who retain their services in the normal course of events, is defending the action.

   - The number of days where Deputy Judges have sat is the equivalent of two County Court Judges sitting in a full time capacity.

3. I propose the appointment of two additional County Court Judges.

4. The Judicial Appointments Commission would take a similar approach in relation to the appointment of magistrates.

17

Ethos

1. The new name shall be The North of Ireland Courts Service.

2. Matters are not improved by the appearance of lawyers, clad in wig and gown. The courts are a frightening experience for most people. I do not believe that 17th century costume improves the quality of service in the Courts. If reform of forensic costume does not come from the profession, then legislation may be appropriate.

3. Symbols
    In pursuit of equality of allegiance, I propose the following:

    *   All insignia, presently displayed in premises owned by the North of Ireland Courts Service and crests on Court stationery must be replaced by emblems acceptable to both communities and a neutral legal and cultural environment created.

    *   All oaths, declarations and commentaries must be recast in a form acceptable to both traditions, and must commit the oath taker:

    To serve Justice and the Public, according to Law.

4. Culture
    The present single-culture environment must be replaced by a dual ethos tradition.

5. Training
    Training will play a crucial role in the construction of a new legal regime for the North of Ireland. Current training courses must be overhauled to ensure appropriate treatment of the traditions, history and culture of the Nationalist community. Training in basic Human Rights issues, and in the requirement of equality of allegiancein a peaceful society will be essential.

    These principles must inform all aspects of the new administration of law regime.

18

Sentence Review Commission

1. A confidence building measure and a new departure. This should be a pragmatic Commission with quasi-judicial overtones, not a judicial commission. The dynamic must be to let prisoners out. The prisoners will boycott a full quasi-judicial tribunal. Victim awareness has a part to play; just like other factors but there have been enough judges and we are all victims.

2. The major difficulty is the fact that the British Government do not recognise political prisoners. Recognition is academic if the Irish Government procedure is generally adopted. A discretion can be vested in the Sentence Review Commission similar to the discretion vested in the Minister of Justice in the Republic of Ireland, who acts upon advice tendered by officials in the Department of Justice. Consultations with all interested agencies should ensure that cases presented for Review before the said Commission are forwarded at a sensible political pace.

3. It should be noted that Southern Irish Governments have never been sympathetic to the IRA and Sinn Fein. Yet, they responded to the first IRA Ceasefire in a political fashion; not a judicial fashion.

    The Minister, in exercising the discretion, reviews, *inter alia:*

    *   The nature of the offence.
    *   Length of time served.
    *   Good behaviour in prison.

    A programme was devised for all prisoners who qualified for review and a putative release date worked out. The prisoners, who had difficulties in relation to recognition of the legitimacy of the State, worked the process.

4. Implications

    *   It is a cross-community measure so reaction will be at worst mixed.
    *   Nationalist opinion will support it.
    *   Loyalist opinion and the Alliance Party will also support it.
        Trimble can't oppose it because
        The Loyalists support it and
        They will win any public debate on the issue.

- It strengthens the Loyalists politically in their own communities, which benefits the Peace Process.
- The IRA prisoners are not recidivists generally. They are not used again. Many IRA prisoners had clear records in private life. Let out prisoners initially with under a year to serve.

19

5. The present Northern Ireland Life Sentence Review System is inadequate and fails to meet the basic obligations of the United Kingdom Government under the European Convention on Human Rights. Increased judicialisation of the release process, as under the proposed Sentence Review Commission, will ensure that a measured determination is made, balancing public concern and the expectations and needs of the individual prisoner.

20

Mechanisms

21

1. It is Salutary to remember some recent historic events. Unionism has a depressing habit of reneging on Terms of Agreement before the ink is dry.

   * The 1921 Treaty talks allowed for the setting up of a Boundary Commission. It would have ceded large tracts of land to the Southern State if it had met.
   * The Commission was intended to be composed of

     A British Representative

     A Nationalist Representative

     A Unionist Representative

   * Craig reneged on the Commission.
   * The British Government failed to redress this violation of the Treaty and Dublin had no power to deliver. Eoin MacNeill [the nationalist representative] resigned and the Border remained unchanged.
   * The Upper House of the new Northern Parliament was to be weighted as a redress for Catholic concerns. Craig vetoed the proposal. So much for weighted votes.
   * Proportional Representation was the preferred electoral system. Craig abolished PR, announcing the change by resolution in 1923 at an Orange demonstration.

2. The new mechanism must enforce all agreements made and the said agreements must be identified with the mechanism. Trusting Unionism is a Losers Charter compared to International Agreements and a mechanism to guarantee strict compliance with the terms of the said agreements.

3. It is impossible to address the concept of Government by agreement and consent, without considering the allied notion of self-determination. These were the twin concepts in the Joint Declaration. The right of national self-determination ranks, alongside democracy, as the main political principle of the 20th C. It was responsible for the creation of new states in central and eastern Europe after the First World War, as well as Ireland and Finland, and it was the engine of de-colonisation. Partition worked for everyone except the Nationalist people of the North of Ireland who were denied self-determination as part of the wider Irish nation. The Joint Declaration reinstated the right of northern Nationalists to share, as of right, in self-determination.

4. The island of Ireland, not just the North of Ireland, makes up the framework for self-determination following the Joint Declaration. In an ethnic patchwork, self-determination does not have to take the form of unity or independence. It can be expressed by the endorsement, North and South , of any comprehensive settlement that would constitute an Agreed Ireland.

5. On 24 April 1993, Hume/Adams stated that:

   The exercise of Self Determination is a matter for agreement between the people of Ireland..we both recognise that such a new agreement is only achievable and viable, if it can earn and enjoy the Allegiance of the different traditions on this Island.

22

6. The British Government said in the Peace Declaration that they will underwrite and implement any Agreement the people of Ireland can reach and help to achieve such an Agreement. The centre of gravity has moved to the people of Ireland themselves to work out their own accord.

7. Nationalists must be fully protected if the constitutional position remains unchanged. If Articles 2 and 3 are amended to accommodate the principle of Unionist consent, then the rights of Irish citizens in the North of Ireland must also be underwritten by amended Articles of the Constitution, dedicated to the consent principle; and in reciprocal British constitutional legislation. If we change Articles 2 and 3 to guarantee the British rights

of Unionists the same Articles must also guarantee the Irish rights of Nationalists in the North of Ireland. Unionism must understand that consent is not a one way street.

7. I am no longer focused on geographic determinism but on the concept that society must be organised on the basis of rights, duties and obligations. Self-determination, in the 19th century and Versailles sense, of the people on this island as a unit, as outlined in the Declaration, is impossible. What is possible is the rationalisation of relationships between the diverse groups who compete for space on our shores. Our problems are not unique. Ethnic problems trouble many European countries still. They have troubled Austria/Italy, Switzerland, Belgium and Spain. They found a local solution. So can we.

9. The solution must include:

- * Proportionality
- * Irish and British Government Input
- * Dual ethos legislation that underpins individual and community inclusiveness.

10. The Joint Declaration committed the two Governments to:

- A new political framework founded out of consent and encompassing arrangements within Northern Ireland, for the whole island, and between these islands.
- Uphold the democratic wish of the greater number of the people of Northern Ireland on the issue of whether they prefer to support the Union or a sovereign United Ireland.
- Accept that such Agreement may, as of right, take the form of agreed structures for the island as a whole, including a United Ireland achieved by peaceful means.
- Respect the democratic dignity and the civil rights and religious liberties of both communities, including:

23

- * The right to free political thought
- * The right to freedom of expression and religion
- * The right to pursue democratically national and political aspirations
- * The right to seek constitutional change by peaceful and legitimate means

* The right to live where ever one chooses without hindrance
* The right to equal opportunity in all social and economic activity, regardless of, class, sex or colour

11. The Joint Declaration indicated that Northern Ireland will remain within the United Kingdom so long as a majority of its population so wishes. It also stated that the creation of a United Ireland will occur, if and when a majority in Northern Ireland so desires. These principles offer Unionists their present guarantee while assuring Nationalists that they can achieve their long term goal by constitutional means, if the necessary consent is forthcoming.

12. The principle is incorporated in Section 1 of the Northern Ireland Constitution Act 1973. British sovereignty over Northern Ireland is conditional upon the consent of the greater number of the people to remain a part of the UK. There is an assumption that the next generation will opt for the existing status quo. This is not necessarily so and we must base this agreement upon the premise that change may come, and ensure that agreed structures address this reality.

12. Section 1 of the Northern Ireland Constitution Act 1973 needs minor amendments to take account of current realities. Other acts may need amendment to give a statutory basis to any future agreement.

13. The Declaration also stated that the Irish Government will, as part of a balanced constitutional accommodation, put forward and support proposals for change in the Irish Constitution, which would fully reflect the principle of consent in Northern Ireland.

14. Balanced constitutional change involves:

- The registration of the concept of Irish unity by consent of the people, North and South, in any future agreement, alongside Unionist acceptance of cross-border Institutions with defined powers and

- Nationalist consent to the existing constitutional format until Unionist consent is forthcoming; on the basis that any future agreement reflects full equality of allegiance for Irish people within the North of Ireland and that any Nationalist commitment to a mooted Regional Assembly is contingent upon agreement of a comprehensive equality agenda for implementation within the North of Ireland.

16. Both consents to be registered in future reciprocal agreements between

the Irish and British Governments, reflecting the terms of a peace settlement involving the peoples of the North of Ireland.

17. The two governments must agree that, if a devolved Assembly is to return, it must be elected for a fixed term and must be based upon proportional representation. Proportionality must be used to establish the necessary Committee structure; whatever that might be.

18. Proportionality alone will not ensure the consent of Northern Nationalists to any new arrangement. Currently, this would mean majority rule. Recent Committee elections at Belfast City Council amply demonstrate the inability of elected representatives to behavy with generosity. Sinn Fein are the largest group in City Hall. No member of their group Chairs a Council Committee.

19. The pathology of the problem is brutally clear. The political views of both sections of our population are mutually exclusive. Anything that causes political discomfort to one camp has an equal and opposite reaction in the other camp. Consensus and compromise are not part of the political vocabulary. The practice of democracy is unknown in the North of Ireland. We are not ready for democracy.

19. Legislation must underpin every aspect of any future agreement because we must not depend on goodwill to effect change.

20. The Panel proposal in the Framework Document is democratically unworkable. The mooted three person Panel will include an outvoted Nationalist.

22. Committee Chairpersons, who will come from different parties, should have limited Policy making powers.

23. The exercise of limited power must proceed by consensus:

   • Progress on any issue to be conditional upon a majority vote in favour within both traditions. This guarantees cross-community consensus. We must not feed the dream of democracy meaning majority rule in the mind of the Unionist population.

24. The two governments must agree on any powers devolved to Northern Ireland.

25. All detail agreed within the Three Strands and ratified by referendum,

END OF TERM REPORT

North and South, to be agreed matters to be implemented through the Inter-Governmental Conference;

26. It is worthy of note that the bulk of this submission relates to Reserved Matters. In the event of failure of the Talks Process, it is appropriate for the sovereign Governments to agree and implement the necessary changes in Human Rights, Administration of Law and Policing, accompanied by appropriate mechanisms; in line with Paragraphs 39, 40, 41,42, 46 and 47 of the Framework Document.

Mechanism

25

1. Institutionalised British and Irish Dimensions must survive any future alteration in the status of Northern Ireland. The Inter-Governmental Conference, established by the Anglo-Irish Agreement must remain on a Statutory Basis as the vehicle to effect change.

2. North of Ireland Members will take part in the Inter-Parliamentary tier of the Agreement along with representatives from Westminster and Dail Eireann: if the necessary Nationalist consent is forthcoming from the Talks Process.

3. There in a need to establish Strand Two and Strand Three links, especially in relation to policy matters directed by the European Union. Evolving Cross Border Bodies should be set up, in some cases modelled on European structures. Commissions should be appointed by the two sovereign Governments to carry out specific functions. These Commissions should be UK/Republic Agencies or Northern Ireland/Republic of Ireland Agencies: as the need arises.

4. Mechanism Proposals

   The two Governments must establish a mechanism for:
   - Implementing any future Agreement.
   - Underwriting the terms of any such Agreement.

5. The Inter-Governmental Conference must be empowered to safeguard and underwrite the constitutional settlement so that each section of the community has a First and Second Guarantor. Each government in the Inter-Governmental Conference would review legislation, at discussion stage, and have the right to veto any proposal bound for the North of Ireland

which it deems fundamentally to threaten the equality agenda. Northern Nationalists must be confident that the Boundary Commission scenario will not return to haunt them.

- The Mechanism does mean engagement by the British or Irish States in the Governance of the North of Ireland, but provides a formula for effecting change and vetting progress.
- The Mechanism encompasses both communities.
- The Mechanism, to be balanced, must be institutionalised so that it can survive future constitutional change in the status of the North of Ireland. The British Government will have an equivalent function as Guarantor of the Unionist tradition, if and when Northern Ireland becomes part of a federal Ireland, as the Irish Government must enjoy in relation to Northern Nationalists, while the constitutional status quo remains in place. The Mechanism must be completely entrenched. It must be constitutionally established that any future agreement between participants in the Talks Process will remain in operation, if and when the North of Ireland votes to join a Federal Ireland. The entire constitutional package would be transferable, apart from the fact that the two Guarantors of the constitutional arrangements would reverse roles. The Irish Government will become the Sovereign Authority and the British Government will act as Guarantor for the Unionist community, with the right of review and veto pending legislation at the discussion stage, as detailed at 5 ante.

26

- The Inter-Governmental Conference must be placed on a statutory basis. Concurrent Acts in the Oireachtas and the Westminster Parliament will be necessary. The Foyle Fisheries legislation is a useful point of reference. It deals with a statutory resolution of similar matters on a much smaller scale.

27

Equality of Allegiance

1. The two governments must spell out equality of allegiance for the two major traditions. Any settlement, consistent with the Joint Declaration for Peace, must guarantee the two communities in the North of Ireland, full equality of status. Discrimination continues in the recruitment and composition of Government Agencies and Quangos, which are dominated by the Official Unionist Party and the Alliance Party. A renewed commitment to Fair Employment, including Affirmative Action where necessary, and the testing of all public policy against the implications for

equality of status, are political imperatives. The cultural insignia of both traditions must be equally protected or equally unused; both flags, both national anthems or nothing at all. Those who attempt to argue against these propositions should note present demographic trends. We will not live in an Orange statelet and the special position of the Unionist population must be removed from new constitutional arrangements.

2. I am appalled by the political vibrations emanating from senior public officials in particular from local Civil Servants in the Northern Ireland Office during the extended period of direct rule. As stated earlier, while it is possible for Catholics to join the presently constituted RUC, it is impossible for Nationalists to join. The situation is similar in the Civil Service. It is impossible to achieve significant promotion in the Northern Ireland Civil Service, without adopting a Unionist perspective. It is a matter of record that, no Nationalist above the level of Principal Officer, advises the Secretary of State. There may be a Catholic in the higher reaches but no Nationalist. The range of advice, presently received by the Secretary of state, is not conditioned by any view formed west of Dundonald or south of Ballygowan. Is the Secretary of State satisfied with this truncated range, bearing in mind that the Labour Party in Britain has expressed concern about the Oxbridge Factor at the top of the British Civil Service and the lack of Blacks and Asians in influential positions? Is there a policy document imminent, addressing the Nationalist deficit in the higher ranks of the Civil Service? The honest answer is in the negative. Nobody will write this policy document amongst the present advisers because it would be against their collective interests to do so.

   Nationalists must be reconciled with the Civil Service. They will be encouraged by a transparent commitment to the equality agenda. I insist that the chill factor associated with the Royal Crest on dinner plates and other paraphernalia, is dissipated as an earnest of intent. The process by which decision makers are appointed in the Northern Ireland Civil Service is in need of radical reform. If you join the Northern Ireland Civil Service at present you must swallow the customs and traditions of the British Civil Service; you must swallow the whole ethos. Equality of allegiance, in future, must mean that Catholics can miss this meal without fear of sanction. All Government departments and Public Agencies must be tested against the equality agenda in the context of structures, accountability, ethos, symbols, culture, oaths, Code of Conduct and training to ensure appropriate treatment of the traditions, history and culture of the Nationalist community.

3. The basis for administration in any democracy is a Civil Service answerable

to an Executive which is answerable to the people. For a generation, Northern Ireland, in the absence of a local, representative political structure, has witnessed an increasing level of autocracy in the hands of Civil Servants, A situation has been created where accusations of favouritism and preferential treatment are commonplace. Such accusations have caused the Civil Service to become very defensive. Most Civil Servants would welcome a system where the buck stops elsewhere.

28

4. The Civil Service must return to the situation where they tender advice, after taking account of the views of the total gamut of people and politicians. They are no longer answerable to the public. They tend to act as if they are a superior, distant SuperUnit.

5. The relationship between the Civil Service and the Executive is predicated upon the interest and enthusiasm of the relevant Minister. Even a competent Minister will struggle to establish respect because:

   • He/she is not the recipient of the wide range of opinion available in a normal democracy to ground decisions and

   • He/she is dependant upon Quangos and Advisory Bodies formed to assist the running of an Agency or a Section of a Department.

6. Transparency in Public Appointments, internal and external to the Civil Service, is an essential part of any future system.

7. We must reassess the power of senior Civil Servants to determine the future of an Organisation and the policy it adopts.

8. It is vital that scrutiny be given to:

   • The specific process by which policy is formulated and

   • The individuals and agencies involved in the said formulation.in, *inter alia,* Tourism, Planning, Industry, the Environment, Education and Training.

9. Appointments to Quangos and Advisory Bodies are made on the recommendation of Civil Servants, who thrive on the responsibility. Patronage encourages Civil Servants to pursue their own agenda which may/may not accord with local feeling.

10. Local feeling is not necessarily right, just like Civil Servants, but Civil servants are not elected and avoid the sanction of a disgruntled electorate. There is a lack of accountability which is articulated constantly by local politicians to any Civil Servant who will listen.

11. One can relate this contention to particular Quangos, - Labour Relations Agency, IDB, LEDU and Curriculum Council - where problems have occurred. Officials may have been disciplined internally, but externally nobody has been taken to task and Quango members are excused or disowned. Direct rule created this problem and time has exacerbated it. There is a need for public accountability.

12. Nationalists view membership of a Quango as follows:

   * There are no good appointments except one of Ours; no account is taken of ability or the lack of it.
   * Even if it is one of Ours, it is no good unless we nominate the individual concerned.

Unionists take a different perspective.

   * An appointment is acceptable if it is one of Ours.
   * They believe that they have a right to be appointed.

13. The assertion of outright discrimination against the Nationalist people in Quango appointments, is endorsed by the recent scandal, involving Positively Belfast. Some questions need to be asked in the aftermath of this fiasco.

   • Were Board Members appointed on the basis of
       Who they were.
       Not what they can do?
   • If this was not the reason why were they appointed?
       Was Social Fund money involved?
       Is Portrush in the Greater Belfast area?

14. Local Government appointments work on the basis of Buggin's turn. An individual councillor of the dominant grouping can express an interest and make the Board. Basic ability is not a factor in appointment.

15. Recently changes have been effected in a flawed system. In general,

Quango appointments, at a minor level, are the subject of public advertisement. Individuals apply and Civil Servants shortlist and select future members. The system remains fundamentally flawed. This is a stratagem to delay change by a Civil Service alert to individuals who might make trouble.

- The same people with the same agenda make the selection.
- Once the advertisement is placed, private canvassing takes place to ensure that the 'Right People' apply.
- Chairmen and Commissioners are excluded from this process. They are selected out of the ether. Generally they are Official Unionists and Alliance Party supporters. For a small party, the Alliance Party holds down an inordinate number of key Quango appointments.

16. The Establishment has contended that Chairpersons should have served on the relevant Board before appointment to the key position. This is a laughable contention, designed to protect a flawed system from Nationalists.

17. The Government must deal with the matter on a professional basis. An external agency must be appointed to vet interested individuals, who would apply through the medium of newspaper advertisements placed by the NIO. The following measures will help:

- An independent headhunters type agency to be retained to deal with all appointments.
- Ability to be the criterion for appointment; not party affiliation.
- Individual posts would be the subject of Ministerial ratification but the selection would be in external, objective hands.
- The Chairmanships should reflect the spectrum of N. Ireland political opinion. No applicant should be excluded on the basis that he/she would fail the Establishment attitude test.

18. There is a Golden Circle in operation in Quangoland at the present time. It is a squalid arrangement that reflects badly on Government and the so called political process. The old Unionist Party ruled on the basis of extensive patronage. The present Quango appointments system would have been a major Civil Rights issue if it had been in existence in 1967.

31

Possible Administrative Model

There are many places we can learn from: Spain, Switzerland, Belgium or Alto Adige. I refer to the latter on the basis of similarities. No model reflects, in detail or scope, the complexities of any other political dilemma. My proposals are outlined in previous pages.

Alto Adige/Trentino/Sud Tyrol

1. Italy got this area in 1915 at the Treaty of London as part of a deal to persuade them not to enter the war on the side of Germany/Austria-Hungary. It is a majority German speaking area, centred on Bolzano in the Alps at one time 91% German. Italians, in the nineteenth century, called it *Terre Irredente* and claimed it. There were very aggressive organisations like the *Deutsches Schulverein* to defend German culture, traditions and schools.

2. To the surprise of the population of Alto Adige and the Italians, Italy got to keep it in 1919, and Hitler disclaimed it in 1938 to keep Mussolini sweet. Once again in 1946, to the amazement of the international community and the deep chagrin of the German population, Italy retained sovereignty over the region.

3. There had been bloody confrontations in the area since the nineteenth century. These increased in the 1930s with the hope Hitler would take the place over and bring the Germans back into *Eines Grosses Vaterland*. In the 1948 Italian Constitution, provision was made for areas like Alto Adige. There were four of them:
    *   Val d'Aosta French speaking.
    *   Alto Adige/Trentino/Sud Tyrol German speaking
    *   Sicily
    *   Sardinia and
    *   Friuli-Venezia Giulia Slovene/ Friulian Speaking Added in1963

4. These areas are known in the constitution as Special Statute Regions because of their specific linguistic and cultural character. A key provision in the constitution made them Autonomous Administrative Regions. The main problem was Alto Adige. Because of a huge German speaking majority, they were not content with the provisions in the 1948 Constitution and clashes continued until the 1950s. Italy was unhappy about any links with Austria for obvious reasons; also because the Red Army remained in Occupation of Austria until 1955.

5. Gradually, by 1969, a deal called the *Pachetto* was hatched. Alto Adige remained part of Italy, but as an Autonomous Administrative Region. Austria had rights to be consulted about matters affecting German speakers in the region. There was Dual Nationality, an important recognition of the Germanness - deutschheit - of the people. Specific legislation which does not apply to the rest of Italy has been brought in. The Constitution prevents legal action to require all Italian legislation to apply to the region. Explicit legislation on job discrimination was introduced. When a German speaker was made redundant, the next person employed in the firm had to be German. People can choose to ski for Austria or Italy. There is a sophisticated power-sharing arrangement to safeguard the rights of the Italian minority in Alto Adige. There have been neo - Nazi rumblings in the last year and some minor violence, but generally the *Pachetto* works.

6. Since Austria is now in the EU, there is even more contentment. They stopped killing each other.

32

1. The Road To A Settlement in Sud Tyrol

- The crucial step forward in the dispute was 28 June 1960, when the Austrians presented the problem at the UN General Assembly. They internationalised the dispute.

- On 5 September 1961, the Council of Europe formed a Sub-Committee on Sud Tyrol. Italy was now under international observation.

- The *Pachetto* - or Package - was recommended on 10 April 1964. The international anchoring of the Package became the main bone of contention. The Austrians and Sud -Tyroleans would not entrust the implementation of the new regulations to internal Italian arrangements.

- A compromise was reached, whereby Italy and Austria regulated the implementation of the Package measures. It was called the Operations Calendar. It was presented on 25 November 1969.

2. It had two aims.
   Ensuring the implementation of the Package and
   Officially ending the Dispute brought before the UN.

3. Three questions needed Clarification.

END OF TERM REPORT

How, in which order, within what space of time were:

Stipulations of the package to be Implemented?

Who would mediate future Disputes?

When and how could the conflict over the Structuring of Autonomy and Minority Rights between Italy and Austria be Officially settled?

33

4. A key feature of the plan.

It did not set Deadlines when certain Measures had to be implemented. Substantive aspects of the Package were placed in order. A new measure could only be implemented if preceding Measures had been satisfactorily Implemented.

- Future disputes on Implementation of the Package to be resolved by the International Court of Justice.

- Procedures to be taken within 50 days of issuing the last Implementation Regulations were stipulated.

- The local Germans voted on it. It was emphasised the Package did not mean a Renunciation of their Right to Self Determination. Austria remained the Protecting Power in Sud Tyrol.

- A new Autonomy Statute came into force on 20 November 1972. Implementing Regulations by the Italian government were produced by Commissions from Sud Tyrol with parity of representation and submitted to Rome. Rome would then approve and draw up a corresponding Decree.

- It took ages. The last Implementing Regulations were issued in 1988. Interestingly these concerned the Courts and the Police. The extent to which Central Government can directly intervene in Sud Tyrol and the Constitutionality of Regional Laws remained contentious Issues.

Which Laws should take Precedence prior to a decision by the Constitutional

Court: National or Regional?

For Sud Tyroleans, Regional Precedence was a *sine qua non*. Rom eventually gave way.

- On 22 April 1992 the Italian Government handed over to the Austrian Government a note confirming the fulfilment of the Package.

It took 28 years. Italy complied reluctantly with the international anchoring of autonomy and enforceability by international legal authorities.

The local Germans voted on it on 30 May 1992, with 82.86% in favour.

The Regional Government in Sud Tyrol voted in Favour on 1 June 1992.

The Regional Assembly voted for it on 4 June 1992.

The Austrian National Council gave its approval on 5 June 1992.

4. There was a formal Dispute Settlement Declaration between Austria and Italy on 11 June 1992.

5. Austria continues to have a function as a Protecting Power in Sud Tyrol and it can seek recourse to the International Court of Justice for serious violations.

34

6. The Settlement contained Three Crucial Elements.

- Enabling as much local administration as possible.
- Achieving this through maximum decentralisation, separate powers and keeping an international aspect in matters.
- Further development must be possible.

7. In October 1994 Luis Durnwalder, Head of the Regional Sud Tyrol Government, said:

Our Autonomy should not be viewed as something static, but as something dynamic, and this is why the Package Conclusion, finalised in 1992, is to be seen as a Guarantee of our Rights, not as a Renunciation of Further Negotiations, which, on the contrary, are particularly important at the present time.

9. It is appropriate that we look to Europe for a solution. Our Continent has seen it all; Plumbing the depths and scaling the heights in the continuing search for democracy, justice and civilisation. Our problems are not unique, though we attempt to portray them so.

10. Some key Points should be kept in mind in relation to Alto Adige.

- Austria and Italy were in dispute over the future of Sud Tyrol.

  As a result of, inter alia, The Framework Document and Other Agreements and Declarations, Coupled with progress on many issues since 1969, the Irish Government and the British Government are not In Dispute. Recent utterances by the two governments indicate that a common platform approach appears certain, on many European issues.

- The time scale for Agreement and the complicated international involvement are not relevant, because friendly Governments are engaged. America is the obvious international presence in our circumstance.

- The Second Guarantor in this Model was seeking Self Determination for a majority culture in the Region involved. This is not a direct parallel of the situation here.

35

- If other European Union partners can resolve Regional disputes, so can we.

- The Model signposts possible difficulties on the road ahead. There will be other difficulties not considered above.

Paddy O'Hanlon
December 1997

END OF TERM REPORT

END OF TERM REPORT